THE STORY OF ARCHITECTURE IN AMERICA

From a lithograph by the author.

A vista of American Architecture.

THE STORY OF
ARCHITECTURE
IN AMERICA

BY THOMAS E. TALLMADGE

Fellow, American Institute of Architects

New, Enlarged and Revised Edition

W · W · NORTON & COMPANY, INC·

New York

PRINTED IN THE UNITED STATES OF AMERICA
FOR THE PUBLISHERS BY THE VAIL-BALLOU PRESS

To the dear memory of
My Mother

CONTENTS

ILLUSTRATIONS

THE STORY OF ARCHITECTURE IN AMERICA

AMENDE HONORABLE

In the preparation of this book I have lightly taken and used many facts and much information which has been painstakingly searched out and gathered by many patient and learned workers in the field of the early architectural history of America. To these I wish to acknowledge my debt of gratitude: to the Metropolitan Museum of New York City for the opportunity of spending many golden hours in the American Wing, and to Messrs. R. T. H. Halsey and Charles O. Cornelius for their "Handbook of the American Wing," which was my constant companion, not only erudite but intensely interesting. The Georgian Period, published by the American architect, the White Pine Series and many others have been of great help. I am indebted to Mr. O. H. Eberlein for much of the information that has led me to make my classifications of the periods of Colonial architecture, even though they did not agree with his; and also to Mr. Aymar Embury for his researches in early ecclesiastical architecture. Mr. Howard Major's book on the domestic architecture of the Early American Republic is invaluable to a worker in the period of the Greek Revival. Though I am not able to subscribe to his enthusiastic conclusions, I have found information and inspiration in his beautiful photographs. My personal acquaintance with the California missions is but slight. I have actually examined only three. Mr. Rexford Newcomb's fine work, "The Old Mission Churches and Historic Houses of Cali-

1

fornia," has been my chief source, and I herewith render grateful acknowledgment to him. I want to pay tribute to Mr. A. D. F. Hamlin, for many years professor of architecture in Columbia University and through his book, "A History of Architecture," teacher and torch-bearer to thousands of students throughout the land. This book contains, unfortunately, little on America, but its chapters on European architecture have been my companion and guide on many a continental excursion.

Other books which have helped me and would help the reader of this volume are: "The Wood-Carver of Salem" by Cousins and Riley; "The Georgian Period" by Ware; "The Autobiography of an Idea" by Louis Sullivan; "The Life of John Root" by Harriet Monroe; "The Life of H. H. Richardson" by Mrs. Van Rensselaer; "The Life of Charles Follen McKim" by A. H. Granger; "The Life of Daniel Hudson Burnham" by Charles Moore and "The Life of Louis Sullivan" by Hugh Morrison.

My principal sources of information, however, have been the files of architectural magazines. The first number of "The American Architect" was published in 1876, and the first volume of "The Architectural Record" in 1891. The pages of these magazines "hold like full garners the full ripened grain" of the story of architecture in America. Some of the harvesters are men well known and loved in their profession. Those in whose words I delighted are: A. D. F. Hamlin, Montgomery Schuyler, Russell Sturgis, Peter B. Wight, N. C. Curtis, George C. Nimmons, Glenn Brown, Harvey Corbett, William H. Crocker.

I am deeply indebted to many friends for much original information and active help. Among these is that grand old Nestor of the fine arts, Mr. C. Howard Walker; also Mr. Ernest R. Graham and the late Martin Roche—never too busy to help another. Professor Thomas E. O'Donnell of the faculty of the University of Illinois gave me free access to his valuable thesis on the Greek Revival. To Mr. and Mrs. Victor Stewart of Petersburg, Virginia, I am indebted, through their kindness, enthusiasm and hospitality, for personal acquaintance with the lovely examples of Virginia Colonial abounding along the historic banks of the James River, and to Dr. Goodwin, the dynamic rector of Bruton Parish Church, Virginia, for my introduction to the spirit and the architecture of Williamsburg and to a share in its restoration.

I am deeply indebted to the Art Institute of Chicago and to Marion Rawls of its staff for active aid and the use of a number of photographs in the illustrations.

I have quoted, often in slightly varied form, from articles which I have written on occasion in "The Atlantic Monthly," "The Architectural Record," "The American Architect," "Art and Archæology," "House Beautiful" and others. For permission to do this I am grateful to the editors of these mazagines.

To the memory of John W. Norton I render thanks for assistance and advice in the preparation of the lithograph and the illustrations, and, more than to any other, to my sister without whose active aid and encouragement this book, while it might have been commenced, would surely never have been finished.

As I read over the manuscript and recognize the source of so many of my allusions and figures, I cannot refrain from paying humble homage to that bright star "in lone splendor hung aloft the night," John Keats.

THOMAS E. TALLMADGE

FOREWORD

THE high sea on which we are now afloat and which has
borne us to the leadership of the world in architecture
marks the culmination of a voyage of three hundred years
—a voyage now beset with calms and now crowded with
adventure, and, curiously, a voyage of which no log has
been kept and no account published. Of the earlier days,
which produced what we call our Colonial style, many
books—some of them excellent—have been written (there
is even an extensive bibliography on old bottles). At least
one book has been published covering the style known as
the Classic or Greek Revival, which followed the Colonial. But of that curious era of bad taste which hovered
around the Civil War, and of that period of high romance
in architecture which filled the epoch between two great
World's Fairs—those of 1876 and 1893—scarcely a word
has been written. Nor has the sudden right-about-face
from Romanticism to Classicism, executed in 1893 and
continuing up to the World War, received any consistent
treatment in printed form. In fine, no connected story or
history of architecture in the United States had ever been
given the public at the time this book was first published.

These considerations, together with the fact that at no
time, perhaps, except in those leisurely and courtly days
of our early history, has the public shown as much interest
in architecture as it does today, have emboldened me to
undertake a continuous story of architecture in America—
a story that should begin with our earliest settlements and

5

continue to the year of our Lord 1927. The book is written principally for the layman, but not without the hope that my fellow-workers in architecture, who are often more proficient in the technique than in the history of their art, may find something of interest and value in it.

There is a further consideration which I hope will make the book of value. The author is himself an architect engaged in the active practice of his profession. For this reason he feels that he is in a better position to understand the wants and the point of view of the building public than the archaeologist or the teacher to whom the happy task of writing books is usually vouchsafed. This position, however, has its drawbacks. It has prevented him from spending long periods of time in archaeological research, although there is consolation in the fact that a great part of any such research now-a-days, especially in the Colonial period, would be but a repetition of the masterly work done by Millar, Edgerly, Kimball, and others. I have endeavored, however, to examine all the important architectural monuments. With but few exceptions, I have had personal acquaintance with the buildings mentioned in these pages.

I have thought best not to make the book a catalogue of buildings or of names, but to dramatize the story of architecture and its champions, and the vital part this art has played in the development of America. Hence the pivotal buildings alone are described in detail, and only those few greatest personalities who, like mountain peaks, elevate themselves above the foot hills. These men are the "heroes" of architecture, and their names will live long after their earthly works have perished. It is to be regretted that in a work of this character and scope a more extensive mention of the "little masters" is impossible, for often in isolated cases the work of lesser men equals or surpasses the work of a master, and the great sum total of it furnishes not only the background for the work of genius, but often its sustenance as well.

In dividing history into epochs and architecture into styles one must realize that no sharp demarcation can ever be drawn, any more than one can say today winter ends and spring begins. But spring, in its average course or at least at its high point, is surely a different thing from winter. So an architectural period in its typical phase or at its culmination has such peculiar and unmistakable characteristics that we are as fully justified in classifying and naming them as is the author of the almanac in marshalling the seasons. Nothing has cultural value until man has named it; not till then does it become part of human knowledge.

The active participation of the public in architecture has been too little recognized. In every building operation the public, represented by the owner, determines the location, the size, the cost, and often for better or worse dictates the arrangement, construction and style as well. These restrictions, or programs as they are called, are not a detriment to the architect. They are a distinct aid, giving him a problem that must be solved, an obstacle to overcome. For him " 'twas pastime to be bound," and architecture, unlike painting, has never "felt the weight of too much liberty." I think it may truly be said that in the creation of a building the owner is the father and the architect the mother; at least, it is certain that while the mother gives the building form and beauty, the father pays the bills. If I have succeeded in this book in augmenting the parents' interest in the life history of their offspring, I shall be content.

I have a still further purpose, and that is to awaken interest in our ancient buildings. That the public is interested, even though private generosity has borne the brunt, is evidenced by the tremendous popularity of restored Williamsburg. Other restorations through various agencies have been the settlement at New Salem, Illinois, the Puritan Village at Salem, Massachusetts, the Moravian Village at Schoenbrunn, Ohio, the Spring Mill Village in southern Indiana, etc. There is no good reason why a nation-wide restoration of our pioneer culture could not be undertaken. The log house of the early settler complete in every detail along our highways, Indian forts in the Western Reserve, plantations in the old South, pueblos in the Southwest, and missions and presidios in Alta California would be far more grateful to the eye than signboards and hamburger stations, and their ultimate service in the preservation of our institutions by awakening interest and pride in our past is beyond our reckoning.

An eminent critic, in reviewing the First Edition of "The Story of Architecture in America," wrote that the author "ran with the fox and rode with the hounds." I freely acknowledge the truth of the assertion even though I am sure that he did not intend it to be a compliment. In fact, I cannot see how history can be written fairly unless the narrator sets forth both sides of the question. When one side only is espoused the writing becomes propaganda. So in this new edition, which adds the interesting progress of architecture during the Depression, the author, with a clear conscience, will continue to admire both the clean-cut vigor and high ideals of the "New Architecture" and the beauty and human appeal in the architecture of our fathers, and will point out a proper place for each in the present American scene.

CHAPTER I

INTRODUCTORY—

In Which the Reader is Given His Stool by the Fireside.

THE idea of an introductory chapter which should trace the course of architecture from its beginnings down to its appearance in America emanates from my good and wise publisher—not from myself. There is a sufficiency of such histories already, but he argued that readers of this book, if such there be, might be ignorant of the general course of architecture, and to such this chapter would be valuable for an understanding of what is to follow. The opportunity, therefore, of writing a chapter which would be the world's shortest history of architecture and of combating therein what appear to me to be fallacies occurring in other histories offers an irresistible temptation.

The first mistake the architectural historian usually makes is to begin the development of our architecture with Egypt; then he traces it to Babylonia and Assyria; then to Persia and Greece. Architecture as far as it concerns us begins only with Greece, "that point of light in history." The architecture of Egypt, Babylonia and Assyria, or any other African or Asiatic land, has had and is having little more influence on our architecture than the palaces and temples that doubtless line Schiaparelli's canals on the planet Mars. One of the paradoxes of art is that the great palace-temples of Egypt could have existed in their magnificence without in the slightest degree affecting the art of Greece, which was then just awakening into conscious-

9

ness in Crete and later learning to walk in Mycenae. So in our little history we shall eliminate every architecture outside of Europe.

Histories of architecture will tell you, or at least give you the impression, that architecture is a mighty river rising obscurely in the prehistoric past and flowing through the ages to some unrevealed ocean. To float on its bosom with the current is the most that man can hope for, and to watch on its surface, now clear, now agitated, the true reflection of the age and times through which it flows, his sole privilege. This conception of architecture leaves no place for originality, fashion or caprice. Every manifestation, it says, had its beginning in previous ages, and will affect what comes after. In this view architecture is another phenomenon of evolution governed by unalterable laws. But architecture, it seems to me, is more like a series of vases, each filled at the river of life by human hands —a few exquisitely fashioned, many broken and rude, but each an expression of the hands that fashioned it and of the souls that conceived it.

Few architectural histories are willing to admit the factor of originality. When they see a black lamb born into a flock of snow-white sheep they say, "There isn't any such animal." Originality and invention may come either from intention or from accident. The discredited story of the origin of the Corinthian capital seems to me highly sensible and probable. It was to the effect that Callimachus happened upon a basket—or was it a jar?—with acanthus leaves growing up about it. Why not? If so it would be an example of invention by accident. In explaining the rounded apse of the French Gothic cathedral, the learned Dr. Cram thinks he must go back to the fifth century and into remote Syria, where he finds an early Chris-

tian dome; but then he has to bisect this dome and trans-
mute it through a dozen different styles and ages until he
gets it into France and the thirteenth century. Would it
not be far more sensible to assume that some young monk,
tracing on his parchment the outlines of the new abbey,
drew a semi-circle instead of a square as the proper form
of structure in which to house the mysteries of the holy
Eucharist? Every architect and painter has the experience
of spinning lines or colors more or less at random until out
of this tangled skein of uncertainty a new fact that he can
establish, a nova in the milky way, suddenly blazes forth.
It is hard to realize that the ancient Romans, for instance,
or even the Crô-Magnons of Pleistocene days, were as intelligent as we are. Yet the advantage we have is merely
that of accumulated data and experience. If we can invent
reinforced concrete, why couldn't the Etruscans invent the
vault or the Franks the pointed arch?

Another human instinct which the historians of architecture pass by is the universal desire to be in fashion. By
aping the manners, the dress, the house, of our superiors we
feel that in some degree we are putting ourselves on their
plane, or that we are making obeisance to authority, or, at
the very least, avoiding the stigma of being thought "different." The gorgeous raiment of Tutankamen was no
more slavishly copied by the nobles than were the great bell
columns of the Temple of Karnak by the priests of the
later and lesser shrines. The elegancies of the buildings on
the Acropolis set the style for all construction in Hellas,
and to have a statue in the manner of Praxiteles stamped its
owner as one of the élite. The sight of Italy herself in the
Gothic of the thirteenth century, which was at variance
with every one of her traditions and tastes, is no more eloquent of the power of fashion than the sight today of

Turkish women in short skirts and with bobbed hair, or of the Japanese in cutaway coats and plug hats. Italy had to be Gothic to keep in style. So we see the Germans of the thirteenth century copying Amiens, the English of Queen Elizabeth's time bringing over German and Dutch artists, the American colonists importing the smart Adam mode, and ourselves today leaping from style to style like architectural chamois in a wild attempt to keep up with the mode. "Is it being done?" has been a potent phrase for the human race since the dawn of adornment.

Little comedies of style are enacted often before our very eyes. Sixty years ago in the days of the Victorian Gothic the popular and fashionable stone in the Middle West, especially for churches, was Niagara limestone, locally called Joliet stone. This stone is very white and brittle, and cannot easily be carved; it was in consequence used with very rough exposed surfaces. When laid up with broken courses in rough blocks it was called "rubble stone." It was universally used for churches, and college buildings and town halls. In the eighties it was displaced by rough-faced, gray Bedford stone from southern Indiana. In the early nineteen hundreds the rough-faced Bedford stone had been succeeded by smooth-faced. Fifteen years ago the old Joliet stone was so completely out of style and forgotten that stone masons could scarcely be found who knew how to cut and lay it. But drive out through fashionable suburbs today—every golf club, every gate-lodge, every villa is, in part at least, built of the erstwhile despised Niagara stone. It is used far more skillfully, with different textures and different mixtures, than it was sixty years ago, but it is the same old stone. This is an example of the normal swing of the pendulum, but there are other factors that cause quicker changes in fashion.

The usual life history of an architectural fashion is this: first, it is introduced by a skillful architect, often at the instance of a client of unusual daring and taste; second, it is imitated by other architects for other appreciative clients; third, it is adopted by commercial builders of no taste at all for customers with less than no taste; fourth, it is dead. A good instance of this is the polychroming of iron, plaster and various materials. The little red and green shades, in wrought iron, plaster and wood, when first done were very charming; as done yesterday by anybody and everybody everywhere they were simply nauseating. To-day, thank Heaven, it is not done at all.

This brings to mind one of the banes of architectural practice and one of the greatest obstacles to architectural progress. The building of houses, apartment buildings for sale, the manufacture of lighting-fixtures and of stained or leaded glass, and (I shall extend it to my favorite bête noir) the manufacture of tombstones, with many others, require, distinctly, taste and artistic ideals as well as business acumen. But too often these useful crafts are conducted by men well-meaning enough, but of no taste or artistic training whatsoever. There is nothing that helps an architect more than a skillful craftsman, and there is nothing that lowers the taste of the public more than ignorant and unscrupulous manufacturers who "give the people what they want."

I am mentioning fashion in architecture in some detail because all architectural histories will tell you that the architecture of every age is the perfect reflection and expression of the culture and life of the time. It often is—perhaps usually is—but it is not always. It is curious for instance that the Niagara limestone should be expressive of cultures as different as 1876 and 1936. Certainly the

Gothic of France, born of mediaeval and unreflecting ecstasy, and reared in tortuous, unlighted and unpaved
streets, was not the proper garb for urbane and humanistic
Italy with her cobble-stone pavements and *torchères* projecting from every *palazzo*. It was but a world-wide fashion thrust upon a protesting state, which dubbed it
"Gothic"—barbarous—in derision. Neither was our architecture from 1820 to 1850—a thing of Greek temples
and porticoes—a true reflection of the pioneer spirit of
young America or of the culture Mrs. Trollope writes
about so annoyingly. In our contemplation of the progress
of architecture, we must not forget that we are dealing
with the work not of some mysterious destiny, but of
human hands,—hands that, inspired or in very bravado, or,
again, by mere chance, now fashion a new thing, now idly
copy the old.

So, also, architecture is a language, a vernacular, in
which the architect expresses himself and which the people
understand. It is a thesaurus of architectural idiom packed
with treasures, from the Parthenon to the Tribune Tower.
A writer, such as an architectural critic, expresses himself
in the current vernacular. If he used old English or the
vocabulary of the Faërie Queene, he would be regarded as
pedantic; if he invented new and original words which he
thought better expressed his ideas or the spirit of the times,
he would be unintelligible. So if the architect tries to put
a Greek temple of the fifth century B. C. to use as a filling-
station, he may well be accused of pedantry; on the other
hand, if he builds a church of entirely new forms, such
as the Church of the Holy Family in Barcelona, people will
not only not understand him, but will think he is a lunatic
to boot. Originality is strong medicine,—an overdose is
often fatal.

But architecture, like language, must live and grow, and that means change. New forms inevitably appear, through necessity, accident, or genius. A new invention, a new science, a new step in human progress call forth a host of new words. The automobile, the aeroplane, the World War have extensively enriched our vocabulary. So, in architecture, a new thing like the sky-scraper or reënforced concrete must eventually be expressed in appropriate architectural forms. In both cases, however, to make the analogy more complete, we usually go to the great storehouse of the past for our needed word or form, and then remould it to our heart's desire. The very words "aeroplane" and "automobile" are eloquent of such dependency. When the philologist exhibits this human frailty it is never questioned, but when the architect does so it brings down upon his head the wrath of the critics.

If there were no exceptions to this custom of going back into the past the future of language and of architecture would indeed be depressing. But there are. Tongues are enriched with original words by the people through the humble agency of slang. In architecture original forms spring from a different source. They are the gifts of genius. A Richardson, a Sullivan, a Saarinen have appeared at critical periods, have given us new forms and breathed new life into our architecture, in the wise providence that shapes our arts and our ends. Such apparitions must always be exceptional but they are those inspired exceptions which when they do occur give an impetus to creation and without which architecture would run from sterility to decadence.

One of the best definitions ever coined is that which describes architecture as frozen music. Consider the colonnade. The spaces between the columns are the measures.

These spaces are divided regularly by smaller architectural features which are the beats. A resulting rhythm pervades the whole. Repeat the feature and the rhythm, and style is born. (The word "style" is a very familiar one in art, and we shall find it especially useful in architecture; we should be as helpless without it as the zoölogist without the word "species" or the young preacher without the word "challenge.") Fashion, which causes the repetition of the building itself, spreads the style. Economy preserves it, for in a great work like a building it obviously costs far less to copy and repeat the pattern than to keep on inventing and constantly changing it.

Style may have at least two different significances: it may be "decorative-constructional-historical," or else purely "decorative." Previous to the fifteenth century, for instance,—in fact, in large part down to the middle of the nineteenth century—only one style of architecture prevailed at any given time; so that when we speak of Chartres Cathedral as "Gothic" we mean not only that its arches are pointed, but that certain structural peculiarities of concentrated strains and balanced thrusts are present, certain flying buttresses and groined vaults that could not exist in any other than a Gothic building, and further, we mean that it was built some time between the twelfth and fifteenth centuries, a period in which every building throughout Christendom was built in like manner. When we speak of Sancta Sophia as "Byzantine" we mean not only that its walls are encrusted with a particularly lovely kind of mosaic, but that its dome is supported by that marvelous invention of old Isodorus known as the pendentive; and we also know that it was built in that twilight time between the fifth and tenth centuries. The style of these buildings is of the first significance.

During the last hundred years, however, particularly in America, a certain eclecticism has prevailed in which, for reasons which will be explained later, all styles are used with equal facility, if not with equal felicity. So that today when a building is spoken of as "Gothic" or "Byzantine" the term no longer has an historical or even a structural significance; its meaning is entirely decorative. Let me illustrate. We see a great skeleton of steel going up on the next corner where once, perhaps, in other days we played ball or rolled hoops. We know it is going to be an apartment hotel because of the huge ugly sign, but unless we examine the architect's drawings there is no possible way under heaven of even guessing at its architectural style. Some day the workmen will come along and begin to hang up terra cotta cornices, columns, and other decorative features. If these are ornamented in the same manner as Chartres Cathedral we will call the building, when it is finished, "Gothic"; if, on the other hand, their surfaces are decorated with the flat and intricate ornament of Sancta Sophia we will call our apartment hotel "Byzantine," even if its name is the "Ritz-Broadmoor"! Such nomenclature is absurd, of course, but we must put up with it until some future historian with a better perspective than ours can properly sort out and label the work going up under our noses, with labels which, we may be well assured, will have the proper structural and historical significance.

Viewed as decoration only, architectural style is very simple, for there are only three basic styles—the Classic, the Romanesque, the Gothic. There are countless varieties of these three styles but they are the three great fountain heads.

Viewed historically, the matter is almost as simple. Begin

with the rise of Greek art or culture—which is the same thing—500 B. C., and divide the history of Europe into five hundred year epochs, and see what you have. These half millenniums are very strange. Perhaps the "so-called human race," as Bert Leston Taylor loved to call it, in the restless sleep which we call life turns over every five hundred years. Perhaps there is a seventh inning in the exciting game of existence in which a merciful providence allows us to get up and stretch ourselves and even throw a few things. Perhaps life is a rhythm with its fullest expression as the node reaches its highest pitch, sinking almost to nothingness as the internodes at five hundred year intervals start us off for another ascendency.

The period of 500 B. C. to 1 A. D. is the age of philosophic democracy with its godlike expressions in Greek art; from 1 A. D. to 500 A. D. is the age of imperialism, and its pragmatism expressed in Roman art; from 500 A. D. to 1000 A. D. is the age of feudalism—the Dark Age—with its deep-browed art of the Romanesque; from 1000 A. D. to 1500 A. D. is the Middle Age—the age of ecclesiasticism, of religious fervor, of the Crusades, incarnate in the ecstasy of Gothic art and the cathedral; from 1500 to the World War is, in its sense of modernity, the Renaissance—the age of science and capitalism—and its art is known as Renaissance.

For a watcher of the skies to see a new planet swim into his ken is a thrilling thing, but to stand on a peak of the past and stare at a new era stretched out before us is far more wonderful. Yet that is surely what we are doing. What the new era will bring we do not know. We can, like Cortez' men, but look at each other with a wild surmise.

The architecture of the first and second of these five hundred year periods is termed Classic. Classic architecture is based on the use of the famous three orders—the Doric, the Ionic, and the Corinthian. An order is composed of a column with its base, shaft and capital, while the part which rests upon the column is called the entablature and is composed of architrave, frieze and cornice.

The orders are best identified by their capitals. The Doric capital is very simple, strong and masculine—a block with a bed mould beneath. The Ionic capital is the most graceful and feminine; it is easily recognized by its pair of curious but beautiful spirals called volutes. The Corinthian is the most splendid; its capital is covered with acanthus leaves—the discovery, you will remember, of the meticulous Callimachus. These orders were "invented" by the Greeks, who used them very simply in a post and beam construction. The Romans conquered the orders and made Roman citizens of them, but considerably changed them in the process. They invented or borrowed from the Etruscans and added to the original orders the arch with its products, the vault and the dome.

The fall of the Roman Empire meant the fall of architecture as well, and the style that arose like a dank fungus out of the bones of the Classic carcass is called the Romanesque. It lasted throughout the entire third period of five hundred years. It was a strong barbaric style with little use of the orders, whose broken forms, cast down by the Visigoths and overgrown by the morning-glories of the Campagna and the grapevines of Provence, had almost disappeared from memory. It used the arch extensively, particularly in a heavy recessed form, and employed the vault to cover the aisles of the rude churches.

A brilliant offshoot of the Romanesque was the Byzantine. In its dully glowing hues it reflected that after-glow of the Roman sunset which shone about the court of

Justinian. It depended upon color, not upon light and shade, for its architectural effects; hence the beautiful use of marble and of mosaic, the best that the world has ever seen. The great gift of Byzantine art is the pendentive. A pendentive is a spherical triangle, and, by the use of four such triangles tucked in between the tops of arches erected on a square, you can bring the square at the bottom to a circle at the top. This enabled the builders of Sancta Sophia, the first and greatest monument of Byzantine art and one of the three most precious buildings in the world, to crown a space square in shape with a round dome—something that the Romans with all their engineering skill and common sense had never thought of doing. Sancta Sophia is in decay. America, if others will not, should restore and preserve it.

From the Byzantine, branching farther and farther from the parent stock, sprang the Moslem arts of Arabia and North Africa. Carried into Spain by the Moors, we see its most beautiful example in the Alhambra, begun in 1248. The Byzantine closer at home we find along the east coast of Italy at Ravenna, where Byzantine ornament was applied to Italian basilican plans, and in glorious St. Mark's in Venice, a church roofed with domes resting on pendentives much after the manner of Sancta Sophia.

The early Romanesque churches of western Europe were roofed with wood, and the chronicles of the Middle Ages are filled with accounts of terrible fires that destroyed these ancient fanes. In Italy and in France at about the same time persistent efforts were being made to fire-proof these buildings. The earliest method used was to cover the nave and side aisles with what are called "barrel" vaults of stone. A barrel vault is a half cylinder like a nutmeg grater or the top of a prairie wagon. It required very heavy walls to keep it from spreading, and it made the church very dark. Undaunted by failures, the monkish architects kept on trying, and their next improvement was the introduction of the groin vault. This is a highly ingenious and scientific device which is, in effect, the intersection at right angles of two barrel vaults. By a repetition of these groins the whole length of nave and aisle could be covered. The groin vault allowed of the use of high-up windows, and concentrated the weight of the roof on successive points of support, which were strengthened by buttresses. One more invention was left for the Romanesque builders, and that was the vaulting rib. No ribs had been used previously, even by the Romans. By building the ribs first and laying in between them the stone surfaces of the groins, greater beauty, stability and ease of construction were effected.

I mention these steps in the method of construction in considerable detail because each one of them was leading inevitably to the glorious dénouement of the thirteenth century—the Gothic cathedral—that marvelous architectural paean which without them would have been unsung.

The Gothic style is usually dated as beginning with the construction of the choir of the Abbey of St. Denis near Paris in 1140, or with the beginning of the Cathedral of Amiens in 1220. Leaving aside the important political, ethical, and social causes of this mighty era in human inspiration and progress—of which Dr. Cram says in effect that the thirteenth century is the greatest century in human history, for here alone we find the perfect union of religion, philosophy, and art—we find that the Gothic style owed its existence to three inventions. The first of these was the ribbed vault already mentioned. This made possible the rapid construction of the stone coverings of the vast interior. The second invention was the flying buttress. This astounding device, counteracting the thrust of the vaults, enabled the mediaeval builders to run their cathedrals up to unbelievable heights. Beauvais is one hundred and sixty-five feet in the clear. The third and most familiar invention of all is the pointed arch. Originally used for structural reasons, it was soon adopted for ornamental forms, and has become the hall mark of the Gothic style.

Equipped with these devices, the Gothic style burst into a radiance that illuminated the thirteenth century as with a light from heaven. It is no wonder that old Abbé Suger, on beholding the choir of his own church at St. Denis, exclaimed, "When the house of God, many-colored as the radiance of precious stones, called me from the cares of this world, then holy meditation led my mind to thoughts of piety, exalting my soul from the material to the immaterial, and I seemed to find myself, as it were, in some strange part of the universe, which was neither wholly of the baseness of the earth, nor wholly of the serenity of Heaven, but by the Grace of God I seemed lifted in a mystic manner from this lower, towards that upper, sphere. And I was accustomed to ask travelers returning from Jerusalem, those who had seen the riches of Constantinople and the splendors of Sancta Sophia, whether these marvels surpassed St. Denis."

Gothic art rapidly spread to England, Germany, Spain, and Italy. In England the long, low cathedrals, slumbering in green pastures and beside still waters, are only second to those mighty fanes across the channel. The Gothic art of Spain and Germany was largely imitative, and that of Italy was purely decorative—witness the beautiful stage scenery of Orvieto, and Siena; but Gothic art as typified in the master cathedrals of Chartres, Amiens, Paris and Rheims, ranks shoulder to shoulder with the Greek art of the Periclean Age. "Je sens deux hommes en moi," wrote Victor Hugo. Two spirits fight for control in the fabric of the cathedral: the vast destructive power of the weight of the great vaults is held by the throat and pushed back by the upholding strength of the flying buttresses. Is not the conflict akin to this in every one of us the mysterious bond that joins our hearts to the heart of the cathedral?

The Renaissance, as its name implies, was a rebirth—a rebirth of every human art and faculty airily assumed to have been lying lifeless since the days of Greece and Rome. In architecture it was a definite abandonment of Gothic art and principles, and a distinct return to the Classic, particularly to the Classic style of Imperial Rome. In it every intellectual effort was clothed with the vestment of beauty. If you have the enthusiasm of the humanist you see in the Renaissance the sun rising in Italy, and spreading light and warmth in succession throughout the countries of western Europe, finally to set beyond an ocean in America.

The Renaissance in Italy is associated with great names rather than with styles: the daring Brunelleschi, who, it may be said, almost invented the Renaissance in the Duomo of Florence; the versatile and virile Alberti; the cultured Bramante; the gentle Peruzzi and the mighty Angelo. Charles VIII and Louis XII, with their roving eyes and their good taste in such matters, saw the Italian maiden in some of their trans-Alpine forays, were enthralled, and took her back to France and made her chatelaine of countless châteaux and palaces.

The Renaissance in France is a far different thing from the Renaissance in Italy. It is distinctly a matter of styles, and it is distinctly French. The styles are named after the kings, and they follow in glittering sequence: Francis I, Henry II, Henry IV, Louis XIII, Louis XIV, Louis XV, Louis XVI, the Directoire, the Empire. Go to the Louvre and in its pavilions and colonnades you can read the continuous story of the "rebirth" in France.

The sun continues on its westering march. With midday in France, in Italy the light was fading in the Baroque of the men who came after Michael Angelo, while in England dawn was breaking in the ruddy style of Elizabeth. But there the skies were never cloudless and blue as in France and Italy. The succeeding Jacobean style was stormy and disordered, and fair weather came not until the day of the great Sir Christopher Wren, who, like a Georgian Joshua, commanded the sun and moon to stand still! In this Georgian style, as we shall discover, the Renaissance, in its strictly architectural sense, came finally to its end in our own American colonies, and it is this fact, whether we like it or not, that indissolubly binds us with the art history of Europe.

CHAPTER II

THE COLONIAL PERIOD 1630–1800

Architecture in the Spring-time

THE EARLY AMERICAN STYLE

THE historian of architecture is fortunate in at least one respect—he can always start his story with his best foot foremost. Architectural movements have almost always a rise, a culmination, a decline, and it is the first period, the rise, that is invariably the most attractive and interesting part of the tale. Innocence, childhood, youth—even their stumblings and mistakes are fascinating. Who does not turn to them with tenderness and kindly envy? An analogy has often been drawn between the life of an architectural period and that of a human being; and, as in the human span, it is the spring-time of an architectural style that is most appealing. How unattractive it would be to have to begin the story of the Renaissance with such pompous bores as Bernini and Palladio instead of the lithe and sprightly personalities of Donatello and Brunelleschi! So with our own architectural growth the Colonial is our youth, the architecture "with the school-girl complexion," and, carrying the metaphor to an ultimate conclusion or rather an ultimate beginning, the "Early American" is its infancy, a style that can hardly walk and which talks to us with the baby-talk of helplessness.

Had the beginning of our architecture been coincident

with the discovery of America it would have seen at its birth wonderful things—the last expiring gasps of the Gothic and the radiant rise of the Renaissance. So hard did the Gothic die in England that in 1492 Henry VII had not yet built the almost unbelievable vault in his chapel in Westminster Abbey, while in France Gothic architecture was giving up the ghost in the flaming traceries of the Palais de Justice at Rouen and the northern tower at Chartres. In Italy, the Renaissance in its ruthless exuberance of youth was tearing down the Coliseum to build the Cancelleria, St. Peter's was begun, Lorenzo de Medici was dying in Florence, and what long, long thoughts were shaping in the mind of the boyish Angelo!

But architecture in America does not properly begin for another one hundred and fifty years, and of the buildings which we have left to us today few were built before yet another fifty years had elapsed. By that time many changes had taken place in the old countries.

In Italy the men who came after Michael Angelo were now lining the city streets with churches built on that robust variety of the late Renaissance which is known as the Baroque. In France the light of the Roi Soleil was being dimmed by the English under Marlborough, and the gay and joyous architecture of the châteaux of Blois and Azay-le-Rideau had grown up into the dignified orders of the Invalides and Versailles. In England—and this is of paramount importance—we find Sir Christopher Wren at the height of his fame. St. Paul's, begun 1675; the Library, Trinity College, Cambridge; Hampton Court; Greenwich Hospital; St. Bride's—these all not only attest his genius, but establish the type of design which we call the Georgian style. In Sweden, Germany, and Holland we find a form of Renaissance practiced in many respects common to all three, rejoicing in high stepped roofs, rather rough and swollen Classic detail, and the use of brick almost to the utter exclusion of stone.

Turning our eyes back again from the old countries to the new, we shall observe that colonists from all these countries settled in America. In 1700,—hardly two score buildings built before that date are now standing—we find New England occupied by the English under the Massachusetts Bay Company; Rhode Island by English, who, under the leadership of Roger Williams, had founded a colony for freedom from the austerities of the Puritans; Connecticut by the English; New York by the Dutch, who had lined the banks of the Hudson with the enormous estates of the kingly patroons. Delaware had been settled by the Swedes in 1638, but in 1655 had surrendered to the Dutch under Peter Stuyvesant and later had fallen into the hands of the Duke of York along with New Netherlands. New Jersey, originally Dutch, became English in 1664, first under the Duke of York and later in part under William Penn and the Quakers. In 1702 New Jersey had become a royal province with her own government. In 1682 William Penn arrived in America and with his Quakers began to settle his great estate of Pennsylvania. Philadelphia was founded in 1683. Virginia, the first of the English settlements in America (Jamestown was settled in 1607) was from first to last thoroughly English in character, reflecting the aristocratic side of English society as opposed to the democracy of New England. Virginia condemned the executioners of Charles I and welcomed to her shores the Cavaliers fleeing from the vengeance of the Protector. She was rewarded by Charles II, and her governors and the House of Burgesses up to the Revolution were distinctly loyal to the Crown.

To a group of persecuted Catholics under the leadership of the Calverts it was given to found in Maryland the only colony in America where complete religious toleration was allowed, and later the Lords Baltimore governed Maryland under a form of proprietorship similar to Penn's personal ownership of Pennsylvania. The Carolinas seem to have been settled by emigrants from various colonies and from England. Charleston, founded in 1670, proved a valuable buffer to Spanish aggression from the south. The Carolinas differed considerably. North Carolina contained many Quakers, Scotch Presbyterians, Irish, and others, but few negroes. Its settlers were small farmers. In South Carolina those settlers who were not English were largely French Huguenots. They had rice and cotton plantations on a large scale, and many slaves. The owners of the plantations lived in Charleston, which became the center of social life in the South.

Georgia, the last and most southern of the colonies, was not settled until 1734, when General Oglethorpe conceived the idea of founding an asylum for debtors in the New World. It was at once successful and grew rapidly. It resisted attacks from the Spaniards in 1739, and became a royal province in 1752.

Florida was discovered in 1513 by Ponce de Léon, and the first permanent settlement in North America was established by the Spaniards in St. Augustine in 1565. The honor of an earlier settlement also lies with the Spaniards, who founded Santa Fé, New Mexico, in 1582. Later Spain planted missions in southern California.

The contribution of France to what is now the United States is confined to the settlement of Louisiana with its capital in New Orleans, founded in 1718, and, before this, to the explorations of Champlain, Marquette and La Salle, whose colonizing efforts were limited to the erection of forts and outposts stretching from the mouth of the Mississippi to the St. Lawrence. In the fall of Quebec in 1759, France saw the end of her dreams of a colonial empire.

We have, then, to examine what the men of these various nationalities coming from the cultured and busy capitals of the Old World to the primeval solitudes of the New effected in architecture. Theoretically, two courses lay open to them: either to evolve a new kind of building, a new style based upon the limitations and stern necessities of their condition, perhaps taking for its inspiration the Indian wigwam, or to copy in the New World as closely as circumstances would allow the homes so recently forsaken in the Old. To quote Hale's oft-repeated aphorism, "Man with difficulty creates, even in a new world," and we find the colonists, far less independent in matters of art than in religion and politics, without hesitation and apparently without thought that any other course was possible, immediately trying to reproduce the beloved homes of their fatherlands.

We once thought, or rather assumed that when the spinning-wheels and the grandfathers' clocks were safely landed, the colonists laid low the forests and built for themselves log houses in which the logs lay horizontally one on the other, keeping their position by their roughly-squared shapes and their interlocked ends. But in this we are probably mistaken. Mark Twain, not so much interested in architecture, claims that the Pilgrims fell first upon their knees and then upon the aborigines. But they surely in any event needed immediate shelter from the rigors of a cruel climate and the unappreciative Red Men, and the higher criticism holds with good reason that, as log houses were unknown in England at least, the English colonists built what was common among the peasants at home—huts of staves and saplings, the spaces filled in with wattles daubed with clay. One of the first of the New England settlers describes these huts half buried in the hillside, and says, "In these poor wigwams they sing Psalms, pray and praise their God, till they can provide them houses." Very soon, however, frame houses began to appear, and it is to these frame houses that our term "Early American" applies. We shall find, I think, that in their original condition these very early buildings must have been entirely mediaeval in appearance.

The fact that the Early American houses, as we know them, do not bear any striking resemblance to the houses of the same age in England or in other parts of Europe seems to contradict this statement, but if we could have walked the streets of Salem or Boston in, say, 1675, the resemblance of the half-timbered and gabled houses to the humbler homes of the Elizabethan and Jacobean periods in England would have been striking—"like an English village badly transplanted," said Lowell. After the first necessity of building temporary shelters had passed away, the colonists began constructing permanent homes, and these are the houses which, more than any that came later, resembled the old homes across the seas. That they did not exactly conform to their prototypes was due to the necessity of using new and strange materials, and to the lack of skilled workmen, certainly not to any conscious effort to be different.

We used always to be told that the Colonial style could be definitely separated into several geographical divisions, and that within these divisions buildings, especially houses, were built in certain definite manners that gave a particular and easily recognizable character to each. The favorite divisions were New England Colonial, Dutch Colonial, and Southern Colonial; sometimes Pennsylvania Colonial was added. There is some basis for such classification, but the effect of it is deleterious, not only on the inquiring mind, but on the practicing architect, who has almost succeeded in designing a type house whereas none existed in the eighteenth century.

The geographical differences in Colonial architecture are so few that they may be listed in a single paragraph: a great fondness for wood in New England, the use of field stone in Pennsylvania, a preference for brick in the South on account of the omnipresent clay. In the South, also, we find a greater use of carving and of mahogany in the interior finish. The approach to the mansion is more often guarded with elaborate wrought iron gates, and little local peculiarities, such as the two-story piazzas in Charleston or the free-standing and enormously wide chimneys in Virginia, are observable. The Dutch Colonial houses have been prime favorites for standardization with the modern architects. These usually have shingled sides with a huge gambrel roof comprising the second story and often extending out in front or rear to include the porch as well. The stories are low, and casement sash are usually used in the grouped windows. These houses certainly are not like anything ever built in Holland, nor, curiously enough, are the houses the Dutch themselves built in this country. The gambrel roof seems to be a New England invention. Nevertheless, the old streets of Hurly and Kingston-on-Hudson, with their comfortable and low-lying houses, certainly look Dutch. Perhaps the wish is father to the thought with us.

The main features of the Colonial style appear in all sections of the colonies. Wood, brick, stone we find from

Maine to South Carolina. Gable, hip or gambrel roofs collect moss along the Santee River or snows on the shores of
Cape Cod, indifferently. Sliding windows with their little
square panes of glass looked alike upon the black man
singing in the cotton fields and Mistress Chew tripping
along the cobbled streets of Philadelphia. Great logs
crackled in the same sort of fireplaces the while William
Byrd warmed his legs after the hunt at Westover or John
Hancock sipped his mulled wine in Boston and discussed
with Adams the presumptions of the Crown. The same
beautifully carved balustrades which aided and supported
the grandsire in his gouty ascent of the staircase, and
furnished the grandson a means of swifter and more ex-
hilarating descent, existed in North and South alike. Youth
and beauty were reflected from the same mirrors, danced
under the same chandeliers, made love in the same parlors,
in every one of the thirteen colonies.

So great was the community of interest, so excellent the
communication between the colonies, and so unanimous in
persons of quality the desire to be in style, that differences
of climate, occupation, ancestry, even building material,
did not prevent a general uniformity. When we consider,
in addition, that the center and fountain head of fashion
was in one place only—London—it is small wonder that
you could walk out of the drawing-room of a Charleston
planter and into that of a merchant in New York City
without noticing the difference. The most sumptuous of
our colonial mansions were not comparable in magnificence with the great houses of Georgian England, but, on
a reduced scale, many an American room would have been
the peer in taste and workmanship of a room of similar
character and station in England.

The Colonial Period in America extended over a longish

stretch of time. If we begin it with the oldest surviving building, of which the date is certain, 1632, and end it in 1820, the date of the inauguration of the Greek Revival, we shall have covered nearly two hundred years. There were great changes in England in that time: the rude Jacobean style, covering the reigns of James I, Charles I, Cromwell, Charles II and James II, had succeeded the Elizabethan; William and Mary and Queen Anne had followed, and after them the four Georges. The reigns of each of these monarchs is reflected more or less in the architectural modes of the times, and above them all tower the great figures of Inigo Jones, Sir Christopher Wren and the brothers Adam, with batons in hand, directing the form and tempo of architecture from the score of Palladio before them.

Each of these styles in turn, in a more or less vague way, was exported to the colonies; each in its turn was fashionable and unfashionable, and each has left its monuments. For this reason it has been found necessary for all recent writers on this period to attempt some classification within the period. Ware calls it all the Georgian period; Hamlin divides it into Formative and Republican periods; Eberlein calls all American architecture up to 1720 Colonial, and after that Georgian; Kimball calls all prior to 1779 Colonial, and from that date to 1857, Early Republican. In this volume we hope we shall not make confusion worse confounded by still another classification. From the earliest settlement to 1800 we shall consider as the Colonial period. This will be divided into, first, the Early American from 1630 to 1700; and second, the Georgian, from 1700 to 1800. A subsequent chapter will treat of the Post-Colonial or Transitional style, from 1790 to 1820. The Georgian and the Post-Colonial overlap about ten years.

I shall advance no argument for this classification other than the contents of the chapters themselves, nor shall I break a lance with any of my predecessors over their chronologies, great as the temptation or diverting as the spectacle might be. The reason for this classification in the broadest sense is given by the architecture itself—as it looks to the author, at least. There is obviously a tremendous difference in the architecture on either side of 1700. Before this period the few buildings are crude, humble and almost without architectural embellishment. They are distinctly Elizabethan, almost mediaeval. After 1700, slowly at first and then more frequently, buildings increase in size, but—more important—they are suddenly adorned with ornamental architectural forms. This treatment is not at the beginning weak and timid, but starts out immediately robust and confident. We call it Georgian. It can, if we please, be divided within itself. Its earliest phase shows the virile influence of Queen Anne and Christopher Wren, as in the Hancock House, built in 1737, Boston, and in the well-known door of the Dummer House, Byfield, Massachusetts. Its middle phase, down to the Revolutionary War, is the developed Georgian, vigorous, consistent and complete. Excellent examples are Westover in Virginia, Mount Vernon, and Independence Hall. Its last phase, from the beginning of the Revolution and extending clear through it into the first decade of the next century, shows the Adam influence. Slender columns and delicate ornament are here characteristic, as in the Russell House in Charleston and the Nichols House in Salem.

Architecture throughout all this period seemed entirely dependent on the information then available. This information came from three sources: memory, architectural books, architects themselves. With these distinctions in mind, we may very well characterize the three types of the Colonial period as follows: Early American—the age of memory; Georgian—the age of architectural books; Post-Colonial—the age of architects.

It was once generally taught and believed that the Colonial style was the work of carpenters. These useful members of society were represented as a race of supermen— mute, inglorious Bramantis and Michael Angelos in aprons; men without education or resources who, in some mysterious way, with pea augur and jack plane called into life the lovely doorways of Salem or the stately panelling of Carter's Grove. It is now known that the carpenter of those days would have been as helpless without his handbook as without his ripsaw. It was once thought that, with something of the unerring taste of the Periclean Greek and the logic of the mediaeval Frank, his soul revolted at the thought of copying stone in wood, and that for this reason he attenuated his proportions and refined his ornament, to let all the world know that pine was his material and that he gloried in it. Perhaps a few men like Samuel McIntire in Salem, had some such vision, but, for the most, these carpenters were but intelligent and skillful mechanics, not philosophers or architects.

This is best shown by the usual procedure in building a house in those days. If the owner was something of an amateur and dabbled in architecture, he might sketch out the rough outlines of what he would like; if not, he wrote a brief specification. Such a document is quoted by Fiske Kimball. In it the owner, Deputy Governor Samuel Symonds of Ipswich, in 1638, instructs the builder concerning the size and the location of the chimneys, doors, windows: "For windows let them not be over large in any rooms, and as few as conveniently may be." The arrangement of the rooms and often the disposition of the façade were dictated by local custom—in New England, for instance, five windows in a range on the façade with the door in the center, while in the Carolinas the entrance was likely to be on the end with a two-storied "piazza" on the south façade. The owner, then, and the master carpenter pored over the handbooks together. These handbooks were numerous and varied, and appeared from time to time. There was the architectural Bible, Palladio, published in 1663, and Scamozzi, published in 1669. Inigo Jones's designs were spread abroad in 1727, and were followed by the Vetruvius Britannicus, a most popular book. There were other works by James Gibbs, Isaac Ware, Robert and James Adam. Still simpler handbooks for the carpenter were published by Robert Morris, Batty Langley and William Paine.

A favorite and cruel amusement of the modern critic is to run to earth these old doorways, mantel-pieces, etc., of these venerable carpenters and show from what particular designs they were filched. Doubtless, as today, the carpenter was sometimes instructed to copy from some adjacent house this cornice or that balcony. This he would do as nearly as he could with great skill and diligence; and if he was often forced to vary from the Palladian rules in regard to proportions and detail it was because the limitations of his material, wood, obliged him to do so. In the latter part of the 18th century columns and architectural motives were attenuated because this fashion had been dictated by the brothers Adam; but in the early days of the Georgian style, as in Westover and Carter's Grove, Virginia, the pilasters, mouldings and other features, were in their full Palladian size, and might just as well have been carved from stone as from wood.

A generation ago the Early American style received short shrift from the historian, but now, thanks to the careful and scientific investigations of Kimball, Isham, and Jones, Donald Millar and others, the growing interest in the style and its greater popularity, it deserves more attention. Kimball lists in all some two score houses now standing as built in the sixteen hundreds; there are, besides, three churches, and that is all.

In what sort of house did Miles Standish so vicariously court Priscilla? In size it was very small; in arrangement, extremely simple. You entered a low door in the center of the long side which faced the street. In front of you in a short hall was a narrow winding stairway upward bound; on either hand was a squarish room, each with a huge fireplace. These fireplaces were served by one huge chimney through the center of the house. This plan was subject to slight variations: often the house was enlarged by the sweep of the roof carrying down in the rear, and creating thereby an ell or continuous addition; sometimes there was but one room with the chimney at the end, and sometimes—a great improvement—there were two chimneys, one at each end of the house. Almost touching the top of your broad-brimmed hat were the bottoms of the hewn summer beams. Under your buckled and square-toed shoes the floor was of wide oak boards, and you leaned your blunderbuss against walls either roughly plastered or exposing the laths or wattles that filled the spaces between the wooden uprights.

On the second floor were two rooms of the same size and disposition as those below. The second story rooms were for storage purposes, while of those below one was the kitchen and dining-room, and one the parlor, which was used in part as a bedroom.

Often one or more of the walls of the first story rooms

was boarded with wide boards chamfered or moulded along the edges and running either vertically or horizontally. This rough wainscoting, with its knots and tool marks tinted and shaded by time to the softest of cinnamons and umbers, is painstakingly emulated today by decorator and architect alike, who take a short cut with lye, dirty water, vinegar, and wax, to give their knotty spruce and pine the Early American flavor! These slight mouldings were not the only surrender to the lusts of the eye. Sometimes the great oak lintel over the fireplace opening was chamfered and checkered as in the fine old example in the Metropolitan Museum, where the ornament seems to show the influence of the art of the red-skin. The balusters of the diminutive stairway were often turned in a sturdy fashion, or cut to a pattern out of flat boards, and the bottoms of the summers were sometimes simply checkered or chamfered.

The furniture which is worth a king's ransom today was then the simplest and cheapest obtainable. The best place to visualize the interior of one of these ancient dwellings is in the American Wing of the Metropolitan Museum in New York, where original furniture is placed in what approximates authenic settings. It was the custom in those distant days to make careful inventories, and if one is out of reach of the American Wing or other repository of Early America, one may use one's imagination on one of these lists. The list of Governor Eaton of New Haven is typical of the more pretentious houses. It was compiled in 1657, and contains, besides furniture, fabrics of upholstery, hangings, Turkey rugs and needle work; metal work of iron, brass, silver, and pewter; books, pottery, glass, and even a globe!

The furniture of this interesting period is as characteristic as the architecture, and as great a gulf separates it
from the succeeding Georgian. There were not many varieties. Chests were a favorite form. There were chests of
drawers with curious Jacobean spindles and mouldings ap-
pliquéd to the drawer fronts; and later there were a few,
more advanced in style, with smooth drawer fronts and
turned legs of the William and Mary type, desk boxes with
carved faces almost Gothic in form, cupboards with heavy
and stolid turned legs, wainscot chairs with massive backs
carved in Elizabethan fashion, and the more familiar slat
or spindle back rush-bottom chairs. Stools there were, and
benches called "forms," and trestled tables, cradles, and
beds.

Before seventeen hundred all of these are distinctly
mediaeval in character. Crudity and heaviness characterize
their straight and simple forms, but these characteristics
have not divorced charm nor even beauty. One feels that
they were first made for use and durability, and then
ornamented as much as time, pocket-book, and religion
would permit—a very sensible way to approach the making of furniture.

To quote from the Metropolitan Handbook on the
American Wing: "From all this it will be seen that before
the first half century of colonization had passed, in fact
before the great Puritan immigration was over, the American colonists up and down the seaboard were well equipped
with most of the necessities and some of the luxuries of
comfortable living. Their houses were cozy and pleasant,
their rooms furnished cheerfully, and their taste was attuned to an appreciation of beauty in textiles, metal work,
glass and pottery. All of these created a domestic interior

reminiscent to a surprising degree of the English or Dutch homes from which the settlers of New England and New Amsterdam came."

The exterior of these fascinating old-timers was equally characteristic. It is a moot question whether they ever stood in the good Elizabethan manner with ribs exposed, the filling of clay and plaster uncovered by the warm coat of clapboards that we see in every case today. It is most probable that when first built these houses were in appearance as in fact "half timber," but that experience of a winter or two with the rigors of a New England climate speedily called forth the covering of heavy siding that becomes from then on a principal characteristic of the colonial house of the North. The gable roof was steep and pointed, and the eaves low—a decidedly mediaeval characteristic and in strong contrast to the flat slope and the higher eaves or cornice of the later Colonial. The house was always broadside to the road with the gables at the ends. The windows carried out the mediaeval picture for they were small, with hinged or casement sash filled with leaded glass in diamond or square panes, in contrast to the wide up-and-down sliding sash with the wood divisions and square panes of the 18th century. This casement sash we know was often filled with oiled paper or parchment instead of glass, and colonists were advised to bring "paper and linseed oil" for their windows. The great chimney was often built of wood, framed in much the same way as the house and covered with clay, though bricks were made from the earliest times in all the colonies. But the outstanding characteristic of the Early American house, the hall mark at least in New England, is the over-hang of the second story. This had no practical purpose except to increase by a foot or two, where it wasn't needed, the dimensions of the second floor; and it furnishes us an eloquent proof of the mediaeval character and the Elizabethan model of these earliest architectural efforts. This over-hang occurs usually in the front, as in the Capen House, Topsfield, Massachusetts, and the House of the Seven Gables at Salem. Sometimes it occurs at the ends as well. The final Elizabethan touch was in the heavy carved pendants that usually hung from the bottom of the over-hang. These furnished the sole ornament of the exterior as the doorway, which is usually the first stem to bear an architectural blossom, remained barren till the next century. A last distinguishing feature is the lowness of the house on the ground, raised only a step or two on a foundation of boulders.

In the South there were houses built of brick in the 17th century. Those at Jamestown, of which the foundations alone remain, were the earliest. They were destroyed, perhaps in Bacon's Rebellion, and the town was deserted after the removal of the colonial capitol to Williamsburg in 1699. The famous old brick tower of the fourth consecutive church—the fifth was completed in 1922—is all that remains visible of the first English colony in America.

Directly across the broad James, over in the cotton fields, are two other precious monuments of Early American architecture: one is the so-called Rolfe House at Smith's Fort. Dilapidated, deserted even by its negro proprietor, it stood like an old aristocrat, ragged and indigent, begging for alms on the highway. Within are some panelling and pilasters of the early 18th century. A few miles away is its decrepit neighbor, Bacon's Castle. This "ancient" of the old régime is in even worse case, for ignorant and soulless hands have ruthlessly destroyed and altered it in part, and have added excrescences hideous enough to

rouse young Bacon from his grave and start him off on another rebellion. But desecrated as it is, it is extremely interesting. Its curved gables, jutting bays and picturesque
gables are entirely Tudor. These two precious buildings
should be acquired immediately by the State or otherwise
and preserved for posterity.

While we are in this fascinating vicinity let us continue
eastward along the James to St. Luke's in Isle of Wight
County. Here, in a clearing in the pine forest, is an astonishing building, the oldest church standing in the United
States—and it is Gothic! Gothic not only in architecture,
but in chronology! What does that mean? It means that
it is the last legitimate descendant of that glorious race
that arose in Chartres and Notre Dame, the last puny offspring from the stone loins of Salisbury and Durham. It
means that its builders, who may have come over with
Captain John Smith long before the productive days of
Inigo Jones and Sir Christopher Wren, were ignorant of
the Renaissance or oblivious to it.

This ancient fane was begun about 1632. Until about
thirty years ago it had stood roofless, windowless, and de-
spoiled of its interior wood-work since its abandonment in
1836. Up to that time it had been used continuously as a
place of worship for two hundred years. Its restoration
was done with zeal and skill, thanks to the energy and
initiative of the Reverend Dr. David Burr of Washington. In fact, a few thousand of the bricks used in its repair were taken from the ruins of the ancient church at
Jamestown, across the river. Some of the old bricks found
in St. Luke's Church bear the date of 1632, but its architecture is the best evidence of its antiquity. The large east
window and the nave windows have curious blunted
pointed arches and brick tracery. Heavy buttresses uphold

the walls, and a great square tower, almost Norman in its proportions, marks the portal. Its crown was probably battlemented, as the postern wall still is. It is in many respects the most precious building in America. May it be ever preserved!

The two other ancient and honorable churches of the 17th century should also be mentioned. They are the old Ship Church in Hingham, Massachusetts, and the Gloria Dei (Old Swedes Church) in Philadelphia. The first is as far removed architecturally as it is geographically from the lovely Gothic parish church on the banks of the James. It is the Puritan meeting-house to the last nail and shingle. Gaunt and bare, it "lieth four square" to its God and to the sea. Its framing trim and nautical, its lines "ship-shape and Bristol fashion," the lookout on top, and the utter absence of the softer amenities of architecture, bear out the tradition that its builders were sea-faring as well as God-fearing. It is supposed to have been built in 1680. The Old Swedes Church in Philadelphia, dating from the very end of the century, is a comical little building, looking for all the world like an Early American frog about to jump into a Georgian puddle. There is nothing whatsoever about it that seems to be Swedish. Its Colonial ornament is evidently of the early days of the succeeding century.

The 17th century closed with settlements well established in each of the colonies. With the Indian menace abated and the wolf, physical and metaphorical, driven from the door, the colonist at last could sit down in his arm-chair, wipe the sweat from his brow, stretch out his legs, light his long-stemmed pipe, and look about him. What he saw in his house was for the most part neither beautiful nor comfortable, and certainly did not become a man of his position or property. How he set about to beautify his home we shall see in the ensuing section on the Georgian phase of Colonial Architecture.

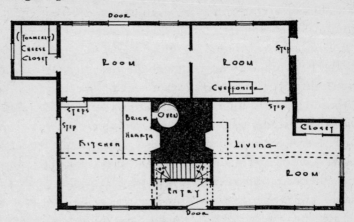

Fairbanks house, Dedham, Mass., reputed to have been built in 1636. A typical example of an early American house.

THE GEORGIAN STYLE

If we look back over our entire architectural history with its ups and downs, its sharps and flats, its lights and shadows, I doubt if we shall find anything more beautiful, more vigorous, more expressive of its times or more harmonious with them, than the good, developed, robust Georgian of about 1750—an appropriate garb for the culture of the day.

With the coming of the 18th century architecture advanced at a lively rate. This, of course, was owing to security at home, the rapid settlement of the colonies, and increasing ease of communication and trade with the mother country. Trade and immigration from England brought over tidings of the great architectural revolution occurring there. The last of mediaevalism had disappeared with the passing of the Jacobean style. Inigo Jones, another St. Augustine, had preached the Classic Gospel of Palladio so effectively that Sir Christopher Wren found England a converted and submissive diocese over which he held sway as a sort of architectural archbishop. In other words, beginning with Queen Anne (1702–14), architecture in England assumed under the direction of Wren that form of the Renaissance which we call the Georgian, and which continued its course until the middle of the reign of George III. This same Georgian was exported to America in books describing it and by men familiar with it.

The earlier aspects of this Georgian style owing their existence to Sir Christopher Wren were the most robust and vigorous, often full of little baroque surprises of which the broken pediment was the most popular. The increased prosperity of the country was directly evident in the expansion of the house plan. The arrangement with which we are so familiar—the house with its length toward the street, the entrance opening into a central hall which ran across the entire house—dates from about 1720. At the end of the hall was the main stair, under the landing of which there was often a rear door. On each side of the hall were two rooms nearly symmetrically arranged. The second story arrangement was similar, only the purpose of the rooms varying. The chimneys, instead of being in the center as in the early American house, were properly placed at each end. Such an arrangement almost invariably resulted in a façade with a central door and two windows on each side, the second story having a range of five windows on an axis with the openings below. Gunston Hall in Fairfax County, Virginia, built in 1758; the Longfellow House in Cambridge, Massachusetts, built in 1759; or, better still, the Dummer House, Byfield, Massachusetts, built about 1715, are examples of this plan.

In any sort of building, throughout the ages, the first

architectural feature to be decorated has been the portal. The lion's skin was nailed on the jambs, probably, before the Mycenaeans carved the beast himself in stone and set him over the lintel. While events in America moved too rapidly to afford, as far as I know, any examples of Colonial houses bare except for the doorway—although perhaps the Parson Williams House, Deerfield, Massachusetts, 1707, is an exception—yet the door received early and loving attention. The doorway of the Dummer House mentioned above is an early example of the hardy and vital influence of old Chris Wren. A famous doorway is that of Westover, 1727, with its baroque broken pediment. Carter's Grove has a curious doorway with a complete pediment all of brick of a different color and kind from the rest of the house, apparently designed and made in England. The streets of Salem, as every one knows, are full of doorways, though mostly dating from the latter part of the century. But the strangest and most picturesque of all is the undated, polychromed doorway from Westfield, Massachusetts, in the Metropolitan Museum. Clearly some ardent soul, some forgotten genius, here grappled with the problem of original design; there is nothing of the copy book, only the struggle of an artist, deprived of learning, to realize an idea. Fan lights and side lights, without which no modern Colonial house could exist, were, as a matter of fact, unknown before the Revolution. They both seem to have been introduced—the fan light first—by Bulfinch, who changed the Adam scheme of a semi-circular light to an elliptical one. So, reader, in building your Colonial house do not introduce a fan light into an Early American design, as I have seen done. Other examples of fine doorways are # 20 Turner Street; the Pineapple House, # 7 Brown Street; the Osgood House; the Lord House,

Washington Street; and # 129 Essex Street—all of Salem.

Next to the door and its frame, the most important architectural feature of the house was the cornice. This starts with almost nothing—merely the eaves trough—and then gradually acquires the accoutrements of Classicism: the cyma, or moulded top member, the fascia, or vertical plain board; the modillions, or brackets; dentils, or little wooden blocks; and the bed mould, or lowest member. The entire entablature, consisting of cornice (described above), frieze and architrave, was very seldom used, but an example exists in the Apthorp House, New York City. If pilasters were used, often a portion comprising the entire entablature broke out from the face of the wall just above the pilaster or column cap. A good example is the famous Craigie or Longfellow House in Cambridge, Massachuetts. Where a house had gable ends the cornice usually continued only a foot or so around the corner, but when it had a hip roof, the cornice extended across the ends as it did along the front.

Window trim was usually simple, though fine cornices or even pediments were occasionally used over the window heads, especially in framed houses. We generally regard blinds—green ones—as essential and as part of the decorative scheme. Not so our ancestors, who used them for utility's sake—sometimes on the outside, more often on the inside, and very often not at all. If the house were brick, the brick or stone lintel was an important feature. It was sometimes segmental, but usually a flat arch, with a projecting keystone and sometimes with skew-back as well.

There was little other ornament on the exterior of the house. If the house was of wood, it would have overlapping or dropped siding, sometimes—in questionable taste—

furnished on the corners with rusticated quoins in imitation of stone or even, as in the case of Mount Vernon, grooved to imitate stone across the entire façade. This baroque touch is usually in the earlier work, the lusty influence of Wren and Queen Anne. Sometimes the quoins were of brick, as in Mount Pleasant, Philadelphia, built in 1761 and occupied for several years by Benedict Arnold, a house in which the exterior walls are plastered. Frequently the front and back of the house were of wood, while the ends where gables occurred were of brick— a very charming treatment. Much more rarely the ends of the house were of wood and the front of stone, as in the Royall Mansion, Medford, Massachusetts, in which pilasters near the corners run the full height of the façade.

Red brick is as characteristic of the Colonial as white woodwork. The hard red brick of Virginia, laid up with a mortar of sand and oyster shells, is as good today as when it was laid. The favorite arrangement of the bricks was in the design we call Flemish bond, composed of stretchers and headers alternating. This makes a strong and beautiful wall. The solemn assertions that the brick for this house or that was brought over from England are, modern criticism tells us, for the most part fairy tales, in the same category with steeples designed by Wren and beds slept in by Washington.

We must not forget the dormer windows. So little use was made of the attic that one wonders if these dormers were not intended primarily as decorative features, much as the staircase was. They are so essential to the character of the Georgian house that a manor without dormers would look as bald as its proprietor without his peruke. The dormers were usually high, narrow, with a simple pediment, and ordinarily spaced on axis with the windows below. In the rebuilding, after the fire, of the old College Building at William and Mary in Williamsburg, Virginia, designed by Wren, the Colonial character of the building was entirely lost by the omission of the dormers.

The magnificent interiors are one of the architectural joys of a good Georgian house. They are far freer from faults of design than the exteriors which, like the four walls of a protecting reliquary, have held the precious contents inviolate through generations. On entering the door the sumptuous note is struck at once by the stairway. Throughout the Georgian period, almost without exception, the stairways were elaborate, evidently a prime feature in the designers' minds to be beautified for its own sake. Turned and spiral spindles, splendidly moulded hand rails of walnut or mahogany, delicately carved brackets under the ends of the treads, newel posts coiled up like a chambered nautilus, are familiar to all of us. Sometimes the balustrade is in the Chinese manner with intricate interlacing rails, as at Brandon or at Battersea House, both near Petersburg, Virginia. It took the practical Jefferson to abolish the stairway as an *objet d'art* and make it a useful object, tucking it away in a side hall, thus giving birth to the canard that he had built Monticello, forgetting the stairway!

A foil for the stairway and a rival to it was the wall treatment of any principal room, which in its simplest aspects always consisted of at least a wood base, a chair rail, and a cornice with moulded trim about the doors and windows. The changes in this scheme, the various lively and vigorous solutions of a problem that is not too easy, inspire with joy any explorer of a Georgian mansion. In the American Wing of the Metropolitan Museum in New York examples succeed each other like so many old masters on the walls of the Tribuna or the Salon Carré. The parlor from Haverhill, Massachusetts, has one wall panelled from floor to ceiling in wood and painted in olive gray, the others papered above the dado with a lively landscape full of trees and hunters. The Samuel Ruggles House has a chaste dado and plaster cornice in oyster white with a paper in brown monotone of a Poussin landscape of temples and Classic ruins. But the room from Marmion, Virginia, about 1730, is the most astonishing: Ionic pilasters supporting a bold cornice, all painted in ruddy hues to imitate marble, while between are panelled walls with painted vases and garlands, the whole room glowing in color and vivacious with its artistic indiscretions. Standing in this room we wonder at the origin of the traditional Colonial interior, all in cold and sickly white paint, with ivory walls and ceiling, as different from the Marmion room as a slice of frosted angel food from a piece of plum pudding with a "stick" in it!

Nobler than any of these perhaps, are the great walls of Carter's Grove, Virginia, 1751, all panelled from floor to ceiling in wood, or the truly palatial parlors and drawing-rooms of the Miles Brewton House in Charleston, with its great coved ceilings and its pedimented and pilastered doors and windows below. This old mansion, started in 1765, had all the vigor and verve of the virile Georgian. So great was the élan of the craftsmen that they even attempted some original design, amusing examples of which may be seen in the detail of the door frames. This Pringle House, as it is called in Charleston, is a grand and lusty old aristocrat. He ought to be a state or national possession, and kept alive forever as an example of virility in architecture. Some of the ceilings in this old mansion, like some of those in Philipse Manor, Yonkers, 1743, and even some in Mount Vernon, are not chaste at all, but are far removed from our traditional conception of Colonial propriety. Broken scrolls, garlands, birds, even busts, appear in their French Rococo—a style smacking of the salon of Voltaire or the boudoir of Du Barry.

So far we have not mentioned the fireplaces, the principal feature of every important room. In no feature of Colonial design is so much variety (one hesitates to say originality) used. What if they were borrowed from Swan's "British Architect" and from Inigo Jones? Like many a healthy emigrant they make fine citizens. Mantels were of two kinds—either a chimney breast that breaks out from the wall and extends clear to the ceiling, or else a fireplace flush with the wall. In the first case there was often a pilaster at each corner that framed the fireplace and made an architectural unit of the whole, as at Carter's Grove. Where the fireplace is flush with the wall the space above it is occupied by an over-mantel. This could be extremely elaborate, as in the Miles Brewton House, Charleston, with a broken pediment, pilasters and frame; or very simple, as in the Nichols House, Salem, where a moulding, broken at the corners, forms a panel. In either event the fireplace opening is seldom more than four feet wide and is usually less in height than in width. Almost invariably there is a shelf, and around the opening a "facing" of marble or tiles. These Georgian fireplaces bear their age plainly stamped in architectural lines on their faces. The early ones are simple enough in form, but with crude mouldings, as in the room from Woodbury, Long Island, in the Metropolitan.

About 1740 there came a craze for copying the elaborate and often rococo designs published in the handbooks. By the time of the Revolution refinement reappears, with its

best expression around Salem in the work of Samuel Mc-
Intire. Then, as the style expires at the end of the century,
we find the brothers Adam refining refinements in their
attenuated colonnettes, their delicate mouldings, their exquisite garlands and urns, a good example of which exists
in the parlor just mentioned from Haverhill in the Metropolitan Museum.

In examining houses of this early period we are lucky
enough if we find a wooden cornice, a turned baluster, a
marble mantel, unchanged by the changing generations.
To expect to find original paint, decorations and furniture
is to expect the unreasonable, if not the impossible. Ten
years is the length of time that ordinarily elapses in our
American life before moth and rust, wear and tear, and
change of style demand that the house be "done over." A
house built in the middle of the Georgian period, therefore,
has probably been "done over," if it has been continuously
lived in, eighteen to twenty times! These restorations,
much as they may pain the archaeological mind, are necessary to keep a building alive. Our foremost architectural
archaeologist admitted to the writer that probably not
more than ten per cent of the stones forming the exterior
of the mighty fabric of Notre Dame in Paris were those
placed there in the thirteenth century. Restorations are
particularly necessary in buildings lying in a latitude where
zero weather occasionally obtains. In Chicago masonry
porches, terraces, etc., are so wrecked by frost that they
have to be rebuilt at least every fifteen years. Southern
houses of the Georgian period therefore show the effect of
restorations less than those north of Mason and Dixon's
line, but in any clime anything so superficial as decoration
is sure to have been changed many times. In view of this
fact the work done by the Metropolitan Museum in New

York in assembling and furnishing its American rooms with original material and in accordance with authentic descriptions is valuable beyond any power of description, and in the few comments made in these pages on Georgian decorations and furnishings we shall not wander far from the American Wing.

The first impression one gets in strolling into these lovely rooms is that of color. Where is the sickly white or the non-committal ivory with which we, as a matter of habit, cover our modern Colonial woodwork? The woodwork in the parlor from Haverhill is an olive gray; that in the alcove from Alexandria is grayish blue; that in the room from Portsmouth, Rhode Island, is stained and glazed with a reddish tint. The extraordinary marbleized and polychromed interior of Marmion we have already mentioned. The room from Oriole, Maryland, is an oyster white, and that from Woodbury, Long Island, a dull blue. There were white rooms, of course, especially in the latter part of the period, but the evidence is that they were not usual.

Our Georgian forbears decorated their plaster walls much as we do. They were hung with fine materials such as damask or chintz; they were papered or they were painted. The fabrics and papers were usually imported— the paper from France and England, which also furnished Chinese paper hand-painted in China. "Le style Chinois" was very *chic* among the best people at home and abroad in the middle eighteenth century. You will remember the stairway at Brandon, and the slat balustrades on porches and roofs. Often the papers bore portraits of Englishmen like Pitt and Burke who had espoused the cause of the colonies against the crown, or were imitations of textiles called "flock" papers. The French papers often had Paris views or romantic scenes of ships, classic ruins and picturesque peasants, sheep, goats, and other bucolic felicities.

Probably no branch of Americana has been as well studied and thoroughly written about as furniture. These pages can add nothing to all this lore and erudition; they may only epitomize. As in architecture, a tremendous change occurred in the design and construction of furniture at the beginning of the eighteenth century. In the Early American work walnut had been the favorite wood, and turned work, as in the William and Mary mode, the favorite method for its decoration. All this is now changed. Mahogany is *de rigueur,* and all the lines must be curved and all ornament carved.

To attempt an inventory and description of the furniture in a Georgian house would be a task too comprehensive for this volume. As I look about the room in which I write there is nothing, except the resplendent radio and the "period" orthophonic, that my Georgian forbears did not have and have better—lovely and graceful chairs with cabriole legs, some with open backs carved in the delicate interlacing of the Chippendale manner, and some with backs upholstered in old velvet or damask, calicoes and chintz or decorated with needlework; lowboys and highboys with the broken pediments and turned vases that we see over the doors of the period; sofas of various kinds, some with gracefully curved silhouettes, entirely covered with velvet and some with open backs; tables of all kinds, round, pie-crust, and square, tiptop or stationary, and some with various ingenious arrangements for collapsing and extension; desks and secretaries, rococo, inlaid or Chinese; "grandfather" clocks, more standardized in design, perhaps, than any other article of furniture; mirrors in all sorts of charming shapes with broken scrolls and eagles, or edged with rococo ornament in gilt; footstools, chests of drawers, four-poster and canopied beds; fire screens—everything, in fact, that human beings of culture and wealth would require for comfortable and polite existence. If we divorced modern plumbing, electricity and central heating from our modern establishments, we should be in exactly the same situation as the Georgians of the eighteenth century. Candles and lamps furnished the light, and what is more beautiful than the light of candles tossed back and forth from a myriad of shimmering lustres? The buffets and cabinets, to use the proper technical word, "groaned" with their fine services, silver platters or tankards perhaps from the hands of Paul Revere, as skillful with the burin as they were with the bridle; "table setts" from China and far Cathay, and fine English porcelain from Derby and Worcester; Chelsea-Derby statuettes of William Pitt and John Wilkes, and Stegel glass that would drive a modern bottle collector absolutely frantic.

Pictures and prints hung on the walls. The painters of the period were Smibert (1684–1751), the earliest of note; Copley (1737–1815), the much tooted and tiresome Benjamin West (1738–1820); C. W. Peale (1741–1826); Trumbull (1756–1843), whose pictures have given, or used to give, every boy his vision of the Revolution; and Gilbert Stuart (1755–1828), the best portrait painter of his time, and fortunate like Peale in having the great Washington often as his model. Of course, pictures by these great men didn't hang on every man's wall. The average citizen was content with prints of various sorts. This was the golden age of mezzotints in England. "To be sold at Mr. Smibert's in Queen Street on Monday, the 26th instant, A Collection of valuable Prints, engraved by the best Hands, after the finest pictures in Italy, France, Holland

and England. Some by Raphael, Michael Angelo, Poussin, Rubens and others"—so runs an advertisement in 1734 from our friend John Smibert, who sold prints in addition to painting portraits. Pictures burned on glass, as terrible in their time, doubtless, as our Indian heads burned on leather, miniatures, and silhouettes—all were popular. Decorative maps were the fad in 1749 as they are in 1936; so were engravings of famous places like Harvard College and later Mount Vernon. We of today, however, may take all the credit for discovering the sofa cushion and the stuffed fish.

The architecture of the latter part of the Georgian period in America, from the close of the Revolution to the beginning of the following century, and in many cases a decade or two beyond, is dominated by that extraordinary family, the brothers Adam in England. More than Inigo Jones or Sir Christopher himself did these rare Scotchmen rule the taste of two nations. The only parallel that occurs to me is the architectural sovereignty of our own H. H. Richardson seventy-five years later, and his was confined to his own country. As the glories of the Athenian Acropolis had inspired Stuart and Revett and in the following period will give birth to the Greek Revival, so in the case of Robert Adam it was the rediscovery of an ancient art that gave him the touch of Midas. Excavations at Herculaneum and Pompeii in 1748 had thrilled all Europe, and especially our young friend, who shortly thereafter was sojourning in Italy, that hothouse of artistic seedlings. On his return to England, Robert and his brother conceived the canny idea of founding a complete architectural system that should comprise the planning and exteriors of buildings and their interior decoration also, not only in its architectural features, but in the furnishings and furniture as well. This system of design seems to have had a dual inspiration: the great ruins of the Palace of Diocletian at Spalato, which Robert reconstructed in a remarkable book, and the excavations at Pompeii. From the first he got sound ideas of planning, of the element of surprise in contrasting rooms of varying sizes and various shapes, square, round, oval, and octagonal. From Pompeii he acquired those extremely delicate motifs so characteristic of his style—the wreaths, the pateræ, the honey-suckle and the fan.

On his return to England he immediately occupied the public eye, first by his appointment as sole architect to the King, and secondly by the construction, with his brother James, of that great edifice, the Adelphi ($\dot{\alpha}\delta\epsilon\lambda\phi o\acute{\iota} =$ the brothers) of Portland Place, and of whole city blocks and scores of famous country houses which we have no space to mention in an account of architecture in America. And as though this were not enough, the brothers blossomed out as inventors and took out patents on the manufacture of "compo" ornaments. I wonder how often the harassed or witless architect, or the wily contractor, in thumbing the pages of the catalogues of compo ornaments, offers up thanks to the brothers Adam for another opportunity to fool the public.

No sooner was the ink dry on the Treaty of Paris than British bottoms were laden with books, furniture, and even the famous compo ornaments of the new style. The Adam mode became the fashion. What more can one say? So much did it become the fashion that to the amateur today and to many an architect this later manifestation of the Georgian is more typically Colonial than the robust mode of pre-Revolutionary days. To many the slender columns, the result not of carpenter philosophy but of fashion, the fan lights, the charming festoons, the delicate pateræ, and those lovely mantels with their medallions of "fair youths, beneath the trees" and "heifers lowing to the skies," constitute the whole gamut of Colonial architecture. In reality they form only its last phase.

While we have awarded the palm to the earlier and more vigorous type of Georgian, there is much about this younger scion, the last of the race, to make it especially interesting and appealing. It sees, for instance, the best of the architectural craftsmen and the first of the professional architects.

The far-famed, the fabled, the almost legendary, carpenter-architect comes before us in the flesh in Samuel McIntire. He is a beautiful specimen—a museum piece—and, knowing his habits and methods of work, we may rightly draw conclusions covering the whole species, although he was undoubtedly the most remarkable member of it. The turning tide of business has left Salem much as it was in the eighteenth century and the great fire of 1914 spared every one of McIntire's masterpieces, so we might say of this *rara avis* that we have the nest and the eggs as well! His thirty years of work were entirely confined to Salem, Massachusetts. Here he was born; here he died. He came of a family of wood carvers, housewrights and joiners, into which he was born in 1757.

His life ran its course side by side with the golden days of Salem's prosperity. Not only was this lively town an important seaport, but it contained ship-building yards second only to those of Boston. Brigs from Salem cruised the Ivory Coast, and, braving the Malay pirates, rounded Marblehead. The good brig "Grand Turk," owned by Elias Hasket Derby of Salem, was the first to make a commercial trip to China, while Captain John Carnes of the same port made a fortune by his secret expeditions to

Sumatra, taking out rum and salt codfish, and bringing back shiploads of precious wild pepper. With the Revolution came prosperity for Salem, and her shipyards rang to the strokes of adze and hammer as they fashioned the timbers of American frigates and privateers. This good fortune was repeated in 1812, so that Salem became famous in her day for the wealth of her merchants and ship-builders. An aristocracy similar to that of Charleston was established, and all was merry as a marriage bell.

The ship-building brought many skillful carvers and much good white pine lumber, and the union of the two is evident in many a lovely cornice and exquisite mantel. McIntire's first house was built in 1782 and his last in 1810, so that this work lies exactly within the limits we have set for the later phase of Georgian in the Adam vogue. McIntire himself was a great Adamite. Not only in the delicacy of his ornament did he follow the dictates of fashion, but in the sterner matters of plan and elevation he pursued a new mode—a mode probably established by Bul-finch, the first architect of the Republic and himself an ardent disciple of the "Adelphi."

The typical Salem house was certainly not beautiful in form. It was big and cubical, three stories in height, and all of white pine. Its roof was so low pitched as to appear flat and was edged about with a wood balustrade. Often it was surmounted by a cupola and captain's walk. The doorway, usually its most beautiful feature, was located in the center and facing the street, though McIntire built some "end to the street" houses. The plans, often with halls bisecting the house in two directions, were usually ama-teurish and inconvenient. Sometimes McIntire in a timid way essayed the grand manner of Bulfinch and Adam with a projecting bay and an elliptical staircase, as in the Waters

House where it is picturesquely likened to a pulled-out shaving, with which (how can one resist the temptation to observe?) McIntire was supremely familiar.

The question of McIntire's right to the title of architect is merely academic. His epitaph, a form of evidence never highly reliable, says "He was distinguished for genius in architecture, sculpture, and music," but Dr. Bently, his best friend and patron, describes him only as a wood carver and housewright, and so also does his death notice in the Salem "Gazette," although a highly complimentary obituary in the same paper refers to him as an architect and versatile musician. He never seems to have had the social status of a professional man, perhaps through lack of a polite education. He was always the respected and well-liked mechanic, his modesty and "sweet manners" never presumed beyond what he regarded as his station in life, and we do not find him knocking at the beautiful portals which he built for the Peirces, the Nichols, the Crowninshields, or the Derbys. He did make one bid for national recognition as an architect, and that was in the competition for the National Capitol in Washington. His design does not indicate great gifts as a designer, and, as we know, he was not selected. The measure of his disappointment we do not know. He might well have taken consolation in the fact that Thomas Jefferson fared no better than himself.

With his several brothers, Samuel McIntire operated a large wood-working shop back of his home. When a patron stalked into his shop with a commission, Samuel undoubtedly sketched out a scheme and drew the plans—and they were badly drawn, too—which always followed the type we have just described; then the construction and framing of the house were given over to his brothers, while Samuel himself put all his efforts and great talents on the design and execution—often by his own hands—of the entrance, the mantels, and the interior trim, of which the door-casings were often extremely elaborate. In the details alone, the glory of these old houses exists and without exception they are charming in proportion, excellent in execution and impeccable in taste.

The porch of the Gardner Pingree house, 1810, has an elliptical plan, very slender Corinthian columns, fan and side lights, and a cast iron balustrade. This is McIntire's last and best house. The wide horizontal bands of white marble separating the stories give it an architectural character lacking in the ensemble of his early work. "Oak Hill" contains lovely mantels and exquisitely carved door-casings. Among his other houses are the Peirce-Nichols, the Tucker-Rice, and the Derby houses, and his largest and handsomest work, the Cook-Oliver mansion. McIntire did not confine himself exclusively to dwellings, for we find him building the Salem Court House in 1785, collaborating with an architect named Bancroft. This building was destroyed in 1839. In 1804 he built Old South Church. Many charming things come from McIntire: the square fence posts with the little attached pilasters and the delicate urns on top; the federal eagle with his short wings and long neck; the baskets of fruit in low relief. They were good when McIntire first chiseled them, and, humiliating as the admission is, we have never been able to improve them. I am inclined to believe after all that McIntire was an architect.

The late Georgian died hard, and years after Jefferson had built his capitol in Richmond and his beautiful Monticello, we find the delicate Adam columns and the exquisite

Adam urns and festoons being erected here and there entirely oblivious of the fact that the Georgian style was officially dead.

An example of this is the Nathaniel Russell house in Charleston, South Carolina, built as late as 1810. It is the perfect norm that the scientist likes to get hold of. Here are no embarrassing exceptions and uncatalogued idiosyncrasies to explain. To the architect the plan is always his first interest, and in this case it is highly satisfactory—no uncertainty and amateurish scheme of hall and stairs, but a compact and clearly articulated arrangement that would do credit to all the accumulated knowledge of an accomplished practitioner of the twentieth century.

The two principal features of the plan are the oval dining-room and the elliptical staircase. The oval room, as mentioned before, was an innovation of Robert Adam and a favorite form with Bulfinch and the Post Colonial architects, the best known example being the famous "Red Room" of the White House, designed by Hoban in 1792. The elliptical stairway is a *tour de force* in grace and fearlessness. It is free standing in a square hall, and it rises, like Jacob's ladder, apparently without terrestrial support to a plaster sky covered with a resplendent sun-burst of delicate rays and streamers. The turned and twisted balusters of "Carter's Grove" and "Westover" have given way to plain thin rods, and the hand rail is a simple encircling band. The façade of this lovely building is typical throughout: three stories, the first low and plain; the second a *"piano nobile"* with high windows ensconced in shallow archways and opening on an exquisite wrought iron balcony; the third more or less a repetition of the first; and the whole crowned with a delicate cornice and balustrade of turned spindles entirely concealing the slightly sloping roof. The stories are separated by band courses, a favorite device of Bulfinch and McIntire and the Post-Colonials.

What the Nathaniel Russell House is to the late Georgian expression of urban architecture, "Homewood" is to its expression in the country house. As we know, "Homewood" was built in Baltimore County, Maryland, by Charles Carroll of Carrollton. What could be more magnificent? It is now a treasured possession of Johns Hopkins University, an example for other great institutions to emulate. Its outstanding characteristic is its sheer beauty—beauty of proportion, beauty of detail, beauty of color and material. If one cares to analyze this architectural lily, its Adam germination is evident in ensemble and detail. The center building with the flanking wings, the low roof, the slender graceful columns with their palmetto capitals, the Palladian windows then fast going out of use, and the marble panels over the windows, are of the right shape, size, and position to a hair's breadth. The carpenter-architect, whoever he was, who carved the facets on this gem, was as good a man as McIntire.

The case of Charles Bullfinch presents difficulties to the classifier, if not to the Classicist. Most of his work is of the Adam or late Georgian tradition, but his work on the Capitol in Washington and his unquestioned status as a professional architect place him in the "upper form" of the Post-Colonial; so, if I may, I will discuss his work, or at least part of it, here and now, and postpone his biography till the later chapter.

Bulfinch's early life and maturity belonged to Boston. Compare him to Sir Christopher Wren, if you like, but the comparison is a feeble one for there was nothing of the gusto or originality of the great Englishman in the refined and meticulous Bostonian. Bulfinch was another Adamite, the most distinguished high priest of the cult, and he stuck to his divinity long after the other Post-Colonials had turned their faces to Rome. However, his work is full of charm and seldom lacks distinction. It was his disastrous experience with the building of Franklin Crescent in Boston in 1793 that made a professional architect of him, as this ambitious scheme which he largely financed as well as designed—another Adam idea—threw him into bankruptcy. The thought of rehabilitating one's fortunes by becoming an architect would be whimsical in any age, but in the eighteenth century it was unprecedented as well. In Bulfinch's case, however, it was highly successful.

Unfortunately, there is little domestic work of Bulfinch left, but the region in Beacon Hill around Mount Vernon Street and lying in the shadow of his greatest work, the State House, is redolent of his memory and influence. The second Otis House, number 85 Mount Vernon Street, is very typical. It used to be a mulberry color, but has long since been painted gray. The house contains the shallow arched niches with their high windows and iron balconies, the three stories, the flat roof with its open balustrade, with which we became acquainted in the Russell House five hundred miles away. On the garden side, however, are some delicate Corinthian pilasters extending through the second and third stories—features that Bulfinch used in the end pavilions of his Crescent, and that Robert Adam had used in Manchester House and other places long before. Three other old houses near the State House on Beacon Street were built by Bulfinch.

If you will remember, the brothers Adam had introduced a complete system of design, decoration and furniture along with the construction of a building. This our late Georgian housewrights attempted to do as well, but less rigorously, perhaps. The change of style is the most marked in the furniture. In the earlier Georgian you will remember that the Chippendale style, with curved supports, and cabriole legs and the rococo chair back, was the mode. All of this suddenly changes about 1790. Sheraton and Hepplewhite become the rage, each with its square or delicately turned legs and its chaste outline. The two famous London cabinet makers based their designs on the precepts and examples of Robert Adam. The Hepplewhite guide was published in 1788, and Thomas Sheraton issued his catalogues between 1791 and 1804. Our American cabinet makers, of whom the most famous was Duncan Phyfe (we shall have more of him later) combined more or less loosely the designs of these manufacturers, producing charming work in entire harmony with the American Adam environment. Sofas, sideboards (of which Adam designed a new form with side pedestals and urns) secretaries, chests, tables, even the ubiquitous grandfather clocks took on a new and chastened character. The good old swashbuckling days of the full-blooded Georgian were over. Refinement and suavity were the mode, which, by the way, did not in any sense imply austerity or Puritanism.

The changes in fabrics, wall hangings, draperies, and so forth, were hardly sufficient to record here. One charming room, the parlor from the Eagle House in Haverhill, Massachusetts, will suffice. The walls are covered above the dado with a French wall paper brilliantly depicting a hunting scene. The windows are hung with plain green silk hangings, draped over a curtain rod in the classic form of a heavy golden arrow. The color of all the woodwork is a light grayish green. In an adjoining room the woodwork is ivory, and the curtains of "toile de jouy" are hung from charming wooden cornices painted ivory with little medallions of musical instruments picked out in gold upon them.

In our discussion of the Georgian period the emphasis has been chiefly upon domestic architecture for the very good reason that it is vastly the most important in volume, and the most interesting in character and quality as well. Next to the houses in architectural and social importance were the churches, and to the lover of architecture they smile like so many babes against the august parenthood of London City and the Wren churches.

Those London churches! Who can resist their appeal or gainsay their pallid beauty? The "city" when Wren, the great architect, strode its cobble-stone lanes and supervised his fifty churches, all rising at once, was a city of homes and church-goers. Today it is a metropolis of warehouses, deserted by night, and by day echoing to the noise of vans and trucks. Seventy-five years ago Charles Dickens on a Sunday morning made a visit to the churches and wrote, "As I stand at the street corner, I don't see as many as four people at once going to church, though I see as many as four churches with their steeples clamoring for people." He was listening to the bells that fascinated me as a boy—perhaps the old London cry that began

"Oranges and lemons," say the bells of St. Clement's;

and ended

"Here is a candle to light you to bed,
And here is a chopper to chop off your head."

rang in his head.

Rather than have this happen he goes into one of the old churches and sits down in an ancient deserted pew. He seems to inhale some "strong kind of invisible snuff." "I wink, sneeze and cough. The clerk sneezes, the clergyman winks, the unseen organist sneezes and coughs (and probably winks), all our little congregation wink, sneeze and cough. The snuff seems to be made of the decay of matting, wood, cloth, iron, earth and something else. Is the something else the decay of dead citizens in the vaults below? As sure as death it is! We stamp our feet to warm them, and dead citizens arise in heavy clouds. Dead citizens are in the very bellows of the organ. They stick upon walls and lie pulverized on the sounding-board over the clergyman's head, and when a gust of air comes tumble down upon him."

But the ancient churches gave forth something more than the dust of dead citizens. They exhaled the sober beauty and the prim loveliness that was drawn in so gratefully by every one of our meeting-houses; for every empty pew in London they filled a dozen in America, and today their spires beckon us irresistibly to Wren's city.

If these now ancient and hoary English churches warm the cockles of our twentieth century hearts, imagine their appeal to the colonist or to the early republican not separated from his home long enough to have recovered entirely from a national nostalgia. To be more exact, the immediate model for the American church was not so much the work of Wren as the work of Gibbs, his brilliant pupil. Gibbs it was who introduced in St. Martin's-in-the-Fields the use of the portico thereby marrying the pagan portico to the Christian spire, whereas in the Wren churches there is little attempt at architectural pretense about the portal. The three seventeenth century churches, which are all that we possess, have been described in our account of Early American architecture, so we have only to mention the early and late Georgian.

The earliest churches are in the South and they belonged almost without exception to the established Anglican Church. The early eighteenth century church, in addition to being the "house of God," was a little theatre for the display of all the pomp and circumstance that a carefully graded and maintained social fabric required. Bruton Parish Church in Williamsburg, "Court church of colonial Virginia," is an excellent example. We can sit in one of the old box pews and reconstruct a service in colonial days. The gentry arrive by coach and horse and loiter around the door in animated debate on the stamp tax. We notice that the men sit on the north side of the church and the women on the left, by order of the vestry. Pretty soon the students enter—among them a number of young Indians—and are herded up to the gallery and locked in. In the gallery of the north wing, humbly standing, are the servants of the parishioners. Soon, in a hush of expectancy, the tower door opens and the Court procession begins. It is headed by His Excellency, the Governor—Spotswood or maybe Lord Botetourt. With all the dignity inherent in the representative of His Most Gracious Majesty, King George the Third, he enters his pew next the chancel. This is a magnificent affair with a great red canopy over it bearing a valance around which runs the governor's name in large gold letters. After the governor come the Council of State and the members of the House of Burgesses and the Surveyor General, and then the service begins; but, as it is very long and the church very cold, we shall conveniently call a halt in our imagination and steal out.

A very different procedure, far more charming if less magnificent, is described by Alice Morse Earle as customary in some of the smaller country parishes of New England. "Just fancy the flurry on a June Sabbath in Killingly in 1785, when Joseph Gay, clad in velvet coat, lace frilled shirt, and white broadcloth knee breeches, with his fair bride of a few days, gorgeous in a peach-colored silk gown and a bonnet trimmed 'with sixteen yards of white ribbon,' rose in the middle of the sermon in their front seat in the gallery, and stood for several minutes, slowly turning around in order to show from every point of view their bridal finery to the eagerly gazing congregation of friends and neighbors."

There were remarkably few types of colonial churches, and of course each one followed in detail the style of its particular period. Books could be written and books have been written on the subject, the best among them being "Early American Churches" by Aymar Embury. Perhaps we may best epitomize all this material and our own observations by selecting three types of churches for consideration.

The first and earliest is the Virginia type. These Virginia churches, of which St. Luke's has already been described, are usually small, always of brick, seldom have spires—a short tower and cupola sufficing—and never a portico. As they are all of the Church of England faith, the interiors have a simple Anglican chancel with pulpit and lectern on either side and the sanctuary with its altar in the middle. The interiors are usually simple and bare, the ceilings flat or barrel vaulted, and across the entrance end there is a balcony. Churches of this type in Virginia comprise St. Luke's, Smithfield; Bruton Parish Church, Williamsburg, 1715 and 1769; St. Peter's, New Kent County; Blanford Church, Petersburg; Christ Church and Pohick Church, Alexandria, in both of which George Washington served as vestryman; in South Carolina, Goose Creek Church, Charleston, and St. Paul's, Edenton.

The second type is the New England meeting-house. It resembles the Virginia type in the modesty of its dimensions but it is built of wood instead of brick. A high, slender, nervous steeple supplants the squat, sleepy tower of the South, and the interior has the denominational center pulpit instead of the chancel. Side galleries occur more often, perhaps. In this, as in all three types, the woodwork is usually white, the box pews having mahogany rails and bases, while the chancel fittings are sometimes white and sometimes mahogany and sometimes a little of each. The New England meeting-houses are the famous: Old North, Boston, the "nest of traitors" from whose spire with its candle snuffers was flashed the news to Paul Revere; Old South Church, recently flayed of its plaster epidermis and restored to the blush of its first childhood. If Faneuil Hall was the "cradle of liberty," Old South was the perambulator, and of all its associations I like most the sermons preached there by the Rev. Samuel Willard against the delusions and cruelties of the persecution of the "witches." Other famous meeting-houses are those at Dedham, Dorchester and Lenox, Massachusetts; Bennington, Vermont; and, most beautiful of all, the First Congregational at Lyme, Connecticut. This little masterpiece is a replica of the original building burned a score of years ago and restores not only the material but the soul. It is late Georgian of the Adam type, and was built as late as 1815. The exquisite proportions of the spire, the graceful portico, the charming interior, put it in a separate niche in our gallery of meeting-houses. For one must admit that whatever beauty the meeting-houses have must be largely the beauty of holiness, since it certainly is not that of architecture, and that their charm must be in the accumulation of thousands of sunlit Sabbath mornings, and thousands of lovely youthful faces, and thousands of prayers, and thousands of songs, that lie like golden dust on the old mahogany pews and the creaking floors.

The third type is the full-blown Georgian church of the first magnitude. Christ Church, Philadelphia, is the best example. It was undoubtedly designed by Dr. Kearsley, an amateur architect, and was built in 1727–37. It could well be by the same hand that fashioned Independence Hall, and it is one of the same family of stalwart sons that includes Carter's Grove, Westover, and St. Michael's in Charleston, South Carolina. The interior of these churches is vigorous and consistent. Even where columns or piers extend through the length of the church, dividing it into nave and side aisles, a clerestory seldom occurs. The clerestory, which is ever present in Gothic churches, is the space between the roof of the lower side aisles and the ceiling of the central nave, and is usually lighted by small windows. In Christ Church it was suppressed, although the columns occur and with them a long gallery extending the length of the nave along either side. This lateral gallery is almost universal in all but the smallest of Colonial churches. Sometimes the supporting columns or posts extend to the under side of the gallery only, and sometimes, as in Christ Church, they pierce the galleries in their upward flight and extend to the ceiling of the nave.

The only other church in the same class with Christ's is St. Michael's, Charleston, South Carolina. Its corner stone was laid in 1751 and its completion took nine years. Five great conflagrations have devastated Charleston, and ten or more hurricanes, and the great earthquake of 1886—all in addition to the bombardments of the Revolutionary and Civil Wars—but St. Michael's still survives. Its brick walls are covered with stucco, which, together with its extremely massive tower 186 feet high—one can hardly call it a steeple—give the Church an appearance of great bulk, if not of grace. Documents show that in values of today the church cost $33,000, with brick at three dollars per thousand and mechanics at one dollar and forty cents per day.

St. Peter's, Philadelphia, 1758, with its high brick tower and thin spire (Dr. Kearsley was on the building committee, but there is no resemblance to Christ Church); King's Chapel, Boston, of very unusual type and very unusual history; and St. Paul's Chapel, New York, are only less important than these. Certain other great churches, such as the Independent Presbyterian Church, Savannah, 1800; First Church of Christ, Hartford, 1806; St. John's, Varrick Street, New York, 1807, recently destroyed; Park Street, Boston, 1809; Center Church, New Haven, 1812; and St. Phillip's, Charleston, 1835, are late Colonial, Post Colonial, or Greek Revival, more or less as their dates indicate.

I think it may safely be said that the Colonial church is not the equal architecturally of the Colonial house. It may further be said that the interiors of these churches are inferior to the exteriors. The charm is there, but they are full of technical defects in design. English work affords a standard of comparison. A house like Mount Airy, Richmond County, Virginia, for instance, would measure up to any Georgian house of the same period in England, but there is no American church that can compare with St. Bride's, Fleet Street, or St. Martin's-in-the-Fields, nor is there one that boasts such an interior as St. Stephen's, Walbrook. That we had no Colonial cathedral goes without saying. The reason for our inferiority in this particular domain is easy to explain. The knowledge contained in handbooks and acquired from experience was sufficient to enable the amateur and the carpenter-architect to produce the nearly perfect house, but the problems presented by a church of any size required far more technical knowledge and equipment than these. Nevertheless, with all their faults we love them still. We should cherish and preserve them, and with pride say to all men, "See! This our fathers did for us."

Of secular and public buildings of colonial days there are extraordinarily few, but architecturally and historically those that still exist are interesting. The oldest and most interesting is the Old State House in Boston. It was built in 1728, and on each side of its curiously stepped pediment the lion and the unicorn still stand, piquant souvenirs of a king's stupidity and an empire lost. Of all buildings in colonial America except Bacon's Castle, this little court house looks the most foreign. It has been called Dutch, which is, of course, absurd, for it is very much English of the Christopher Wren type. I believe the designs were surely made in London. It yields place in importance architecturally and historically only to Independence Hall, Philadelphia. What Christ Church is to ecclesiastical architecture in the colonies, Independence Hall is to the secular, and both would appear to be by the same hand, though the historians tell us differently.

The main building was erected in 1733 in that splendid period of the Georgian's young manhood. Along with its great dignity and impressiveness, we are carried away by the vigorous movement, originality, élan, of the whole design. The same freshness and exuberance attend the interior, built upon a plan of simplicity and good sense, the principal feature of which is the great east room—a perfect setting, nobly planned, for the signing of the Declaration of Independence and the framing of the Constitution. The two attendant buildings on either side are recent additions, but fit satisfactorily in the original scheme.

Other public buildings of this period are the Cradle of Liberty, Faneuil Hall, Boston, 1741, very evidently home grown, awkward, and gaunt, a kind of secular meetinghouse; the original buildings of Harvard College, quiet and domestic; Carpenters Hall, Philadelphia, 1724; and the Pennsylvania Hospital, reminiscent again of Hampton Court and Christopher Wren.

The classic example of the Adam style in the latter phase of Georgian architecture is Bulfinch's State House in Boston, commenced in 1795. It has been greatly enlarged, but the little round dome maintains its character, and keeps watch and ward over the sacred precincts of Mount Vernon Street and Beacon Hill. May it extend its benign protection over every ancient roof, steeple, or dome, in Massachusetts or any other state, which the hand of modern efficiency and exploitation threatens!

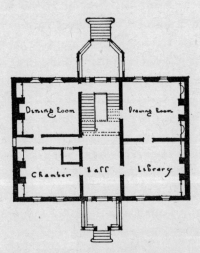

Gunston Hall, Fairfax Co., Virginia, built in 1758. A typical Colonial plan of the Georgian Period.

CHAPTER III

THE POST COLONIAL 1790–1820

The Private Property of Thomas Jefferson

It is hard to believe that the lovely Colonial work in its later Georgian manifestations, about which we wax enthusiastic today and which we endeavor so painstakingly to copy, should ever have been hopelessly out of style and discredited; yet so it was in the last ten years of the eighteenth century. This last decade or so, from 1790 to 1800, is a curious and interesting period of our architectural history. For a long time no one paid any attention to it at all; it was submerged in the general calm and unruffled sea of the Colonial style. But not so many years ago it raised its head, and has claimed a place on every architectural chart and a name of its own.

The historians have differed about this period, some claiming that it is a part of the mainland, merely the closing phase of the Colonial style, and others that it is an outlying reef of the Classic Revival. Two things about it are certain: first, it is a time of real transition, and, second, it is the personal property of Thomas Jefferson. Like Alexander Selkirk, he treads its shores, the monarch of all he surveys.

Some historians would plot our chart as follows: Colonial, 1607–1776; Post-Colonial, 1776–1789; Roman Revival, 1789–1800; Classic Revival, 1800–1855. These critics see the end of the Colonial about the time the influence

75

of James and Robert Adam was made manifest—as for instance in those lovely slender doorways of Salem—and
they would place Bulfinch's famous Capitol Building in
Boston in the same category. Then of these ten years which
we are attempting to describe they make a Roman Revival,
still further separating it from the Colonial stem. Another
name, and a good one, for this debatable period is the
"Republican Style." But it seems to me that the most
sensible classification is something like this: Colonial 1630–
1800; Post-Colonial 1790–1820; Greek Revival 1820–
1850. It will be noticed that the Colonial and Post-
Colonial overlap ten years. This does not rob the Colonial
of some of its most precious treasures, and it makes of the
last ten years of the eighteenth century a decade of real
transition, belonging, however, more to what has been than
to what is to come.

Thomas Jefferson was the first of our citizens to regard
with fine scorn the pallid and provincial beauties of Mount
Vernon and Mount Airy. Even the Adam phase of the
Colonial, the aristocrat of decoration, that last and most
courtly gesture of a society which for taste and refinement
has certainly not since been equalled, he regarded as barbaric because it did not conform to the true forms of ancient design. "The first principles," he wrote in 1781, "of
the art (architecture) are unknown, and there exists
scarcely a model among us sufficiently chaste to give us an
idea of them." It is curious that the great democrat who is
said to have received a foreign ambassador in his dressing-
gown and carpet slippers should have been so punctilious in
regard to the proprieties of architectural raiment. Architecture, as everyone knows, was merely a side line for the
man who wrote the Declaration of Independence, was
twice Governor of Virginia, spent five years at Versailles

as the successor to Benjamin Franklin, was for two terms President of the United States, and who ended his brilliant career as the founder of the University of Virginia.

His fondness for architecture resulted not from any innate artistic urge, but from his profound scholarship, his open and inquiring mind, not second even to Hamilton's, his long residence on his beloved estates where building was a constant occupation, his passion for educating the masses, and, finally, his extensive travels in Western Europe. In 1789, that seething year when he left Paris in the hands of democrats even more ardent than himself, his eyes had watched the construction of the Pantheon, had admired the recently completed buildings about the Place de la Concorde, and had doubtless compared in humiliation the great façades of the Louvre and the Invalides, all grandiose examples of advanced Classicism, with the puny fronts of Independence Hall and the Boston State House. He had not been to Italy, but he had seen and studied that perfect Roman temple, known as the Maison Carrée, at Nîmes in the South of France, and there were other Roman antiquities in Provence that we may be sure he did not miss. When, therefore, Jefferson was recalled to become Secretary of State in the new Federal government under Washington, he carried back with him from the land of Voltaire, Mirabeau, and Soufflot, not only new ideas of manners, morals, religion and political philosophy, but a decided interest and a new knowledge in architecture. The difficult problem he found confronting him in Washington's cabinet and the immediate hostility which sprang up between himself and Hamilton did not tend, we may be sure, to bring him the serenity that lies in the shade of a Roman portico, or the satisfaction that comes from laying stone on stone and watching one's own dream crystallize into a reality.

Nevertheless, Roman though he would be, American and Virginian he remained, and never did his Classic toga cover entirely his Colonial coat-tails. Blood, genius, environment, local building materials, American workmen—all combined to make his creations true sons and daughters of their native soil. It would take an architectural critic of peculiar discernment to see a replica of the Roman Pantheon in Central Hall of the University of Virginia and to the layman, seeing more clearly, Jefferson's dome is merely a fitting successor to the dome of Bulfinch on Beacon Hill. For this reason it seems beside the truth to magnify Jefferson's individual leaning towards the Roman manner into a "Roman Revival," or indeed into a revival of any sort. Another excellent reason for not giving the influence of Jefferson's creations any such exalted title is that it lasted only fifteen or perhaps twenty years, giving place about 1820 to a real revival, which lasted a half century and which will be described in the next chapter.

After the detour on the subject of Jefferson to whom we shall return again, let us continue along the main highway of the Post-Colonial. How can it be identified? What are its monuments? You will remember that the last phase of the Colonial, coinciding pretty well with the War of Independence, was marked by a fine delicacy of detail and proportion—a faint echo to catch which the ear must be attuned to the strains, delicate and rare, piped by the brothers Adam in London. Examples of this most charming phase of the Colonial exist in profusion in some of those lovely doorways in Salem, for instance, or in Homewood near Baltimore, with its slender colonnade. Few Colonial buildings had outstanding porticoes with pediments resting on columns, and when these do occur, as in Homewood or in the Redwood Library in Newport, they never extend entirely across the façade, as was customary in the buildings of the ancients.

In the Post-Colonial you will notice, first of all, that the attenuated proportions of the late Colonial have given place to proportions closely approaching those of the ancient Roman and contemporary French monuments. Notice also that the detail of the preceding period, sometimes prim, sometimes elaborate, reflecting Christopher Wren, Grinling Gibbons, Palladio, Robert Adam, or whomsoever, gives place to sedulous regard for the detail of the ancient Roman buildings. Notice also that the portico, seldom used before 1790, comes into its own and is the characteristic feature of almost all Post-Colonial buildings. It may be tetrastyle or four-columned, hexastyle or six-columned, octastyle or eight-columned; it may be prostyle, amphiprostyle, or peripteral, (terms which you can look up for yourself) or even pseudo-peripteral, which means that pilasters or engaged columns have taken the place of freestanding columns. The interiors show less of the change, and maintain in their fireplaces, door-casings, and cornices, most of the characteristics of their predecessors.

Now to return to Thomas Jefferson as the hero of the Post-Colonial. His earliest work, Monticello, antedates in style as in chronology the period with which we associate his name. Jefferson was only twenty-six when in 1769 he made the first drawings for Monticello, his life-long home. From 1796 to 1809 he worked upon it, and we are told that he acted as contractor and superintendent as well as architect. The building as it stands is of its time, Palladian rather than Roman despite its low dome and stubby Tuscan colonnade. Nevertheless, it shows that the young architect had gone to original sources, which abounded in his ample library, rather than copied the work about him or the designs in the numerous builders' guides that were in every carpenter's kit. His next architectural essays were made when he was Governor of Virginia in 1779, and consisted of drawings for remodelling the Governor's House in Williamsburg. The scheme, though never consummated, makes use of porticoes, front and rear—amphiprostyle, as Jefferson doubtless called it.

It is the Capitol of Virginia at Richmond, however, that made Jefferson's reputation as an architect, that has caused the spilling of more ink than any other building in the land and has been a bone of contention among the critics for a generation. It is the classic norm of the Post-Colonial, the typical example, the measuring-stick by which other monuments may be adjudged. It was conceived in Jefferson's fecund brain in 1785, and completed in 1789, a date which establishes the beginning of the Post-Colonial period. Jefferson designed the building in Paris at the request of the Governor of Virginia. He was not alone, however, in the preparation of the designs. Of this he writes, "The drawings of the façade and other elevations were made by Clérisseau, one of the most correct architects of France and author of the 'Antiquités de Nîmes.'" It is thought that Jefferson in his letters to the authorities in Richmond understated his responsibility for the design, as he wished to convey the impression that this building on which he had set his heart was the work of a professional architect. Some of the drawings Jefferson made in after-years for the University of Virginia, however, show gross errors in draughtsmanship and design, such as the projection of the entablature far beyond the face of the column, a mistake that amateurs to this day invariably make. These errors do not appear in the designs nor the construction of the Capitol building, so that Clérisseau's coöperation must have been considerable.

The building, as Jefferson stated, is frankly based on the ancient Roman temple at Nîmes in France, for centuries known as the Maison Carrée. It is one of the most perfectly preserved monuments of antiquity, and greatly impressed him on his European tour. Jefferson's building surpassed the original almost three times in size, being about 155 by 120 feet in the ground plan. To save expense, the order was unfortunately changed, as Jefferson admits, from Corinthian to Ionic. In 1870 and in 1904 the building was remodelled and restored. It still has a good deal of the appearance and flavor of the old régime. Jefferson, with all his erudition and enthusiasm for Classic architecture, could not make a Roman temple out of a meeting-hall of the House of Burgesses. It has a decidedly French flavor of the mode of Louis XVI, and suggests knee breeches and silk stockings rather than Roman togas.

Jefferson, in the modest epitaph which he composed for himself, says not a word about having been twice President of the United States, but ends with the statement that he founded the University of Virginia. This beautiful collection of buildings at Charlottesville is a double monument to him—two wreaths for his brow, one of laurel and one of bay—for he not only conceived the idea of these halls of higher learning, organized them and by tremendous labor got the state to finance them, but he designed and built the fabric as well.

Jefferson had the ingenious idea that each building should be a living proctor of the art of the architect, a model in full size of some famous ancient monument. So the great Library, or central hall, is a replica, in a manner of speaking, of the Roman Pantheon except that it is one-half as large in all its lineal dimensions, which means that it comes to one-fourth of its area and one-eighth of its volume. The Library building sits at the head of the celebrated professors' houses, a double row of small buildings for all the world—I say it with all respect—like a big red hen, scratching up bits of knowledge for her chicks. These little buildings represent Jefferson's idea of the best examples of the three Classic orders, for instance, Pavilion #1 represents the Doric order of the Baths of Diocletian; Pavilion #2, the Ionic of Fortuna Virilus; #3, the Corinthian of Palladio; #4, the Doric of Albana; #5, the Ionic with medallions of Palladio; #6, the Ionic of the Theatre of Marcellus; #7, the Doric of Palladio; #8, the Corinthian of Diocletian's Baths. Pavilion #9 repeats Pavilion #2, while the remaining pavilion illustrates the Doric of the Theatre of Marcellus. Curious that there are no Greek examples! The buildings are of red brick with white "trimmings." Verily, it is easier for a camel to go through the eye of a needle than for a building of red brick trimmed in white to appear Roman.

It is certainly interesting and not a little amusing to observe the effect of Thomas Jefferson's genius on the architectural critic and historian. The spell of the first democrat permeates Monticello and the University. I confess that I entered those classic groves and porticoes a staunch Hamiltonian and came away a convert of Jefferson's, and yet I knew that my imagination was being ensnared and my judgment put to sleep by the Jeffersonian enchantment. To proclaim a man who certainly was not an artist and but doubtfully an architect "the father of the arts

America" and the founder of the Classic Revival is the usual task of Jefferson's biographers and eloquent proof of his century-old bewitchment.

One of the worst definitions in the language is that which characterizes genius as the capacity for taking infinite pains, and yet it exactly describes the genius of Thomas Jefferson. His interests were universal. Architecture was merely one of them, and in it he evinced the same capacity for taking infinite pains that he applied to the law, to philosophy, to the sciences, to education, to the writing of the Declaration of Independence, and to the governing of the United States. I will go farther and say that in architecture his knowledge was really less fundamental than in the other pursuits of his catholic mind. Had it been otherwise, how could he have scorned Colonial architecture, so beautifully expressive of the life about him, and embraced so faithlessly—he, the lover of liberty —Palladianism with its hidebound formulae and its musty dogmatism? It merely means that while his contemporaries fortunately knew nothing but the simple and natural art about them, Jefferson knew one thing more, and that was architecture in the grand manner—the architecture reposing between the heavy covers of Palladio, gracing the Place de la Concorde, or crumbling in the Roman Forum. His capacity for taking infinite pains had made him familiar with its every detail, but no lightning flash of intuition had illumined its falsity. So we look in vain for any originality or subtlety, any architectural grace such as we find, for instance, in the New York City Hall or the White House in Washington. More than that Monticello and the professors' houses have many technical errors and an unpleasant heaviness. Jefferson's reputation as an architect is saved in spite of himself by the very limitations against which he rebelled, the red Virginia brick which he was obliged to use, the good white pine and the humble and unlearned American hands. If his work is great it is because its author was great. It is a splendid and touching part of him, not a bright star in the architectural galaxy.

Although the radiance of Thomas Jefferson filled the Post-Colonial skies, there were other luminaries who, though of much less magnitude, were far more proficient and sophisticated in their trade. The first of these is Charles Bulfinch. His famous State House makes him forever a part of Boston. In that city he was born in 1763, and he was graduated from Harvard in 1781. In 1787 he made the grand tour and, on returning from Europe, became first an amateur architect, designing houses gratuitously since he was affluent and must have been goodnatured. He soon decided to charge a fee, and by so doing became our first professional architect. Forty or more churches and public buildings are ascribed to him. Dying in 1844, he lived and practiced in three styles. The first was the last or Adam phase of the Colonial, of which the State House in Boston is his best example. The second was the Post-Colonial, in which category should be placed the old Capitol in Washington, which had been burned in 1814 and to rebuild which Bulfinch was called in 1817, remaining until its completion in 1830. The third was the Greek Revival, of which his Maine State House, built in 1828, is an example. Bulfinch was brought up in the Adam tradition, and his natural conservatism and rare taste held him to it long after it had yielded to the Post-Colonial and Greek Revival in other localities.

James Hoban worked in Washington just before Bulfinch. He was an Irishman who emigrated to Charleston before the Revolution. His great work is the Executive

Mansion in Washington, whither he went in 1792. He not only built it, but rebuilt it after the British had burned it in 1814. He erected as well the State House in Charleston. Hoban's work is accomplished and suave, with a strong French flavor. He was a thoroughly satisfactory architect.

The beautiful City Hall in New York claims two architects—John McComb, born in 1763, and Mangin, a Frenchman. We will not enter into the controversy as to who did what. In point of design the building is the finest of the whole Post-Colonial period. Accepting the *parti* and composition of a typical American problem, it is decorated with a charming Louis XVI facing of pilasters and arched windows, and crowned with a lovely cupola (restored). It is by all odds the most sophisticated and stylish building of its time, a proof in stone that "a thing of beauty is a joy forever." St. John's Church, Varrick Street, New York, for which I looked in vain a year ago, discovering only an ugly warehouse on its site, was by McComb's hand.

The father of the first building of our land, the United States Capitol, was Dr. William Thornton. He was a physician, born in the West Indies in 1761, educated in London, and a travelled gentleman. The date of his arrival in America from London is given as 1793. He was selected by Washington to design, on the superb site chosen by L'Enfant, the French architect, the first official home of our government. This original capitol building, burned by the British in 1814, was a typical design of the Post-Colonial School, and, when Latrobe, the father of the Greek Revival, rebuilt it, he adhered, curiously enough, to Thornton's original design. In addition to the Capitol, the good Doctor designed the Octagon House in Washington, now the abode of the American Institute of Architects, and Montpellier, James Madison's home, in Orange County, Virginia.

The city of Charleston, South Carolina, is an architectural history in itself. Architecture is its food and genealogy its wine. If your mansion is a mushroom growth affair of but fifty to seventy-five years, and if you are not a Pringle or a Pinckney, a Middleton or an Izzard, you may pick up a few crumbs, but you cannot sit down at Dives' table. One of the most brilliant chapters in this architectural history is the Post-Colonial. It had its heyday in Charleston, the center of the gracious and luxurious life that a glorious war and the wealth of the rice-planters drew about it, and its monuments of these purple moments are beautiful and impressive. The City Hall, built by Manigault in 1801, is, I think, the finest building of all. It is an "architect's" building. Its white marble façade has the quality that is distinctive of this brief era—a quality foreign even to the Colonial—in that it shows the result of architectural study. The façade consists of a pavilioned wall with a high basement and two stories. It is decorated with superimposed engaged columns, and pilasters with beautifully proportioned arched windows between. The whole is crowned with a pediment over the pavilion, and a fine balustrade on either side. As in many other southern buildings of this period a horse-shoe stairway with a wrought-iron balustrade swings up to its main entrance.

All Post-Colonial work is what we architects call "carefully studied." This is a minor example, perhaps, but it is typical. For a great example go to the old City Hall in New York, which is of this period and was carefully designed by two professional architects. Compare it now with the best similar example of the Georgian phase of the Colonial, the well-loved Independence Hall, designed by an amateur, a doctor. The first is a composition all the parts of which are carefully related to each other and to the whole, in space, scale, and detail. The second, with all its charm, is an assemblage of various architectural forms without any learned regard for their relationship. The two buildings are as they appear—the first the work of a trained architect, the second that of an amateur.

Aside from subtleties and technicalities of style note this more evident phenomenon. In the coming of the Post-Colonial France superseded England in her position of architectural authority.

Such is the scant roster of these our first architects in the interlude which we have called the Post-Colonial—a soft intermezzo between the art of the colonies and that of the Republic. In that sense is it purely transitional, a twilight style that glowed with roseate hues of the old régime and presaged at the same time the dawn of the new nation soon to come up like thunder out of the past.

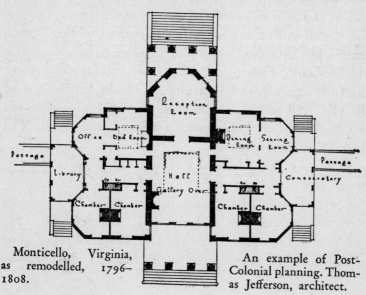

Monticello, Virginia, as remodelled, 1796–1808.

An example of Post-Colonial planning. Thomas Jefferson, architect.

CHAPTER IV

THE GREEK REVIVAL 1820–1860

In Which We Slip a Chiton Over Our Linsey-Woolsey

THE Post-Colonial period found architecture in America innocent and left it sophisticated. Up to the time of Jefferson's building of the Capitol in Richmond and his construction of Monticello, our buildings had been simple assemblages of rooms adorned with architectural ornament, often indiscriminately taken from the handbooks; but the Post-Colonial introduced the professional architect, and with him came the grand manner. Buildings were now designed on axes with expert consideration of circulation, of the *parti,* which means the architectural concept and of the plan as a thing of beauty in itself. Its exteriors had begun with the passionate enlèvement of the Roman temple by Jefferson, but under the expert hands of men like McComb, Hoban, and Manigault the façades became carefully studied and skillfully composed expressions of the plan. All of this architecture you will have observed was Roman Classic, often with a strong French Louis XVI flavor, but never Greek.

While the Post-Colonial was flourishing along the Potomac and in various places from Philadelphia to Charleston, a new style had sprung into being in England. Its birth was spectacular and romantic. Far back in 1762 two young Englishmen, Stuart and Revett, having gone to Athens (one is reminded of Donatello's and Brunelleschi's memorable trip to Rome) and made elaborate drawings of the buildings on the Acropolis, published these under the auspices of the Dilettanti Society of London. The drawings depicted in exquisite graven lines the almost unknown majesty and beauty of those resplendent monuments of the Periclean Age—the Parthenon, the Erectheum and the Propylaea. Wrecked by Venetian cannon and buried through three centuries by the bastions and bulwarks of the Turk, in these books before the amazed eyes of Western Europe they burst through the Moslem dunghill into glorious bloom. England became Hellenic. "The world's great age begins anew, the golden years return," sang Shelley, and the wept-for Adonais cried,

> "O Attic shape! fair attitude! with brede
> Of marble men and maidens overwrought
> With forest branches and the trodden weed;
> Thou, silent form, doth tease us out of thought
> As doth Eternity."

In 1821 the Greek war for independence stirred every man's imagination. "Give me six hundred mountaineers with two pounds of beans and a gallon of whiskey per day for each, and I'll lick the Turks in forty-eight hours," boasted the Pennsylvanian Colonel according to Mrs. Trollope, while over nearer the scene of operations George Gordon Byron, Lord Byron, said much the same thing when he wrote,

> "Earth! render back from out thy breast
> A remnant of our Spartan dead!
> Of the three hundred grant but three,
> To make a new Thermopylae!"

In Germany Goethe, Schiller and Lessing had struck the Sapphic lyre, and Wincklemann with his spade was searching for the bones of Achilles and Agamemnon. In France arose, like a second Alexander crowned with laurels and surrounded by his eagles, the miraculous figure of Napoleon. All of this Greek urge, this Attic complex, had its immediate repercussion in current architecture.

The first Greek building in England, a small garden temple, had the honor of being erected in 1758 by that same Stuart who had led the "return of the Heraclidae." The use of pure Greek ornament and of the Greek orders rapidly increased in popularity, culminating in beautiful St. Pancras's Church in London by the Inwood Brothers, 1819–22. More famous were the great Bank of England by Soane, and St. George's Hall, 1833, Liverpool, by H. Elmes, a young genius who went before his time.

In characteristic and somewhat heavy fashion the Germans adopted the style, and applied to it all their erudition and painstaking care. The result was a series of great buildings which are among the most notable in German architectural history: the old Museum and the Brandenburg Gate, Berlin; the Propylaea, Munich; the Parliament House, Vienna; to mention but a few.

As for the French, with their usual architectural independence and resourcefulness they refused to sign on the dotted line at the behest of Phidias and Callicrates, and their contributions to the Greek Revival insisted on being Gallic, and not Hellenic. The huge Madeleine is Roman, not Greek; the Arc de Triomphe by Chalgrín, the mightiest triumphal arch ever built, is French-Greek, or Néogrec as the books call it; and the Library of Ste. Genéviève by Labrouste is equally original.

Along with this sympathetic appreciation and appropriation of certain elements in Greek architecture, we find an entirely harmonious current of Greek influence in

French life and manners. "Le Style Empire" in furniture, with exquisite tact and skill, takes Greek ornament and applies it with many original features of appliqué and ormolu to the mahogany escritoires and fauteuils of the salons of Compiègne and Malmaison.

The Classic style in painting formed one of the most distinct and brilliant epochs of French art. David, the high priest of Classicism, in his "Oath of the Horatii" did more to stamp the Classic ideal on French life and customs than Chalgrin with his arch, or Napoleon with his vision of himself as a reincarnated Alexander. And, as a final testimonial to the triumph of David and of Classicism, the ladies of the beau monde threw away their ruffled skirts and laced corsets, and the loose flowing robes and simple girdles of the Roman matron became de rigueur. Regnault, Gros, Ingres, continued after the fall of the Emperor the cold formulae of their fiery master, David; while in sculpture the grand tradition was carried on by Rude, with his "call to arms" on the Arc de Triomphe, and Houdon who did our own Washington.

In French letters André Chénier, sacrificed on the altar of the Revolution, and Madame de Staël, fluttering and scolding about the imperial eagle, were perhaps the only ones who purposely expressed themselves in Classic phrase. Chateaubriand, Hugo, Sand, Gautier, de Musset, Dumas, Guizot saw in Classicism itself a high romance, and we have the paradox of Classic art hand-in-hand with Romantic letters.

I have mentioned some of the phenomena of the Classic Revival in France in this much detail to show what a real revival is; to show that to be sincere a cultural movement must arouse enthusiasm and coöperation in every department of intellectual and spiritual activity; and also to show that an ideal with two thousand years of forgetfulness over its corpse may be resurrected and live again if life be breathed into it by all the people. In other lands the Greek image was carried about in its coffin for so much a look.

You will remember that there is a group of Jeffersonian enthusiasts who argue that because Jefferson's Franco-Roman building in Richmond was built in 1789, thereby antedating the first of the Greek Revival buildings in Europe, Jefferson is the father of the Greek Revival both abroad and at home; and in order to make the facts fit the theory, they combine the Post-Colonial and the Greek Revival under one term which they call the Classic Revival. There is only a very remote chance that the creators of the Greek Revival in England ever heard of, let alone ever saw, Jefferson's Richmond building, and the claim that this great European movement saw its birth in America is preposterous. Its lineage is perfectly clear: it stepped directly out of the covers of Stuart and Revett's "Antiquities of Athens."

The lesser but still more insistent claim that Jefferson was the father of the Greek Revival in America is, I believe, equally untenable. The great volumes of the "Antiquities of Athens" reposed, we are told, in the library at Monticello, and Jefferson must have been well acquainted with their contents, yet in no instance did he ever use a Greek order or even a bit of Greek detail. It is really astonishing, when you stop to think about it, that not one of the professors' houses at the University of Virginia—each one avowedly a lesson in architectural style—is Greek; without exception they are Roman. Jefferson either saw no beauty in the perfect beauty of those masterpieces on the Acropolis, or did not understand their significance. Perhaps he felt—which was true—that the real analogy with the infant Republic lay in Rome, not Athens. Nor did any other of Jefferson's fellow architects in the Post-Colonial epoch essay the Greek—neither Hoban, nor Thornton, nor Bulfinch, nor McComb, nor Mangin, nor Hallet. Their work was for the most part a French version of the Roman or the Adam mode of the Georgian.

The Greek Revival in America was a direct importation, as every other architectural fashion had been. In starting a description of it we cannot even begin with the historian's cant phrase, "The germ of the movement may be found long ago, and so forth." In fact, of all the exotic styles that have captured the American taste, the Greek Revival was the most exotic and of our provincialism the most flagrant example. It was brought to this country in much the same way as Dolly Madison's bonnets, save that in the case of this architectural adornment we can be much more definite for we know exactly who was the importer. His name was Latrobe—Benjamin H. Latrobe—and in due course we shall hear more of him and his works.

Whether Jefferson or Latrobe was the father of the Greek Revival depends on whether Latrobe in building the Bank of Pennsylvania in 1799–1801, our first Greek building, got his inspiration from Jefferson's Roman Capitol building in Richmond or from the established Greek vogue in England. To clear this crucial point I wrote to the court of last resort in such cases, Mr. Fiske Kimball, and this is what he says: "I will answer your question about Latrobe as well as I can. There is no question that Latrobe got his stimulus to use the Greek details from Cockerell and the work abroad. On the other hand, I do not find the temple form employed there for buildings of practical use until long after he left. His first important work in America was the completion of the exterior of the Virginia Capitol, and it was while doing this that he made his sketch for the Bank of Pennsylvania. Thus it is probable that the Capitol was not without influence on his adoption of the temple form."

Why our infant republic accepted the Greek Revival in architecture with such unquestioning enthusiasm is a bit of a mystery well deserving of some research. Its vogue in England and in Germany, great as it was, was not comparable in any way to its universal use with us. Greek was, of course, a major study at our few universities, but its intrusion into the literature of the time is not discernible. There is no Hellenic note struck by the lyre of Washington Allston, or later by Bryant, Irving or Poe.

Apropos what a temptation to tell something of the passing of the old Knickerbocker tradition and the coming of that new régime of which Washington Irving was the bright particular star! A sudden activity that took in commercial expansion, mechanical invention, civic pride and a new cosmopolitanism, changed New York from a sleepy Dutch burg to a wide-awake American city. The "Cheshire Cheese" of those days in literary New York was Cockloft Hall, and here Paulding, Halleck, Drake, Cooper, who came in 1822, and Bryant in 1825 and the irrepressible Irving revelled and drank deep. To these intellectuals should be added Robert Fulton and Samuel Morse, who both began their careers as painters, J. Vandelyn and J. Trumbull, whose Washingtons, Pocahontases, and Captain John Smiths populate the Rotunda at Washington. Surely there is nothing very Greek about these men; nor about St. Nicholas, who with his reindeers had to land on a temple roof and slide down a Greek chimney (" 'Twas the Night before Christmas" was written in 1822 by Clement C. Moore, a member of the group).

A history of American literature before me makes no mention whatever of any Greek Revival in letters; in fact, neither the word "Greece" nor any of its derivatives even occurs in the index. The same is true in painting and sculpture. Benjamin West's, Copley's, and Gilbert Stuart's lives were mainly laid in the Georgian period, and their work is closely modelled on the great 18th century English portrait painters, but never even in their latest works did they follow David or Gros or Ingres in a choice of Classic themes. Trumbull painted his huge pictures in the Rotunda of the Capitol in Washington in the grand manner, but with no suggestion of the Greek about it. The geographers and the architects seem to have had the Greek field to themselves. The streets of Elmira, Ypsilanti, Athens, Rome, Cincinnati, Sparta, Corinth, Ionia (to say nothing of New Thermopylae so dismally visited by Martin Chuzzlewit) echoed to the creaking of the ox-carts on their way to the winning of the West or to the shouts of "Tippecanoe and Tyler Too" from long-coated and beaver-hatted patriots. For what strange reason did these frontiersmen line these same streets with peristyles and porticoes? It would be interesting to collect all the Greek names attached to unoffending American towns—towns that have gone through their histories staggering under the same handicap that still affects the lives and fortunes of the Algernons and Percys named by doting and romantic mothers.

Up and down the Atlantic seaboard, through the Western Reserve, along the Gulf of Mexico, up the Mississippi, and over the plains, the Greek Revival spread. I have noticed that the famous tabernacle built in Salt Lake City by that extraordinary man, Brigham Young, has the tell-tale Greek profiles in its mouldings and cornices. In all these localities climate, building materials, and even the habits of the people differ enormously. Yet the style of architecture and even its forms are common to all. For this there is only one reason: fashion. Wherever the warm rays of fashion could penetrate up sprang an acanthus, and every covered wagon, along with the rifle and the plowshare, found room for the porticoes of the Parthenon and the Choragic Monument of Lysicrates. A building that was not Greek in 1827 was as hard to find as a skirt that was not short in 1927.

The costumes, the manners, the art of colonial days were perfect in their architectural setting; and one feels that, however bad architecture may have been in that stuffy and embroidered era which we call "Victorian," the checked pantaloons, the flowing whiskers, the bonnets and bustles, were its proper accompaniment. Even today the sensible attire of men and women which makes for the efficiency that is necessary to keep one's place in our hectic American scene, goes well enough with the clash and clang of the skyscraper, the squeak of the in-a-door bed and the purr of the electric washing-machine. But where is there any such harmony between life and architecture in the thirty or forty years of the Greek Revival?

To use Henry James's description, American society was not only provincial; it was parochial. And if one is to believe Mrs. Trollope, who spent some three ungrateful years with us during the height of the Greek Revival, "the domestic manners of the Americans" had little of the Pentelic polish which we associate with Hellenic culture. Aside from the whiskey drinking and tobacco chewing, the patriotic bombast, the greed for money, the prudery of the women, and the uncouth manners of the men, all of which she gleefully dwells on again and again (mistaking the skin for the soul of the American character), she mentions an utter lack of knowledge and appreciation of the fine arts. "From all the conversations on painting which I listened to in America," she says, "I found the finish of drapery was considered as the highest excellence, and, next to this, the resemblance in a portrait. I do not remember ever to have heard the words 'drawing' or 'composition' used in any conversation on the subject." Especially illuminating and astonishing is her description of the nineteenth annual exhibition of the Pennsylvania Academy of Fine Arts. "The antique statue gallery" filled with plaster casts, was presided over, she says, by an old crone who opened the door furtively now and then to let in alternate groups of men and women, who, we may imagine, with crimson cheeks and downcast eyes hurried by the figures of the Apollo Belvedere and the Capitoline Venus! We agree with Mrs. Trollope that there could be little love of art in a society that regarded the master-pieces of Greek sculpture as fit exhibits for a *sala pornographica*. There were enough virtues in the courageous breasts of the men and women who pushed the border-line of empire clear across a continent without our having to pretend that their simple souls were fired by the Greek ideal or that an architecture that had flourished two thousand years before and five thousand miles away was the natural and spontaneous expression of their culture, the "only true American style."

The examination of these facts and others persuades me that the Greek Revival in America was a fad pure and simple. The real interests of the people in this critical period were politics, exploration, and business—not art. With the exception of literature, art was at a low ebb between 1820 and 1850; not a painter, not a sculptor, not a musician, of note. The undeniable beauty of much of the Greek Revival work lay unfortunately not in the soul of the artist, but in the glory of the ancient models which he so carefully copied. A Rienzi could not but be magnificent in the borrowed robes of the Tribunes, but in the case of the Greek Revival even the robes were for the most part shoddy. The columns that gleam so majestically across the Potomac from Arlington are not marble, but plaster; and the architraves and cornices, with their accoutrements of metopes and triglyphs that appear to bear so heavily on many a sturdy Doric post, are but of wooden boards. The Greek Revival certainly "got away with murder."

What was this Greek Revival, and how did it come about? In it the architects exactly copied, wherever they could, either ensembles, portions or details of Greek temples, applying them to every kind of American building. I know no instance where any sort of originality was used in arranging this artistic loot; it was applied to the American building exactly as found. Exactness in copying was the ideal; any deviation from the model was a barbarism. The buildings thus faithfully emulated were the Parthenon, the Propylæa, the temples of Pæstum, for the Doric; the Erectheum, the temple of Bassæ, and the little temple of Niké Apterix, for the Ionic; and the Choragic Monument of Lysicrates for the Corinthian.

The early Georgian architects were great copyists, too, but they deviated freely from their models. They picked and chose from many sources; they drained the honey from a thousand different blossoms; and when prompted by expediency they freely changed the proportions to fit the material at hand. Not so our Greek Revivalist. He was not content, for instance, with the perfect simulacrum of the profile of the Parthenon cap; he must have the exact proportions of the column as well, so our American-Greek blithely adopts the proportion of diameter to height as one to six, which old Callicrates had figured out to be necessary for the beauty and stability of his column in marble, and sticks to it till death for columns in stone, wood, plaster, cast iron, or what have you.

The portico was the special feature desired in every building, and it is the portico that adds the most beauty and dignity. Porticoes had been used back in the Post-Colonial—the White House, planned in 1792, is a beautiful example—and even before that in the Georgian, as in old St. Phillip's, Charleston, 1723; but these had been always in some form of Roman or its derivatives—never Greek. So characteristic of the Greek Revival is the free-standing portico with its four, six, or eight columns, its entablature and its pediment, that this style has been called on occasion the "portico style."

The portico in this case is usually arranged prostyle, which means projecting from the front of the building only. Hundreds of examples might be mentioned: that of Hibernian Hall, Charleston, South Carolina, dedicated in 1841—which, by the way, is hexastyle (six-columned) Ionic—is an excellent one. The ultima Thule, the final ambition of the designer, however, was the peristyle or colonnade running completely around the building. This is technically known as the peripteral plan. It meant a pediment at each end. Its great prototype in ancient days is the Parthenon. Not often was so magnificent and expensive a scheme achieved, but fine examples exist in the Doric house of Nicholas Biddle, the first American to travel in Greece, at Andalusia, Pennsylvania, built in 1834, and in Stephen Girard's famous college in Philadelphia, built by Walter in 1833–37 in the Corinthian of Lysicrates.

Not in the East alone were there imposing mansions in the Greek style. In Madison, Indiana, on the Ohio River, is the home of James F. D. Lanier, built in 1844 at a cost of forty thousand dollars—a noble building with a tetrastyle Doric Colonnade and the unusual dignity of a great round cupola. During the Civil War Lanier was a sort of Robert Morris to his state, having loaned it upwards of a million dollars. Other fine houses are to be found in Delaware and Vermilion, Ohio; Niles, Michigan; Waukegan, Illinois; and, in fact, in almost every town bordering the Mississippi and its eastern tributaries. Lincoln's home in Springfield, Illinois, for instance, is Greek Revival but without the portico.

A description of a typical Greek Revival house in the Western Reserve, for example, as Ohio was called in the early days, will perhaps illustrate most of the salient points that were characteristic of its kind.

If it were a grand mansion it would have a portico; if not a portico, it might have pilasters on the corners; lacking pilasters, it would have corner boards (we are assuming our house to be of wood), but the wooden siding would never be mitred around the corners as in Colonial work. These clapboards or sidings, by the way, were usually laid flush, not "drop," as shingles are laid, so that the wall presented a smooth surface as like as possible to stone or cement. Even where brick was used, as it was especially in the South, it was painted gray. White plaster or stucco, usually marked off to imitate stone, was a very popular treatment.

The entrance, which in a Colonial house is almost invariably in the center, was as like as not at the side or next the corner. There was much more diversity in plan in the Greek Revival houses than in the Colonial, so that the house might have been built in an L or a T or, more attractive still, in a central cube with low wings symmetrically arranged. The doorway was distinctive, and decidedly different from the familiar Georgian with its elliptical fan light, the lines all being square—Greek Doric pilasters on the side with a full entablature of architrave, frieze and cornice, and the door itself of simple vertical panels, with a long, low, rectangular transom above and thin vertical side lights on either side.

The windows had the sliding sash, as in the Georgian, with the glass divided into rectangles by thin wood strips, but these rectangles were usually fewer in number and consequently larger than in the Georgian houses. The trim around the windows was usually simple, broad and flat with little or no cornice.

The predominating feature is always the main overhang. This was typically a full Greek entablature—architrave, frieze, and cornice. If there was no portico, the gables were at the ends of the house, and here the entablature was likely to return only a foot or two (a Georgian device) instead of extending fully across the end. In many houses, directly beneath the entablature or breaking through it, were small low windows opening into the attic. These little windows were often attractively filled with cast iron grilles of Greek honeysuckle design.

Cast iron ornaments of various kinds, especially window-grilles, balconies and balustrades were very popular and are entirely typical of the Greek Revival. For this the development of the coke and iron industries, owing to the tremendous demand for iron in the extension of the railways, was largely responsible. In the South, towards the end of the period cast iron to a great extent supplanted wood in the construction of the famous two-storied "piazzas" without which no southern house was complete. To the saunterer along Meeting Street in Charleston or Chartres Street in New Orleans it might seem that some gigantic ferrous spider had spun his iron webs across the fronts of the sleeping mansions.

Owing to the need of adhering to the Greek temple form, all of the roofs had to be of very low pitch. The ancient temple pediments had slopes seldom exceeding thirty degrees. In lands devoid of ice and snow and in buildings probably roofed with tile there would have been no objection to this flatness, but in America, especially in the North, such roofs were a nuisance. They were too flat for shingles and, if made of metal, hot and unsightly. They were a constant source of trouble and expense, and the cause of those water stains which form, in houses of this period, the principal decorative motive for the second story ceilings. Greek temples not having any chimneys, our builders, lacking the necessary precedent, left theirs very plain and simple—a most sensible procedure.

The suburban and country houses largely followed the plans developed in the Post-Colonial periods. In the cities interesting new arrangements were developed. Many of these old houses remain. They may be seen today around Washington Square in New York, doubtless shaking in their boots as the tide of modern construction approaches them. Those in Philadelphia had absolutely plain fronts, all of smooth red brick with stone sills and lintels of white marble. These plain lintels of marble, stone, or wood, are always indicative of the style. In Georgian days the lintel was a flat arch of brick, often with a keystone in the center. In the Post-Colonial it had given way in many cases to a panelled lintel with square blocks at the ends, while in the Greek Revival the perfectly plain lintel obtains.

Many attractive houses were built along the old stage routes between Albany and Buffalo and along the Hudson. They retain many Georgian features, such as the dormer window and the red brick. The high basement containing the kitchen, the long narrow hall, the parlor and drawing-room, the dining-room behind, lasted through this epoch and the following.

The interior detail of all of these houses was ordinarily very heavy. Be it said to the credit of our Greek Revivalists, they made no attempt, as far as I know, to copy a temple in its interior arrangements. How would you like to live in a *cella* without windows of any kind, perhaps, sleeping in the *pronaos* and dining in the *opisthodomos?* But while Greek plans were not consistently carried out, the flat Greek profile prevailed everywhere. The stairs were usually simplicity itself, with square or round spindles without mouldings or ornament supporting an unmoulded mahogany hand-rail; very chaste and severe compared, for instance, with the elaborate Georgian stairway of Carter's Grove. In important mansions the ceilings were very high and around them ran complete Greek entablatures in plaster. In the less important rooms there was a plaster cornice of some kind, and usually a rosette around the hanging chandelier. The principal rooms opened into each other, often in stately fashion, and the separation was indicated by free-standing Ionic columns—the favorite style for interior treatment. The wooden panelling and even the dado of Georgian days have disappeared; so also has the wall paper, the walls being simply painted in flat colors.

The fireplace had lost much of its previous importance. The over-mantel disappeared, giving way to the mirror. The fireplace itself, however, was usually of marble, and sometimes elaborately carved with figures taken from Flaxman or Wedgewood. Mirrors imported from France became very popular. Their height and width and the elaboration of the gilt frame were in some degree an estimate of the financial standing of the owner. They occupied important places, as at the end of the drawing-room between two windows or over the fireplace reaching to the ceiling.

Much of the furniture of these houses had doubtless been handed down from the previous period, but the new taste, having swung from English to French, followed the mode of Paris. The Directoire and Empire succeeded Sheraton and Hepplewhite and Adam in the popular estimation. While the French mode called for ormolu ornaments of brass, the American designs usually eschewed them, using mahogany veneer with elaborate patterns in the matched grain or burl of the wood. Great dressers and wardrobes with huge cornices, and chairs that follow more or less Greek or Empire lines but often without carving, are characteristic. The four-poster bed continued in popularity, but the posts are often elephantine in their proportions. Much delicacy and elegance on the other hand is to be found in the work of a man like Phyfe. His "lyre" tables and his side chairs are as fine as the work of the great Englishmen.

Duncan Phyfe is the hero of the decorative arts of the period, and his active life as a furniture designer and maker exactly fills the span of the Greek Revival. He emigrated from Scotland in 1783 and opened his shop in New York City in 1790. He apparently gave his customers, who were the great of the land, whatever they wanted, but it was always the finest that his taste and skill could fashion. A hundred years ago it would have cost you a cool thousand dollars to have decently furnished your drawing-room with Mr. Phyfe's furniture, with chairs for twenty-five dollars apiece and a great pier table at three hundred. A chronological display of his furniture would give a perfect picture of the taste of the time. It would begin with the Sheraton and Adam types (Post-Colonial), then the French Directoire (early Greek Revival), and then the Empire (later Greek Revival), the furniture getting progressively heavier and coarser but being always of the finest craftsmanship, finally to end with the black walnut atrocities of the Parvenu period. We are glad to chronicle that Phyfe retired full of years and honors and, having sold out his business, which employed over a hundred men, went to his final reward in 1854.

While we have been discussing houses, we should note that during this period public construction for the first time assumed in American building the major place. The development of the new western states and the increasing wealth of the national government required the carrying out of a great building program. National buildings and state capitols were now without exception in the Greek style. The greatest of them, of course, is the Capitol building in Washington, the contemporary portion of which is Greek Revival. Even Mrs. Trollope praised it wholeheartedly, and what she says about one part of it is so interesting and significant that it is worth quoting:

"In a hall leading to some of these rooms, the ceiling is supported by pillars, the capitals of which struck me as peculiarly beautiful. They are composed of the ears and leaves of the Indian corn, beautifully arranged, and forming as graceful an outline as the acanthus itself. This was the only instance I saw, in which America has ventured to attempt national originality; the success is perfect. A sense of fitness always enhances the effect of beauty. I will not attempt a long essay on the subject, but if America, in her vastness, her immense natural resources, and her remote grandeur, would be less imitative, she would be infinitely more picturesque and interesting." She did not know that in addition to the "Corncob Capitals" Latrobe had made, in the same building, capitals of tobacco leaves and had designed some with the cotton bole as their decoration!

Other government buildings of the time and style were the Treasury building and the Patent Office in Washington; Custom Houses in New Bedford, Savannah, San Francisco, and New York; the Mint in Philadelphia, and the old Exchange in New York. Many of the states seized upon the Greek style as a proper expression of the power of the commonwealth, and Indianapolis, Albany, Mount Pelier, Nashville, Columbus, have capitol buildings built in it.

The building at Columbus, Ohio, is particularly interesting, and its construction may be regarded as typical. In 1838 the General Assembly of Ohio provided for its Capitol building, and through its commissioners "advertised for plans, offering premiums." From fifty to sixty sets of plans were sent in. They picked out three sets of designs, and appointed an architect, Henry Walter, to "combine their best points"! Begun in 1839, the building was not completed until 1858 after many vicissitudes and much changing of horses in the architectural stream. The building as it stands in use today is of the Greek Doric style, imposing in its dimensions and proportions, and crowned with a huge cupola to which the legislator could proudly point as a dome and which the purist with equal conviction could declare to be not a dome. Banks and Exchanges were eloquent of expanding commerce and credit: Merchants Exchanges in New York and Philadelphia, the old Quincy Market, Boston, United

States Banks in Philadelphia, Erie and Savannah, the Suf-
folk and the Middlesex Banks in Boston, and almost countless buildings of like nature throughout the South. A
typical example is the old Cotton Exchange of Petersburg,
Virginia, now restored and put to civic use. Venerable and
dignified in its Doric habiliments, it stood long awaiting its
cup of hemlock. In every city fortunate enough to possess
any, at least one such building of this period should be
preserved as an historical monument or used as a museum
of history or art, which can usually accommodate itself
to ancient and not always convenient surroundings.

The revival in pagan architecture went arm in arm with
a tremendous revival in emotional Christianity. The Methodists, the Baptists and the Presbyterians vied with each
other in the number and zeal of their revivals and the
number of converts brought into the fold. We remember
the mother in Israel of the Methodist faith who, in commenting on the revivals going on in her western home, said,
"Well, we saved only three souls last night, but, thank God,
the Baptists didn't save any." When Francis Asbury, "the
Father of American Methodism," landed in America in
1771 there were but three hundred Methodists in the
colonies. When he died in 1816 there were over two hundred thousand and more than two thousand ministers,
while in 1850 there were 690,000 members and 9500 ministers! Those were the heroic days of the itinerant preacher
and the circuit rider who carried his Bible, a loaf of bread
and a change of linen in his saddle-bags. The Pauls and
Peters of this day forded the streams and threaded the forests, visiting their flocks in true apostolic fashion; while
their voices urged the sinner to the mourner's bench, their
strong right arms repelled the rowdies and the scoffers.

It is hardly fair to expect such militant Christians to

have paid much attention to architecture, yet the churches of the time, I should say, did not fall far behind the standard of other buildings. Here again the Greek was the chosen style, and the portico, long since introduced into the colonies through the influence of Gibbs and used on many a Georgian church, naturally maintained its place, simply changing from Roman to Greek. The Wren steeple, though reduced in height, and simplified and sturdier, maintained its place above and behind the portico. Some churches, however, adopted the temple arrangement *in toto*. The beautifully proportioned Westminster Presbyterian Church in Charleston, South Carolina, dedicated in 1850, is a hexastyle prostyle fane that might have been erected on the Forum Romanum, its detail being, contrary to the usual rule, Roman and not Greek. The interiors of these buildings are usually cold and uninviting and do not differ particularly, except in detail and in lack of interest, from their Georgian and Post-Colonial forbears.

There was one exception to the general rule of conformity to the Greek style. The name of Upjohn is a famous one in the annals of American architecture. Three—or is it four?—generations of Upjohns have practiced their profession in the United States. Richard, the founder and first President of that august body, the American Institute of Architects, was born in England in 1802. He came to us in 1829, working first in New Bedford, and then in Boston where he labored with Bulfinch on the State House. In 1839 he went to New York, and there he did the work that proved him an exception. Old Trinity Church, a Colonial building, was in disrepair, and Upjohn was employed to remodel it. He proposed, as architects have a way of doing, to build a new building. This new building, the famous

Trinity, is Gothic. It was built in 1846 in the heart of the Greek Revival. Upjohn also built old St. Thomas's in the Gothic style. Following the example of Trinity, or perhaps independently of its influence, other Gothic churches were erected, such as the Huguenot Church in Charleston, South Carolina, built in 1844. Upjohn is often given credit for the parentage of a Gothic revival; but it seems to me that these occasional Gothic churches constituted no revival at all; they are merely sporadic recurrences of the grand old style always before men's eyes in the great cathedrals of France and England. A real Gothic revival came, we shall see, in the sixties, but in character and detail its products were very different from these occasional Goths who strolled in their bearskins among the snowy chitons of the men of Athens.

So much for our barbarous intruder. He is hardly noticeable among the phalanxes of porticoes and pediments. The following are all Greek Revival churches: the First Presbyterian and the Unitarian Churches of Philadelphia; St. John's Chapel, Portsmouth, New Hampshire; Westminster Church, Providence; the Second Presbyterian Church, Albany; the chapel in Amherst College; the First Presbyterian Church, Worcester; and the Congregational Church in Henrietta, Ohio. Both St. Phillip's and St. Michael's in Charleston have Greek touches added after the disastrous fire of 1833. Even a synagogue or two doffed the gaberdine and donned the toga, like the Beth Eloim of Charleston, rebuilt in 1840. Colleges, schools, academies, ladies' seminaries of which there was an especially bountiful crop, prisons, hospitals and even factories appeared in the Greek guise. Some of these were famous for their beauty, such as Girard College in Philadelphia, and some showed remarkable advances in scientific arrangement. There is a tradition that European authorities on occasion visited our penal institutions, finding them an advance on Newgate and Old Bailey.

Architects had come into their own, you will remember, in the brief period of the Post-Colonial, but, while the Greek Revival boasts many an architect, there was also a noticeable backsliding in the direction of the handbook. The reasons were obvious: the Greek style had to be copied exactly or not at all, hence the necessity for the *vade mecum*; and, because of the great expansion of the country, parishes grew altogether too large for the few architectural missionaries. This condition gave birth to that despised species, the carpenter-architect, still extant, indeed, in the contractor who will design as well as build your edifice. The journeyman carpenter (the craftsman) had largely lost the traditions of these master craftsmen of Georgian days, so the job was now done by a contractor who got his elevations from the handbook. Aside from those majestic tomes, the "Antiquities of Athens," which reposed only in the great libraries, there were various lesser and much more convenient sources of information. That ardent Hellenist, Owen Biddle, published a handbook of Greek detail in 1805, and Asher Benjamin kept his own publications up to date by new editions in 1814, 1832, 1833, while Minard Lefever published a book in 1833 called the "Modern Builders Guide." Nevertheless, above these small fry with their squares and handbooks, tower the great figures of the Greek Revival architects themselves.

The first of these is Benjamin H. Latrobe, the man who brought the Parthenon to America in his gripsack. He was born in England in 1764. He studied architecture and practiced his profession in England where he was associated with that celebrated Greek Revivalist, Cockerell Sr., after a

youth spent in Germany where he attended the University
of Leipsic, he became a Prussian soldier and was wounded
in action. After serving as Surveyor of Public Offices and
Engineer of London, in 1796 he came to Virginia at the request of Washington. He was engineer to the State of
Virginia, and superintendent of water supply in Philadelphia. Thomas Jefferson appointed him surveyor of public buildings in Washington with especial charge of the
construction of the Capitol. Owing to the War of 1812
this work was suspended and in 1814 the British burned the
Capitol; but at the close of the War Latrobe was reap-
pointed architect of the Capitol. He retired in 1817 and
lived for a while in Baltimore, later moving to New Orleans, where he died in 1820, just about the time the style
he had introduced into America had become universally
accepted. Latrobe's epochal work was the Bank of Pennsylvania in Philadelphia. This building was pure Greek
hexastyle prostyle, and of the Ionic order. It was torn down
shortly after the Civil War. With the exception of a small
house built in Connecticut in the preceding century, this
was the first Greek building built in the United States. The
size and beauty of the building, the authority of Latrobe,
and the enthusiasm of Nicholas Biddle, the promoter, made
this bank the cynosure and envy of all eyes. Greek architecture was the latest thing, *le dernier cri,* the fashion.

Latrobe's work on the Capitol in Washington was done
between the years 1803 and 1817, and is principally confined to the semi-circular room known as Statuary Hall.
This room was once the Hall of Representatives, and
echoed (they had great trouble with faulty acoustics) to
the honeyed pleadings of Clay, the Great Compromiser,
and to the Olympian utterances of the Jovian Webster.

Now it is the resting-place—though they appear restless

enough—of those unhappy effigies of the great and the near-great, the favorite sons and daughters of their respective states, done into almost every material and ranging from lilliputian to brobdingnagian proportions, which attract smiles from the sophisticated and awe-struck whispers from the innocent—a humorous indictment of our taste and knowledge of sculpture during the nineteenth century. This hall is Greek Corinthian after the charming columns which still cling to the little monument in Athens dedicated to Lysicrates.

In 1805 Latrobe submitted to Bishop Carroll two designs for the proposed cathedral in Baltimore. One was Gothic similar to Peterborough in England, and the other Roman like the Pantheon. The Classic design was chosen and in 1821 the cathedral was dedicated, "the finest Classical church in America."

Latrobe's final work was the Second Bank of the United States in Philadelphia. For this he went back to first principles, copying the Parthenon. It was built between 1819 and 1824.

Of Latrobe's pupils and disciples the most interesting was Robert Mills. As a Greek he would have been a Spartan. No Attic or Ionian softness for him. He almost entirely eliminated ornament, and in the Washington Monument, in Washington, begun in 1836,—his finest work—dispensed with every moulding and other architectural accessory as well. Think of the Draconian restraint of a man who, with that cliff of white marble before him, refused to scar its face by a single scratch. Before this Mills had built the Washington Monument in Baltimore in 1815, introducing the Vendôme and Hadrian Column idea into America. The huge and dignified Treasury Building in Washington, of the Ionic order, built in 1836, is also his work. He seemed to have had a monoply in custom houses, as he built them in Middletown, Connecticut; Newbury Port, Massachusetts; New Bedford, Massachusetts; and New London, Connecticut; Wilmington, North Carolina; Norfolk, Virginia; and Savannah, Georgia. Numerous mints and sub-treasury buildings, filled out his busy life and extensive practice. He was the "court architect" of his time, and in his vigor and simplicity the Sammichele of this Greek Renaissance.

William Strickland, 1787–1854, should be familiar to a student of these times. Also a pupil of Latrobe, he was the antithesis of Mills in style. He liked curves and ornament and cupolas. He has given us the best of the "exchanges" of his day, the Merchants Exchange in Philadelphia, built in 1834. Picturesque and original in form with its swinging colonnade, it is one of the few buildings of the Greek style that can claim much in the way of originality or picturesqueness. Strickland was the inventor of that happy expedient which substituted for the dome on state capitol buildings. The crisis was grave. The legislators called for domes, but domes were never used on Greek buildings. Strickland took the little Choragic Monument of Lysicrates, that veritable life preserver of the Greek Revivalist, and perched it on the highest part of the roof. It is remarkable how well it looks in this location. His fine Capitol Building in Nashville, Tennessee, while superintending the erection of which he died, offers a good example of this treatment. In this connection one might mention the courthouse in Petersburg, Virginia, which bears a sort of spire made of several stories of the Choragic Monument, superimposed, but it is not, as far as I know, by Strickland. Another of Strickland's achievements was the first use of illuminating gas which he introduced in the Gothic Masonic Temple in Philadelphia, built in 1809. Strickland built as well St. Paul's in Philadelphia and the old Chestnut Street Theatre, and in 1828 tried his hand at remodelling Independence Hall.

Other architects there were, like Isaiah Rogers, who built the Merchants Exchange, 1843, in New York city; Young and Rogers, who built the Custom House in Boston in 1847; and Ithiel Town, whose Capitol building in Indianapolis bears the unfortunate addition of a dome, proving that Strickland was right!

The last of the big men of the Greek Revival period was Thomas U. Walter, and he produced what is probably the masterpiece of the style—Girard College, the gorgeous building he erected for that old arch-pagan, Stephen Girard. Walter was born in 1804 and died in 1865. His school was the draughting-room of Strickland, and, as we might expect, his taste tends toward the lighter aspects of the style, the Ionic and Corinthian, in contrast to the sterner Doric manner of Mills and Latrobe. Girard College was built in 1831. It is all of white marble, a great peripteral colonnade of Corinthian columns enclosing four marble walls pierced with little bedroom windows which search as best they may for the sunlight. It was such glaring though beautiful examples of inappropriateness that caused the downfall of the Greek Revival. Walter lived till 1865, working for the most part on the completion of the Capitol in Washington, but this work falls in another epoch.

The fall of the Greek Revival was so sudden that transitional works are rare. Usually the cornice is the first to show the coming change. Drive through the country in Michigan, Ohio, or Illinois—in fact, any state east of the

Mississippi—and if you watch closely you will find frame houses with good Greek doorways and window-casings, but with jig-saw brackets under the cornice; curious and ugly things. Look farther and you will see that the next thing to show change was the porch. No longer Doric or Ionic columns, properly rounded and fluted; instead you will see thin, square posts with the same ugly jig-saw ornamentation. The last were the window and door frames. When these become pedimented and ornamented, we have seen the heels of the Greek Revival.

A fine and monumental example of this transitional style is a grand old mansion at 93 Rutledge Street, Charleston, South Carolina. It has a great piazza in Greek columns, cast iron trellises, and a cornice of the Parvenu type.

So perished the Greek Revival. No great social or natural cataclysm overthrew it. The fad died out. Its end came through what was really an attempt to return to common sense and some practicality, and, if the style that followed reached the lowest point in the artistic expression of architecture, its forms, at least, came nearer to expressing the purposes of the buildings and the nature of the materials in use. The Greek style was frequently attacked by its contemporaries. The absurdity of applying Greek columns and temples *in toto* to the solution of American problems was often pointed out. The anomalies of using wood, tin, and cast iron in imitation of marble was frequently dwelt upon.

Back in 1835 Washington Irving had bought an old Dutch farm-house just above Tarrytown on the Husdon River, and had remodelled it in a picturesque half-Gothic manner. It is described in an old book as "cut up into odd, snug little rooms and boudoirs, according to the signs of promise from the peaked roof and gable-ended exterior. The eastern side of the house is overgrown with ivy presented to Irving by Sir Walter Scott." As "Sunnyside" was a famous place of pilgrimage, undoubtedly its picturesque beauty constantly challenged the popularity of the Greek. "Godey's Lady's Books" of the forties publish, side by side with pictures of ideal "Doric" cottages, designs in Swiss chalet or English cottage style. An article in the "North American Review" in 1836 attacked the Greek style, and in 1842 A. J. Downing, a man who deserves a biography, published his "Cottage Residences," showing houses in what was called the "Downing Cottage style." A curious eddy in this latter architectural stream is indicated by the old "round houses," which were, however, occasionally octagonal. In 1854 a book was published by Mr. O. S. Fowler called "A Home for All or the Octagon Mode of Building." This book proved, at least to the satisfaction of the author, that a house of circular or octagonal plan not only had the smallest amount of outside wall space for the area of the enclosed rooms but also resulted in a building more conveniently arranged and more elegant than the prevailing "Cottage" or "Doric" type of building, of which he was especially scornful. Mr. Fowler, who was also an author of numerous works on phrenology, must have had many disciples, for a number of these octagon houses were built throughout the country. I remember as a boy an old round house in my home town. Its stairs were in a well in the center, which was lighted by a cupola, and the rooms presented an amazing variety of triangles, octagons and trapeziums. Needless to say, the house was haunted—probably by the ghost of Euclid. A little more missionary effort added to these attacks and exhortations induced the fickle worshippers to overthrow their

Athenian idols, and by 1850, except in the far West, perhaps, the "Greek mania" had passed away.

Whether or not a good copy is preferable to a poor attempt at originality is a question of temperament not determinable by any intellectual process. We are certainly blessed with an excellent opportunity to test the point in a comparison between the Greek Revival and the style that succeeded it. As another points out, whether a style is good or bad—and by that is meant logical and appropriate or the opposite—is no criterion of its importance historically, and for that reason alone every monument of the Greek Revival should be carefully preserved and honored. Aside from the regard of the historian and archaeologist, the lover of beauty for its own sake, too, would regret the loss of a single column or pediment. Absurd as these monuments may seem when judged by a logician, they are entirely satisfying to one who believes that beauty is its own excuse for being. On that side, at least, the contribution of the Greek Revival was almost without exception one of charm and dignity.

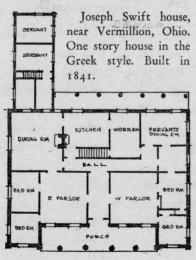

Joseph Swift house, near Vermillion, Ohio. One story house in the Greek style. Built in 1841.

CHAPTER V

SPANISH AND CREOLE ARCHITECTURE

Orchids and Gardenias in Our Geranium Beds

THE SPANISH MISSIONS

It seems curious that all the while we Anglo-Saxons were building along the Atlantic seaboard the Georgian mansions and meeting-houses of which we are so proud, the Spaniards, thirty-five hundred miles away on the shores of a still mightier ocean, were converting the Indians and building other meeting houses. We and they were virtually oblivious of each other. We may well feel a thrill in reading that on July 27, 1776, twenty-two days after the signing of the Declaration of Independence, the first colony of white men pitched their tents and broke ground for the mission of San Francisco de Asís, the future metropolis of the Pacific coast.

These Franciscan and Dominican padres and commandantes belong chronologically in our Colonial period, but what an abysmal gulf separates them from our Colonial forbears in architecture, religion, government, manner of living, and every social and cultural activity! Can you imagine Fra Junípero Serra establishing one of his missions in Salem, Massachusetts, or Jonathan Edwards reading Calvin's Institutes before men-of-arms, friars, and Indians in the chapel of San Diego de Alcalá? The easy-going and, in mundane things, ignorant monks, surrounded by their copper-colored and childlike neophytes in a Cytherean climate, were no match technically for the energetic and highly educated preachers, deacons and vestrymen who built not only for beauty, but for efficiency and protection from the elements. Both styles were well nigh perfect in their harmony with their environments and their reflections of the culture which produced them. In the interiors I should say that the monks of California surpassed the Americans in architectural charm and religious atmosphere. Their problem was simpler, and they were aided by the presence of the altar and its accessories, but on the other hand they had little to work with and poor hands to mould that little. Such interiors as those of Santa Inés with its beamed ceiling, San Antonio de Padua with its delightful surprises, Santa Bárbara with its paintings, have far more color and warmth, even more directness and simplicity, than the prim and often awkward interior of the Colonial church.

But notwithstanding such differences, the Spanish architecture of the missions and the Georgian architecture of the colonies are cousins, for they are both members of the great family of the Renaissance. After a full century of neglect and ostracism, the architecture of the mission has been received into the American family, has become a part of us, and this new old blood, crossed with the Puritan tradition, has produced in the last twenty years in California perhaps the loveliest daughter of our architecture—a daughter with the vigorous constitution of the north and the slumberous eyes and orchid coloring of old Mexico.

Before we enter into any discussion of the architecture of the missions, it might be well to say a word only about their history. The Spaniards had been in Mexico for two hundred and fifty years before they received royal orders from their home land to occupy and colonize Alta California. As was the custom in Spanish conquests, the priest and the soldier went hand in hand; the cross and the sword burst simultaneously upon the view of the astonished natives. The sword was to achieve the land for the King of Spain; the cross was to achieve the natives for the King of Kings.

The settlement of these dual conquerors in California always took a certain form: it was tripartite. There was first the presidio, second the mission, and third the pueblo. The presidio housed the commandante and the soldiers. It was the symbol of temporal power and the King. It was usually an enceinte of four walls with a plaza or courtyard in the center, into which the various offices, dormitories, guard rooms, and so forth, opened. Its walls were moderate in height and strength, and were feebly protected by corner bastions.

The mission was a more complicated structure. It consisted usually of the church, sacristy and baptistery, and often a chapel, and in addition to these (I quote from Rexford Newcomb) "Shops for the industries, such as weaving; carpentry; blacksmithing; soap and candle making; hat, shoe, and rug making were provided, as well as various storehouses for hides, tallow, wool, and grain. Add to these apartments quarters for the major domo . . . a few guest rooms, a hospital or infirmary, and some notion is gained of the various structures that the padres so simply, yet so logically, developed to meet the needs of their educative program." It is the patio, however, that we visualize when we think of the mission. Around its ample area ran the protecting wall; from the adjoining shops came the ring of the hammer, the wheeze of the saw, the guttural laughs of the Indians. Within its shady cloister walked the padres busy with their beads or breviaries, on the sun-bathed stones or clay of the enclosures sprawled the Indian children, and at the well in the center the dusky neophytes filled their jars or slaked their thirst.

The pueblos were a helter-skelter conglomeration of adobe houses and thatched huts which housed the populace, for the most part Indians. They require no description as none of them remains, their sites now supporting, for the most part, the various buildings of the modern California town.

Of these three factors in a Spanish settlement, the mission almost immediately became preëminent. A positive cause for this is to be found in the vigorous administrative ability and wisdom of the first few ecclesiastical presidents of the mission system, and a negative cause in the peacefulness and docility of the Indians, which rapidly allowed the presidios to fall into neglect and decay.

The converted Indians seem to have existed in a state of willing vassalage, hypnotized by the gorgeous ritual and mysteries of the church. They who had seen God in clouds and heard Him in the wind, saw Him now in gilded iconography within the four walls of the church, and heard Him in the sonorous antiphonal or the fairy call of the Angelus. They lived in the pueblos; the bachelors were herded together and locked up at night, while the unmarried girls, were kept in a convent outside. As a convert of the living church the Indian was not to spend his time on flowery beds of ease. He reported at sunrise for prayers and mass; breakfast followed, after which each went to his work; after dinner at noon there was a siesta until two; work again until the Angelus bell at sunset; prayers and the rosary, and then the Indian was free to dance and otherwise express himself until the routine began again the next morning.

The mission priests had no illusions about the Indians:

souls they had to be saved, hands they had to be exploited, but minds or wills to become useful and independent liegemen of his Most Catholic Majesty they had not. Nevertheless, the Indians seem to have had kind masters and to have been contented and happy. History records only a few outbreaks, the worst at San Diego, in the last of which Father Jayme and two others were killed. Comparing these with the fearful massacres and bloody reprisals of the New England soldiery, it would seem that the Catholics in California at least understood the Indians better than did the Puritans.

The whole history of Alta California, the coast line, that is, from San Diego to San Francisco, between 1769 and 1825 is a chronicle of the establishment of missions. It is said that the great and saintly mission builder, Fra Junípero Serra, desired to plant one of God's mile-posts at the end of every day's journey. As these missions are most of them marked by architecture of beauty and interest, and as their names are picturesque and romantic, I cannot resist the temptation of transcribing a few from the records with the dates of their founding: San Diego de Alcalá, 1769; San Carlos de Borromeo, 1770; San Antonio de Padua, 1771; San Luis Obispo, 1772; San Juan Capistrano, 1776; San Francisco de Asís, 1776; San Buenaventura, 1782; Santa Bárbara, 1786; Santa Cruz, 1791; San Juan Bautista, 1797; San Luis Rey, 1798; Santa Inés, 1804; San Francisco Solano, 1823. How Spanish they sound, and how far away! All of these have left more or less extensive and interesting remains.

The golden days of the mission system extended from about 1800 to 1813. Padre Serra, having fought a good fight and kept the faith, and incidentally established a spiritual and temporal domain for the King of Spain, died in 1785. The presidency of the missions succeeded to able hands. Padre Fermín de Lasuén was the dominant figure in their culminating period. "Under his administration," says Newcomb, "the missions prospered and became wealthy estates absolutely and solely administered by the padres, who became, in a sense, not only the preachers of the country, but also its great farm managers, its great merchants, and, so far as the Indian population was concerned, its rulers. The stock multiplied upon the farms; great quantities of grain were produced; the mission orchards and vineyards grew into bearing and throve abundantly. Nearly all the missions erected new and handsomer buildings of brick or stone, provided irrigation ditches and aqueducts. . . . The padres furnished great quantities of supplies to the presidios, and thus the government became the debtor of the missionaries whom it protected."

Clouds appeared in these cerulean skies in 1813, when laws were passed turning back certain lands to the Indians. In 1821 Mexico gained her independence from Spain. Legislation soon followed to "emancipate" the Indians, but the final blow came in 1834 when the Mexican Congress passed the law secularizing all the missions, and passing their control to commissioners always ignorant, usually corrupt. Within ten years only a handful of the Indians remained. The wealth of the missions had disappeared, and the great structure built up by Serra had toppled to the ground.

However, as is usually the case, there were compensations. The mediaeval, almost feudal régime of the missions could not have lasted for long in the face of Anglo-Saxon immigration. With the fall of the missions began the rise in importance of the presidio, and the growth of commerce and society.

We cannot pause to consider the few remains of Spanish domestic or civil architecture in California, except to recall that in the eighteen twenties and thirties, just before the coast became Americanized, a charming and brilliant social life centered about Monterey and San Francisco. The patio with its soft-voiced monks, its droning bees, its humble Indians—the last gesture of mediaevalism in the New World—has been succeeded by the busy plaza with its color, noise, and life—the promise of an imperial future.

The student of the Renaissance in Spain will discover that the first style to emerge from Gothic mediaevalism was that curious and fascinating mode known as the Plateresque, or silver-smith style. Whether the name was derived from its similarity to repoussé metal work or whether silver workers who emigrated to Spain from Holland fashioned some of its models, is immaterial. It was a mixture of Moorish, Gothic and Classic forms—the famous hospital of Santa Cruz in Toledo is a good example—and it is usually supposed to have flourished between 1500 and the accession of Philip II in 1556. With the reign of this monarch architecture executed a right-about face. The style became cold and formal. The chilly and depressing Escorial arose to house and entomb a royal and cruel fanatic. This style is known as the Griego-Romano, and its course proceeded evenly enough until 1665. It was then overwhelmed by one of those architectural freaks that upset the critics and add to the joy of nations. This outburst was the invention of an otherwise obscure architect with the unpronounceable and almost unspellable name of Churriguera; and the style he brought into the world is called after him the Churrigueresque.

It was an outlandish fashion which violated every architectural canon and broke every commandment of taste.

It maintained the old Spanish principle of contrast, however. What does a Spaniard love more than a great, barren, tawny wall, be it granite or adobe, and, bursting out in the center of its aridity like a tropical oasis in the midst of a desert, a vivid, gorgeous splash of scintillating ornament? This principle of contrast is carried to the last degree in the style of Churriguera. The ornament itself is a confused and writhing mass of broken cornices and squirming volutes, of columns with their elsewhere fair surfaces broken out in a thousand architectural excrescences, of entablatures tortured and twisted as though upon the rack of Torquemada—niches, shields, saints, cupids, "rotting fruits and swollen garlands," all stirred up into an architectural phantasmagoria impossible to describe. There is a sort of orderliness underlying it all, nevertheless. For instance, it is always on axis—that is, symmetrical on either side of a certain line—and it is usually spread on the surface with a constant thickness. It is, moreover, always contained within a boundary eminently architectural.

Along with this characteristic spasm of decoration, which usually occurred about the main portal, the Churrigueresque possessed other features easier to understand— domes of beautiful colored tiles; belfries and cupolas of charming silhouette and detail; delightful star-shaped windows; great swinging volutes that can be traced back, I dare say, to Alberti's Santa Maria Novella, built as the dawn of the Renaissance was breaking in Florence.

This style was in the ascendant in Spain during the conquest of Mexico, and it was exclusively employed in the great rebuilding of the Aztec cities, while the indigenous Mayan forms were totally ignored. We see it in the cathedrals of Havana and Mexico City, at Chihuahua, at Gaudalupe; and the magic hand of Bertram Goodhue again called it into life in the beautiful San Diego building in the Panama Pacific Exposition of 1915. Naturally it was this style that Fra Junípero packed over the hills as he set forth on his painful journey to Alta California, and it was this style that was employed with modifications in all the missions.

These modifications consisted for the most part in leaving off much of the elaborate ornament. Volutes, cartouches and garlands could hardly be evoked from the childish minds and fumbling hands of the Indian artisans, who could, however, build long, sturdy walls, very simple arcades, belfries of modest dimensions, and even small domes. Occasionally, as at San Luis Rey de Francia we have a naïve attempt at an ornamental gable; at Santa Bárbara, a pediment supported on six engaged Ionic columns that look for all the world like work of the Mycenaean Greeks; at San Carlos Borromeo a star-shaped window, and some little domes above it. At Santa Cruz, at Santa Bárbara, at San Buenaventura, the companario or open belfry is a characteristic feature. A beautiful one exists, also, at San Gabriel Arcángel, where the bells in separate niches, like deep-voiced monks each in his pensive cell, awaken the morning with the Angelus and in the evening toll the knell of parting day.

To describe each mission with its church, patio, and all its complication of parts would be far beyond the scope of a single chapter. Yet one should be familiar with the outstanding examples of mission architecture.

The most elaborate, the most architectural, and the most advanced in type is the mission of San Juan Capistrano. It lies nearly half way between San Diego and Santa Barbara, located, as most of the missions are, in a picturesque and commanding site. Behind are the foot hills of the Santa

Ana mountains, and at one's own feet break "in a sound like thunder—everlastingly" the waves of the Pacific. San Juan is one of the foundations of the tireless and devoted Junípero Serra, himself far more worthy to be canonized than the San Juan for whom the mission was named, an inquisitor and a persecutor of the followers of John Huss and other heretics. Serra founded the mission in 1776—an easy date to remember. Within ten years—taking the figures from Newcomb—there were five hundred and forty-four inhabitants in the settlement. Thousands of sheep roamed over the mission pastures, and the adobe granaries were bursting with the stores of the padres.

The plan of this mission furnishes an excellent type. The long, narrow church rising above the plaza, together with its tower, baptistery, and sacristy, dominates the scene. To the west stretches the great square of the patio with its cloisters and numerous shops and work-rooms. Connected with the patio and extending parallel with the church, and with it bounding the busy plaza, is the hospice with quarters for the major domo and rooms for guests. Behind the church is a little patio for the padres, their private quarters, a garden, and the cemetery. This splendid establishment, rivalling works of similar character in Europe, enjoyed but a brief maturity, for the disastrous earthquake of 1812 did more damage than any inroad of the Goths and Vandals—overturned its tower, threw down its proud vaults, and left it practically in ruins. The church and patio have never been rebuilt. Within the gaunt arches and broken traceries "the moping owl doth to the moon complain" (if there be owls in California) and through the ruined nave and deserted sanctuary walk with wondering or unconscious feet the tourists and the trippers of whose presence in California there can be no doubt.

Architecturally there are some curious things about San Juan,—the absence, for instance, of any Christian symbols, which is explained by the local tradition that the master mason was a heathen Aztec. Some of the ornament, such as the handles of the baptismal font, is certainly Mayan. The main cornice and base of the sanctuary and nave and the mouldings about the sanctuary door are such as never came out of Christian Spain, and their prototypes, doubtless, in some altar to the sun, saw the painted priests, the gleam of the obsidian knife, and the dying struggles of the captives at the feet of the magnificent Montezuma.

Santa Bárbara is probably the best known of the missions. It was established in 1785. It is notable for its façade —a pediment and false portico, undoubtedly copied, as Newcomb points out, from a Spanish translation of Vitruvius, illustrated with Roman buildings. The church is of noble proportions, one hundred and seventy-five feet long and forty-five feet wide. Two great towers announce the entrance. The interior is injured by the flat wooden ceiling that covers up the ancient beams, but much color and interest are contributed by the Stations of the Cross and the many other paintings. The lovely garden and basins, the cloister, and the holy ground where rest the padres "each in his narrow cell forever laid," make Santa Bárbara one of the famous historic, romantic, and architectural shrines in the land.

One should visit Carlos de Borromeo near Monterey, often called the Carmel Mission, for the tomb of Padre Serra, for the curious restored interior with its flattened barrel ceiling, for the lovely *fachada* (façade) with its charming dome and its star-window. The doorway to the chapel goes back long before the Churrigueresque for its inspiration. It is Moorish-Gothic, with just a dash of the

Renaissance.—Plateresque, you will remember, that spicy dish is called. Carmel appeals to the architect in one of his softer moments. Rules and styles are thrown aside, matters of construction and materials can go hang; the poet in him is refreshed, revived, and uplifted.

Then there is San Gabriel Arcángel near Los Angeles. How difficult it is to leave any of them out; San Gabriel is one of the oldest, having been founded in 1771, though the present church was begun in 1794. It used to be famous for its fine wines and brandies, but now its fame rests on two things: the magnificent campanario with its range of bells (one of those inevitably beautiful things that makes one suspect its creator, man, may be but little lower than the angels; perhaps the archangel himself whispered in the ear and guided the hand of the forgotten artist!) and the range of extraordinary buttresses that, as Newcomb points out, were doubtless inspired by the Mosque of Cordova in Spain. Other interesting things to be seen are the fine collection of vestments, a charming outside stairway, and a rare collection of books.

The mission of San Juan Bautista is interesting to the architect as the only example of the three-aisled basilica, albeit the aisles have been walled up. There is little left of the venerable mother mission of San Diego, nor of the missions at the other end of the chain around San Francisco bay. They fell prey alike to disestablishment, neglect, time, and the arch-enemy of missions, the earthquake. We shall end our list with the mission named after the canonized King of France, San Luis Rey de Francia. This is the largest in point of size, and one of the first in architectural interest. The plan, always of primal interest to the architect, is strikingly similar to that of its neighbor to the north, San Juan Capistrano. The plan of the church itself discloses a long and narrow nave, which was usual with well-developed transepts, but most unusual in the mission type. It also had a lantern or dome over the crossing, unique in the mission type. Its tower is graceful, rivalling Santa Bárbara. San Luis is not startling, but it maintains a high average of excellence, and its design throughout comes nearer to the professional standard than perhaps any other.

Our love for the Californian missions must not blind us to the beauty and interest of those in Texas. As a matter of fact, the Texan missions, while fewer in number, are in many cases more elaborate in architecture and richer in decoration. This is due to the fact that they were nearer civilization, and that they were built by Mexican rather than Indian hands. Their purpose, arrangement and general aspect, however, are very similar to the missions of California. San Antonio harbors most of them. Of these the Alamo is the most famous. Here, as every boy scout knows, perished David Crockett and his American frontiersmen in their desperate battle with Santa Ana in 1836. It has a heavy and elaborate portal in Spanish Mexican style. San Antonio has four other missions of interest and beauty. That of San Juan Capistrano, built in 1731, was evidently copied, in its façade at least, from San Francisco Espada, which was erected in 1690; both have lovely open campanarios. The mission of San José is the most beautiful of them all. Its sturdy cloister, its lovely chapel, and, above all, its rich façade and portal are eloquent of a knowledge of architecture and its technique far beyond the simple suspicions of Serra and his dusky followers. This mission is reputed to have been built in 1701. The Conception mission, also in San Antonio, was built from 1732–52. Its two west towers suggest Santa Bárbara, and it boasts as well a central dome. The sculpture about the portal is far more delicate than is usual, and the steep gable of the portal it-self is unusual and most interesting. The San Antonio missions possess occasional little souvenirs of the vanished Gothic, such as the pointed arches in San José and the flying buttresses in the mission granary nearby.

So, falteringly, stand the missions, once young, lusty, and self-confident like ourselves. Now the silver cord is loosed, and the pitcher broken at the fountain. Is it the wind in the Vale of Carmel stirring the pines and the cypresses? Is it the ghostly voice of the padre sleeping beneath the stones? Or is it the ancient church itself that whispers to us in appeal, "I have been young and now am old, yet have I not seen the righteous forsaken nor his seed begging bread"?

THE FRENCH AND SPANISH INFLUENCE IN LOUISIANA

Louisiana furnishes, next to California, our most brilliant example of exotic architecture. In New Orleans we have a whole city, an *urbs in urbe,* of a past civilization and of an almost extinct people set down in a frame of towering skyscrapers, clanging trolley-cars, and whirring automobiles. The Vieux Carré, the old city, founded in 1718 by Sieur Jean Baptiste Lemoyne de Bienville, is composed of one hundred or more little squares separated by narrow, straight streets, and arranged about an imposing civic center, the first in America. The great square, dubbed originally Place des Armes, is now called Jackson Square, but the little streets still bear in abbreviated form their original and mellifluous names—Duc de Chartres, Duc de Burgoyne, Duc d'Orleans, Madame Royale, St. Louis, Ste. Anne, St. Pierre. Originally French, the city became Spanish in 1769, and remained so until 1799, when it returned to its Gallic allegiance. In 1803, by a stroke of the pen and the payment to the needy Napoleon of fifteen million dollars (the cost of a modern skyscraper), Thomas Jefferson made it American together with a territory imperial in its extent and regal in its richness. Fascinating and instructive as the history of this savory and romantic city is, we must pass it by for the consideration of its architecture.

Two obliterating fires, one in 1788 and another in 1794, swept away the greater part of the eighteenth century city with the exception of the buildings about the Place des Armes. The buildings in the "quarter" now standing were erected for the most part in the first half of the nineteenth century. They are usually called French. Creole would be a much better name, for they are a perfect mixture of French, Spanish and American. They are to architecture exactly what the steaming *bouillabaisse* and *poulet créole,* which one eats in their purple shadows, are to cooking.

> "This bouillabaisse a noble dish is—
> A sort of soup or broth or brew,
> Or hotch potch of all sorts of fishes,
> That Greenwich never could outdo."

The earlier eighteenth century buildings have not the American ingredient. They are entirely French, and to the writer, at least, the Spanish element is hardly discernible. Especially charming is the old Convent of the Ursulines. It is said to have been built in 1730–34. It looks later, but as it stands it might just as well be demurely resting on the side of a little square in Rouen or any other French town. With its center pedimented pavilion and its shuttered windows with their sunken panels, its high roof, its rusticated quoins, its picturesque concièrgerie, it is perhaps our best example of Bourbon architecture. Romance, equally Gallic, lurks behind its walls, for here young women sent by France, each with a trousseau from the French king, awaited their prospective husbands. When built it was the largest structure in the Mississippi valley.

The famous Cabildo, flanking with its counterpart the Cathedral, is much more provincial. With all its charm, the proportions of the Cabildo are heavy and the mouldings coarse. It shows its Spanish ancestry, but it is not the elaborately ornamented Churrigueresque that we found in California Missions. It is rather of the *Griego-Romano* type of Herrara and the Spanish Classicists, and even at that the influence of French environment is plainly discernible. The charming wrought iron balconies, erected in 1795, are French, as is the general disposition and orderliness of the composition. The high roof with its unusual dormer windows we are told was added in 1851, though it appears to be a part of the original design. In the Salle Capitulaire, the great audience hall, took place the ceremonies of the transfer of the Louisiana Territory, first from Spain to France and afterwards from France to the United States.

The Cathedral in the center of the composition, flanked on either side by the Cabildo and its counterpart, is not of great architectural interest. A center tower and the choir were added in 1819 to an older construction by the father of Greek Revivalism, Benjamin Latrobe. In 1851 the tower fell; and the façade was rebuilt by Depuilly in its present uninspiring form, except that his openwork tower has been encased in a still later one.

The character of the old city comes not so much from these imposing monuments as from the hundreds of lesser

domiciles. They appear to have been built anywhere between 1800 and 1860. This throws them for the most part
into the Greek Revival period of American architecture,
and if you will examine carefully the detail, especially
about doors and windows, you will find the Greek mouldings, the acanthus ornament, the Doric capitals, that were
the vogue throughout the length and breadth of the land.
There are, however, some curious and notable exceptions.
The Grima House in St. Louis Street, probably contemporary with its cast iron water tank on which the date
1831 is plainly moulded, is all of good Georgian architecture. A lady who lives in and maintains the fine traditions of the Vieux Carré, advanced the interesting
conjecture that its builder was a Harvard man, and that
he brought back from Cambridge an enthusiasm for the
Georgian which he crystallized in his mansion.

The most curious of all is a big three-story house at
920 St. Louis Street. To have looked up at its gaunt façade
from the stone streets of Vicenza or Verona would not
have surprised one, but to find in old New Orleans an
Italian Palazzo in the manner of Palladio or San Michele
is a refreshing shock. The basement is heavily rusticated
with arched windows. Above rises an order two stories in
height of pilasters with composite capitals resting on pedestals. The upper windows under the main entablature are
arched and have keystones sculptured in the form of old
men's heads. A high attic story surmounts the composition. I could find nothing of the history of this strange
exile, but the design was obviously copied from some venerable edition of Palladio.

Benjamin Latrobe in his fascinating memoirs vividly
describes the Vieux Carré of his day. Here he lived for
many years, and here he, and his son also, died of yellow

fever. Curiously, his observations on New Orleans mosqui-
toes are followed by his chapter on yellow fever. It took
another eighty-five years to write them into one. Latrobe
says that most of the houses of his day were one story in
height. The roofs were steep and their edges projected out
over the sidewalk as much as five feet—an admirable device as it assured shade in the summer and dry feet in the
worst rain. He speaks of the Spanish tile roofs brought
from Cuba, and particularly of the Americanization of the
European plan which demands individual accessibility by
corridors or otherwise to each room. Several of these one-
story houses with their wide projecting eaves still remain.

Most interesting of all are the ancient half-timbered
houses which he found. These were built in the mediaeval
fashion of sills and girts and studs of sturdy timbers extending clear through the wall. The open spaces were
filled first with mud or adobe, and later with soft (bat-
ture) brick, and plastered outside and in, the exterior
stucco completely covering the timber as well as the brick.
This is exactly the construction of the Early American
houses of New England, if we substitute the wooden siding for the stucco. Evidently the French settlers had memories similar to the Englishmen, for the streets of the little
towns of France are lined with ancient houses not less
rich in their faded plaster and carved timbers than those
of England.

The typical Creole house of the old quarter as it exists
today is something like this: The façade is flat and rises
straight from the lot line. The windows are French casements, extending to the floor; often those of the first story
are arched, as in the Old Absinthe House; they are always
covered with shutters. Around the middle of the house, like
a French ballet skirt, projects a lacelike iron balcony, often

continuous. These balconies are very typical; we shall return to them. The whole composition is crowned by a cornice, sometimes simple, often elaborate. Above the cornice rises the steep roof of slate or tile, usually pierced with rather large dormer windows. These dormers are puzzling. Invariably they are well proportioned, and usually Georgian in design—delicate Georgian, almost Adam. They are all as like as so many peas, and their gabled brows have nothing in common with the square-headed dormer window of France.

The whole façade is plastered, and the plaster painted. The pinks, ochres, yellows and even greens of these plastered walls give the old buildings much of their character. These colors have been called Spanish, but as I got a lovely shade of pink in some very wet paint on my coat sleeve one can hardly call them ancient; but, new or old, they have faded, become discolored and streaked, so that the magnolias and roses in the old courtyards are almost lost against these tender, glowing backgrounds.

To the architect these façades have great technical interest in the beauty and charm of their proportions. The French, more than any other people, have what we call the "architectonic sense," which might be described as a nose for proportion and detail. It is this surety of design that more than any other element is unmistakably French. This is especially evident in the Napoleon House, built, you remember, for his reception should the eagle escape from the rocky cage of Sir Hudson Lowe; in the Paul Morphy House, the home of the Napoleon of chess, and in the house at the adjacent corner of Royal and Conti Streets. The detail is often of the soil. One must remember that these houses were built in the full tide of the Greek Revival, some of the most celebrated exponents of which lived in

New Orleans; so that, if one examines carefully the mouldings, particularly about the portals, one will usually find
the flattened surfaces and subtle profiles of the Greek
style. Some houses are completely and frankly of the Revival. There is a very fine one on St. Peter Street opposite
the Cabildo, which is Greek inside and out, with magnificent doorways carved with the Greek honeysuckle and
pateræ.

Equally interesting and significant with the façade is the
plan of these houses. The typical plan comprised on the
entresol a large room in front with windows on the street,
which one entered from a wide hall or drive that extended
on the side from the street to a court. This court is often
urged as an evidence of Spanish design. From what Latrobe says, however, the courtyard or patio arrangement existed in New Orleans before the Spanish régime, and,
besides, it is quite as common in France as it is in Spain.
The courtyards in New Orleans with their lack of cloisters
and fountains are far more French than Spanish; whatever
their nationality, they are beautiful features of these lovely
ensembles. What old-world glimpse is more charming than
these courtyards within our doors—the royal palms and
magnolias hurtling their violet shadows against the opal
walls of the Grima gardens, or the shadowy arches, the
winding stair, the casual balconies, and the big pots bursting with their oleanders? In that stony courtyard on Royal
Street are impressions just as poignant as the vistas through
other doorways in Assisi or Seville. The front room often
had a room of equal size behind it, and behind this was
the stair opening off the drive and continuing to a similar
range of rooms above. Around the edges of the courtyard
were the shallow kitchens, the service rooms and cistern,
and above them the slaves' quarters. The lower room in

front was usually a shop and the rooms around the court-yard as often work-rooms and factories.

The interior woodwork is almost always Greek Revival, and the same mouldings, evidently made from stock knives, are to be seen over and over again. Plaster cornices of Classic form occur and re-occur, and big rosettes from which the chandeliers hung were prime favorites. Frescoes are sometimes found, as in the "Haunted House" on Royal Street, which, by the way, has a magnificent "Empire" door, apparently made in France. Even as I write some beautiful frescoes in chiaroscuro in the style of Canova are being denuded of their layers of wall paper at 435 Royal Street. The fireplaces are not elaborate—usually of simple marble slabs with a shelf above.

Finally, and deserving of special mention, there is the iron work. It is of two kinds and two periods. Iron work on the older houses and before 1850 is always wrought. These wrought iron balconies are of great delicacy, beauty and variety. They are seldom of the rococo form, but follow the chaste models of Louis XVI. Especially lovely ones occur in the Old Absinthe House, in the Grima House, at 910 and 628 Toulouse Street, the State Bank Building, and so forth. There is a wrought iron doorway with transom and side lights at 832 St. Louis Street that is a joy to behold. The iron gates of the Cabildo with turned iron spindles are cited as examples of Spanish work.

Cast iron balconies, erected after 1850, exist in the greatest profusion. They are usually supported on the slen-derest posts arising from the sidewalk. Often the "posts" are cast trellises. The earliest cast iron is on the Cantalba buildings flanking the square and bearing the monogram of the countess who built them. Cast iron designs are to be found of the greatest variety and originality, but the finest of them all exists in the remarkable fences in front of the Leeds and Gallagher Mansions. These are composed of native vegetable forms. Maize, rose vines, tulips and live oaks, all unite in a design of extraordinary vivacity and richness. When we remember the capitals of Indian corn in the Capitol at Washington, the only work of art that Mrs. Trollope found to admire in the new world, we can make a shrewd guess that our old friend Benjamin Latrobe was the designer.

The sword of a Damoclean commercialism has long hung over the lovely head of the Vieux Carré. Several fortunate circumstances have granted it reprieves. The first are the difficulties of the terrain itself—from the point of view of the promoter. The streets are ridiculously narrow and the sidewalks little ribbons of stone. The squares themselves, though perfectly regular and uniform, are hardly a fourth the area of an ordinary city block. This bijou arrangement hardly appeals to the promoter of skyscrapers or other commercial structures. So, repelled by the barricades of art and tradition and geography, business has turned for its expansion and exploitation to another direction. The promoter with a good-natured shrug of his shoulders has said, "Let those artists and old-timers fry in their own sauce-créole," but we know that the truce is not forever. Already here and there ugly modern structures profane streets sacred to a mellifluous past. Unless civic pride be aroused and action taken, the greedy city will in time sweep the phantom barriers away, and the Vieux Carré will live only in the pages of Lafcadio Hearn and in the fading memories that the years so pitifully hold to their hearts.

CHAPTER VI

THE PARVENU PERIOD 1860–1880

The Age of Innocence (Or Where Ignorance Was Bliss)

THE Classic Revival had become a classic senescence five years before the Civil War broke out. Wars have various and curious effects on architecture. The glorious blooms that sprang out of the barren rocks of the Acropolis were watered and fertilized by the golden shower descending from the defeat of the Persians. The Crusades brought to Western Europe possibly the pointed arch, certainly the pendentive. The wars of Philip II against William of Orange imported the plateresque or jewelers style from the dykes and lowlands of Holland to the sierras and orange groves of Spain. But in general the effect of war is to stop all building for the time being. If a period of expansion and national élan, financial or spiritual, follows, there will be a great revival in building, but usually in a different style. This is what occurred during our Civil War. The Classic Revival was lost to view in the smoke of cannon and the glare of burning towns, and when the war was over men refused to turn backward to the old and faded love.

The period of fifteen years or so following the war was one of great financial and industrial activity. The flotation of the United States loans brought us in contact with the great financial houses of Europe, gave rise to the house of Morgan and brought about the Jay Cooke failure of '73. The principal phenomenon of this era, however, was the expansion of our railway systems. The great trans-continental railroads were built, and huge fortunes were made (and lost) in stock operations and real estate speculation. The Bessemer process had been invented, and its exploitation by Carnegie and Frick not only made possible the rails for the new railroads, but laid the foundations for the world's greatest industrial corporation. For the first time in the history of our country people were born into and lived in an atmosphere of speed—not a speed that would oppress us, but one in decided contrast to the celerity of the covered wagon or the velocity of an Erie Canal boat—into a life far more strenuous than Thoreau's at Walden Pond, or even that of the pioneer, whose struggle was with nature and not with business competitors.

Such a period had little time for the acquisition of culture, and yet with the possession of money came a growing avidity for it. The royal way to culture and the arts was via the check-book and the greenback; hence our rather harsh title of "Parvenu" for this interesting, if not beautiful, period in our architectural and social history. Our architectural styles were purchased along with the other amenities—and where if not over the counters of those eternal centers of fashion and authority to provincial states, London and Paris? So in considering the architecture of our Parvenu period we find two great influences of almost equal popularity and éclat, the Victorian Gothic and the French style of the Third Empire.

What social diagnostician can explain the mysterious artistic plague that swept over England in the middle of the last century, and was imported, as all reputable plagues are supposed to be, by shipboard? The guilty persons

carrying these germs were the first American tourists, for
were not these the days when the clipper ships, a convey-
ance by far too hearty for the tourists, had but lately been
supplanted by the new side-wheelers, the first of the ocean
liners? The American invasion of Europe was on. When
our countrymen found—seated about the throne of the
good but somewhat obvious Victoria—Tennyson, Carlyle,
the Brownings, Ruskin, George Eliot, Macaulay, Dickens,
Thackeray, they would have looked in vain for stars of
equal magnitude in the fine arts. Why in such a brilliant
galaxy should art and taste have glimmered so feebly or
have been so utterly eclipsed? I don't know why the Victorians "were right on questions of morals and wrong on
questions of taste," perhaps it was the Prince Consort. But
we do know that Tennyson and the Brownings and the
rest of the elect exchanged wax flowers, Paisley shawls and
antimacassars without a qualm; that Canova was the favorite sculptor and Landseer the popular painter; that
young ladies laced and had the vapors; and that young men
wore Dundreary whiskers.

The architectural situation in England in the fifties was
something like this: England had been the pioneer in the
preceding Greek Revival, and her porticoes and peristyles
had profoundly influenced the art of Europe as well as that
of America. But about 1850 there had come in England
the Gothic Revival—a protest, the critics would call it,
against the exotic and inappropriate Classicism, but a protest
so belligerent that the resulting conflict became known as
the "Battle of the Styles." Who invented the Gothic Revival? I cannot say. Perhaps it was Ruskin, who brought
out the "Stones of Venice" in 1851, and with his pen for
a shuttle wove out of Italian Gothic art and the English
language a fabric that glowed and glimmered in misty

England as bewitchingly as the façade of his beloved St.
Mark's in a Venetian sunset. Perhaps it was the Pre-
Raphaelite brotherhood with William Morris's frank
contempt for Classic art, and the mystical revolt of Burne-
Jones and Rossetti from the banal sentimentality of contemporary painting. Perhaps it was the Oxford Movement
with Newman, Keble and Pusey exhorting the Victorians
in the Church of England to the higher spiritual life of the
cloister and the cell, *pro vita monastica*. Perhaps it was Sir
Gilbert Scott, who went raging about the cathedral towns,
seeking what he might restore. Perhaps it was Pugin, who
gave to the revival of Gothic art not analysis, but passion.
At any rate, a group of architects arose who worked in a
revived Gothic style: Sir Charles Barry, the architect of
the Houses of Parliament, whom the English regard as the
greatest since Wren; G. E. Street, pupil of Barry and author of the fine nave of Bristol Cathedral; Sedding, a Pre-
Raphaelite; Waterhouse, who built the great bulks of
South Kensington and the Manchester Law Courts; G. F.
Bodley, who evolved a style which is still characteristic of
English work; and a host of architects who were hatched
out of the Crystal Palace from whose prolific shell emerged
most of the men who dominated Mid-Victorian art.

Now let us look at the situation as it was across the
Channel. Those Frenchmen are extraordinary fellows, at
least in architecture. We have seen that during the Classic
Revival, ignoring the slavish imitations of Periclean temples going on across the Channel and across the Rhine, they
had raised the stupendous Arc de Triomphe and the magnificent Madeleine, both inevitably French. So while the
Gothic Revival piped to them from England, and in their
very midst the great symphonies of Rheims, Chartres, and
Notre Dame, rang the call of the thirteenth century in

their ears, the French calmly proceeded with the orderly and logical development of their architecture. Historically, this is the period particularly associated with the rise and fall of Napoleon III. The Emperor was a great lover of architecture and out of his own pocket paid the vast sums that rehabilitated the castle of Pierrefonds and immortalized the indefatigable archaeologist Viollet-le-Duc. While the beautiful Eugénie was setting the feminine world agog with her crinolines and bonnets, her energetic husband was making Paris the most beautiful city in the world. From the great boulevard system of Baron Haussmann, a string of pearls about the neck of Paris, hung like a flashing pendant the opera house of Garnier. Near at hand rose the extraordinary iron church of St. Augustin by Baltard, while upon Montmartre, out of the white lights and the red windmills, slowly loomed the Byzantine basilica of Sacré Coeur. Other great buildings of this brilliant period are the Palais de Justice by Duc, the École des Beaux Arts by Duban, the new buildings of the Louvre, and most interesting of all, the Bibliothèque Ste. Geneviève by Labrouste. It was not a period of the greatest purity nor of great simplicity. It proved to be, in fact, as we shall see, an architectural repast altogether too rich for our innocents abroad.

So, then, the two principal and almost exclusive influences at work in America in this period of a full generation from 1850 to 1880 are first the English Gothic Revival, often called the Victorian Gothic, and secondly the contemporary Renaissance work done in France.

I have an old book. It is of the type that was once, and perhaps still is, called a gift book. It is very large, not designed, obviously, for a student's shelf, but intended to be laid slightly askew on the marble-top parlor table. Its leaves

are genteelly gilded and across its blue cloth cover in large
and picturesque letters runs the title, "Homes of America."
Its glossy pages, illustrated with skillful woodcuts, fall into
three divisions—"Colonial Homes," "Later Homes," and
"Modern Homes." These last establishments were the latest
word in fashion and elegance when this tome was published
in the seventies.

In the mind of our author evidently the American home
was the home of the rich, the distinguished, the elegant. For
society in the age of innocence was divided into three
classes—the rich people, whose insignia were a mansion with
a cupola and a victoria with a span of horses; the "hard
up," often sitting at the rich man's table, composed of
professional people, people on salaries, and unsuccessful
business men, and whose insignia often were the perambulator and the boarding-house; and the poor people. The
poor as like as not had to be helped by the rich at Thanksgiving and Christmas, and included in this enormous class
were the mechanics and skilled laborers—those who now
own their own houses, drive their own automobiles, and
often send their boys and girls to college.

Even today, when a new and chastened point of view
has largely wiped out these undemocratic distinctions,
one pronounces the names of the merchant princes who
dwelt in these "American Homes" with something of
the unction of our gift book's author—"Ogontz," the
home of Jay Cooke with its mansard roof and seventy
rooms; "Rockwood," the home of W. H. Aspinwall; the
great villa of Samuel Colt; the Swiss chalet of Albert Bier-
stadt, dean of the Hudson River School of painting; and
way out on the shores of Lake Michigan the gold fish castle
of Potter Palmer. There were a few smaller, but scarcely
simpler, dwellings of the distinguished, such as those of

Nathaniel P. Willis, E. E. Church, and Charlotte Cushman.

Houses built fifty years ago are familiar enough to all of us, but they should be viewed only in the woodcuts of their own day to be sympathetically appreciated. The great mansion, with mansard and cupola and porches, oriels, bays, porte-cochères and green-houses attached, dominates the scene. Around it are lugubrious bays and weeping willows which somehow remind us of Christina Rossetti and of Napoleon's tomb at St. Helena. In front is the broad and very smooth lawn, policed by the famous cast iron dog and his companion, the notorious cast iron deer, and sure to be dotted with flower beds of cannas and gladioli curiously fashioned by the German gardener in the forms of stars, crescents, and anchors. Out of a shining victoria drawn by two "spanking bays" languidly steps Elsie Dinsmore with her buoyant skirts and bonnet and her lace sunshade. She is casting an arch but maidenly glance in the direction of Uncle George, who, equipped with side whiskers and a high hat, tight pantaloons and a Prince Albert, is expounding the wonders of nature to, we have to fear, the deaf ears of little Rollo, who appears to be shying a stick at the good dog Dash. In the distance are the broad reaches of the Hudson, reflecting the extraordinary clouds that top this scene of refined and sumptuous felicity.

We must confer on the architects of those days, however, the jewel of consistency, for the interiors are exactly what you would expect. The straight narrow hall, the stairway in one run except for a sharp turn at the top where in a niche, presumably to warn you of the winders, stood Canova's Hebe or Powers' Greek Slave. High narrow windows, high narrow rooms, high narrow porches, and

St. Luke's, Isle of Wight County, Virginia. Built in 1632; restored in 1888. The oldest church in America and the last of the Gothic.

PLATE 1

The Parson Capen House, Topsfield, Massachusetts. 1683. Mediae-val in aspect and typical in every respect of the Early American house.

A Colonial house of about 1750 near Petersburg, Virginia. The huge brick chimney is characteristic of a Southern house.

PLATE 2

Westover, Charles City County, Virginia. About 1730. A splendid
example of the robust Georgian phase of the Colonial.

PLATE 3

King's Chapel, Boston. Perhaps our best Colonial church interior. Built in 1754.

Independence Hall. 1732–52. The fully developed Georgian in a civic setting.

PLATE 4

First Baptist Church, Providence, Rhode Island. 1775. Shows influence of Wren in design and of Adam in detail.

Nathaniel Russell House, Charleston, South Carolina. About 1810. A lovely and typical example of the last or Adam phase of the Colonial.

PLATE 5

Old City Hall, New York City. 1803. Mangin and McComb, architects. The masterpiece of the Post Colonial. The little dome of the Parvenu period has been removed, and the cupola and interior restored.

Monticello, the home of Thomas Jefferson. 1796–1809. Designed and erected by him.

PLATE 6

The White House, Washington. A sumptuous example of Post Colonial architecture. Built in 1792 and rebuilt in 1818. James Hoban, architect.

The Library, University of Virginia. Thomas Jefferson, architect. Built in 1818.

PLATE 7

The old Court House, Petersburg, Virginia. Pure Greek Revival using the Corinthian order. It was built in 1835, and the architect was C. Pallard who also designed the old Custom House.

A Greek Revival house in Racine, Wisconsin. Built in 1853.

PLATE 8

Girard College, Philadelphia. Built by Thomas U. Walter in 1833–47. The masterpiece of the Greek Revival. In form an octostyle peripteral temple in the Corinthian style.

A house in Washington Square, New York City. The Greek Revival as expressed in a city mansion.

PLATE 9

Dementi.

Entrance hall, Wickham-Valentine house, Richmond, Virginia. Robert Mills, architect. Built in 1812.

Living room, Lanier House, Madison, Indiana. Built in 1844. Architect, Francis Costigan.

PLATE 10

Santa Barbara Mission, California. 1785. A typical example of the
missions built by Junipero Serra.

Photograph by Whitesell.

The low building in the center is Madame Johns Legacy in Dumaine
Street, the old quarter, New Orleans. Built about 1800.

PLATE 11

Old Art Museum, Boston, 1876–78. A fine example of the Victorian Gothic. Sturges and Brigham, architects.

Photograph by Fuermann.

The McCormick house on Rush Street, Chicago. Built about 1875. The mansard roof and ornamentation show the influence of Charles Garnier and French architecture of the Third Empire.

PLATE 12

Women's pavilion, Centennial Exposition of 1876 at Philadelphia, Pa.

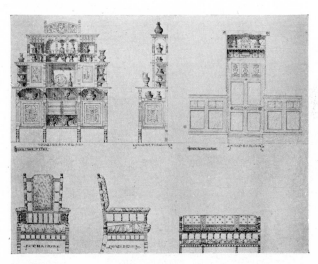

Eastlake Furniture, designed by Peter B. Wight, architect, 1869.

PLATE 13

Trowbridge

The unchanged dining room of Mr.
Kellog Fairbank, Lake Geneva, Wisconsin. The style is Eastlake and the
material yellow pine. Built in 1874.

An interior of 1880 with mingled Eastlake (fireplace) and Queen Anne
motifs.

PLATE 14

Trinity Church, Boston, 1877. The masterpiece of the Romanesque Revival. H. H. Richardson, architect. Porch by Shepley, Rutan and Coolidge.

PLATE 15

Richardson's Best

One of its sons—and occupying its site—
the Marshall Field Office Building, 43 stories
high, built in 1933. Graham, Anderson,
Probst and White, architects.

The Home Insurance Building, Chicago, built in
1884, the father of the skyscraper. The two top
floors added later.

PLATE 16

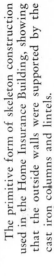

The primitive form of skeleton construction used in the Home Insurance Building, showing that the outside walls were supported by the cast iron columns and lintels.

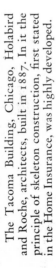

The Tacoma Building, Chicago, Holabird and Roche, architects, built in 1887. In it the principle of skeleton construction, first stated in the Home Insurance, was highly developed.

PLATE 17

A suburban residence of stone, wood, plaster and brick,
built about 1888. Queen Anne in style.

A typical city house of the Romanesque Revival, built of rock face
limestone about 1891.

PLATE 18

Interior, residence of the Hon. John Hay, Washington,
D. C. Henry H. Richardson, architect. Built in 1884.

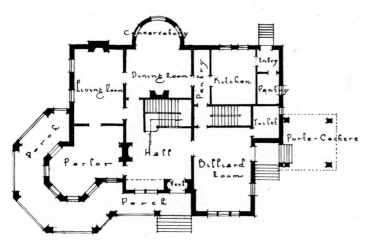

A Romanesque plan by Burnham & Root, built in 1889.

PLATE 19

The Court of Honor, World's Columbian Exposition. 1893. The figure of the Republic is by Daniel C. French. At the end of the lagoon is the Administration Building by Richard M. Hunt.

The Palace of Fine Arts, World's Columbian Exposition. 1893. Charles B. Atwood, architect. Our most brilliant example of Greek ornament applied to a modern building.

PLATE 20

The Transportation Building. World's Columbian Exposition.
1893. The great work of Louis Sullivan that gave his school of original design its first impetus.

The Midway Gardens, Chicago, by Frank Lloyd Wright.

PLATE 21

The doorway of the Getty Tomb, Graceland Cemetery, Chicago.
Designed by Louis Sullivan in 1890. As near perfection as mortals
are allowed to approach.

PLATE 22

Photograph by Henry Fuermann & Sons.

A small house, Oak Park, Illinois, exemplifying at their best the principles of the Chicago school, built in 1906. Vernon S. Watson, architect.

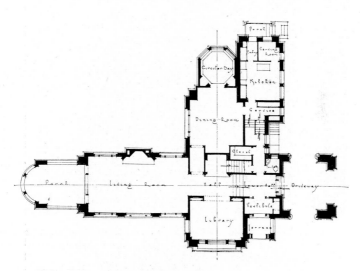

A typical plan of the Chicago school. Tallmadge and Watson, architects. Built in 1912. Oak Park, Illinois.

PLATE 23

The Public Library, Boston. Completed in 1895. McKim, Mead and White, architects. Italian Renaissance in style.

PLATE 24

Main Portal, Union Station, Washington, D. C. D. H. Burnham & Co., architects. Designed by Peirce Anderson, and built in 1913.

The main waiting room, Pennsylvania Station, New York City, McKim, Mead and White, architects. This used to be called "the best interior in America."

PLATE 25

The Woolworth Tower, New York City. Cass Gilbert, architect. Built 1911–13. The first of the super skyscrapers.

PLATE 26

St. Thomas's Church, New York City. Cram, Goodhue and Ferguson, architects. A building the equal of any Gothic structure in Europe of its size, in beauty of proportion and originality and vigor of detail.

PLATE 27

A house by H. T. Lindeberg, architect, typical of the discriminating taste of the Eclectic period.

The Goodman Memorial Theatre, Art Institute of Chicago, a rich example of the art of Howard Shaw, architect, built in 1926.

PLATE 28

A house in Santa Barbara, California, by George Washington Smith. A beautiful example of the brilliant architecture of the California coast.

PLATE 29

The High School, Evanston, Ill. Built in 1926 by Perkins, Fellows & Hamilton, architects.

Memorial Gateway, Harkness Memorial, Yale University, New Haven, Conn. James Gamble Rogers, architect. Built in 1920.

PLATE 30

New York Public Library. 1897. One of our best examples of a public building exemplifying the principles of design as taught in the École des Beaux Arts. Carrere and Hastings, architects.

PLATE 31

Photograph by J. W. Taylor.

The Blackstone Hotel, Chicago. Marshall & Fox, architects. Built in 1910.

Photograph by Chicago Architectural Photographing Company.

First National Bank, Chicago. 1903. D. H. Burnham and Company, architects. The typical skyscraper of the Eclectic period.

PLATE 32

Ford Engineering Building, Dearborn, Michigan. Albert Kahn, architect. The design is governed by common sense, originality and artistic ideals of a high order.

Ziegfeld Theatre Building, New York City. Joseph Urban and Thomas Lamb, architects. A brilliant attempt to bring the stage in stone onto the street.

PLATE 33

The Tribune Tower, Chicago. John Mead Howells and Raymond Hood, architects. The first prize design of the "Chicago Tribune" competition. The detail is Gothic, but the spirit is entirely American. The steel skeleton is indicated in the unbroken piers.

PLATE 34

Lithograph by T. E. Tallmadge.

After the design by Eliel Saarinen which won second prize in the
Chicago Tribune competition in 1922.

PLATE 35

New York Telephone Building, New York City. Voorhees, Gmelin and Walker, architects. A great building, showing in its offsets the effect of the New York zoning law. Built in 1926.

PLATE 36

No. 333 N. Michigan Avenue, Chicago. Built in 1928. Modernism brilliantly applied to the design of the skyscraper. It might be called "clean architecture." Holabird & Root, architects.

PLATE 37

Lounge, The Tavern, Chicago. Holabird & Root, architects. Murals by John W. Norton. The color scheme is blue, grey and silver. Modernism in repose.

A doorway in Cranbrook School, Bloomfield Hills, Michigan. Built in 1927. Eliel Saarinen, architect.

PLATE 38

The Cathedral of Washington, Mount St. Alban. The choir from the Bishop's Garden. Henry Vaughan, Robert Bodley, Frohman Robb and Little, architects.

PLATE 39

Interior of the nave, Cathedral of St. John, New York City, Cram and Ferguson, architects.

House at Syosset, Long Island, Delano and Aldrich, architects, built
in 1929.

Library, House for Max Epstein, Winnetka,
Illinois, Samuel Marx, architect, built in 1931.

PLATE 40

Empire State Building—84 stories high, 2 million square feet of usable area, 50 thousand tons of steel, Shreve, Lamb and Harmon, architects, built in 1929.

Radio City of Rockefeller Center—70 stories high. When completed it will comprise 12 buildings, 4 million feet of floor space, 125 thousand tons of steel—the largest private building project in the world, Hood and Foulihoux, Corbett, Harrison and MacMurray, Reinhard and Hoffmeister, architects.

PLATE 41

A Century of Progress—view from the skyride looking east—A vision of a new order.

The Science Building by Paul Cret, architect.

PLATE 42

A Prefabricated House as built by General Houses, Inc.; steel frame, asbestos-cement board.

Interior of the same with furnishings by Sears, Roebuck & Co.

His own house as designed in 1934 by William Lescaze, architect, New York City. The first floor is the architect's office.

PLATE 43

The "air plane type"—3 story apartment. Julia C. Lathrop Homes—a typical floor.

Julia C. Lathrop Homes, Chicago, P.W.A. Project, Robert S. De-Golyer, chief architect; contains 975 living units, cost $6,000,000, and occupies 35 acres.

Associated architects:

Hubert Burnham
Edwin H. Clark
Quinn and Christiansen
Hugh M. G. Garden
Lowenberg and Loewenberg

Ernest and Peter Mayo
E. E. and Elmer C. Roberts
Tallmadge and Watson
White and Weber.

PLATE 44

A typical Post Office designed in Washington under supervision of a board of advisory architects—Modernized Classic.

Photograph by Gottscho.

The National Archives Building, Washington, D. C., built in 1935, designed by John Russell Pope. It splendidly carries on the tradition of a governmental Classic style.

PLATE 45

The Governor's Palace, Williamsburg, seen
from the Palace Garden.

The parlor of the Raleigh Tavern, Williamsburg. The furnishings are by Susan
Higginson Nash who directed them for the
entire restoration.

PLATE 46

high narrow bathtubs, where there were any, carry out the high and narrow motif.

We all know these houses. To many of us their ugliness is now covered with the veil of honorable old age, and memory blows about them the mist of loving forgiveness.

Safely intrenched behind the ramparts of the ages, who of us wishes that Falstaff had been a Volstead or that Aimée McPherson, instead of Cleopatra, had ruled in Osirian Egypt?

Two types, then, in accord with the influences we have mentioned—one the Victorian Gothic, the other the French Mansard—prevailed. The Gothic was the better, for bad Gothic is invariably better than bad Classic. Perhaps this style was not entirely alien to our blood; at any rate, there were fewer rules about it. But the Victorian Gothic that we practiced was a curious affair. It was not the good old Lancet or Decorated or Perpendicular Gothic that every traveller knows. It was not even the Gothic of Pugin and Sir Charles Barry which we see in the Houses of Parliament. It was a weird, naïve adaptation of the work of Scott and Shaw. It had a decided Italian tinge which was surely Ruskin, but Ruskin probably as digested by the other Englishmen. Now in addition to the Victorian Gothic of England and the Napoleonic Renaissance of France, there is one other influence which I have not mentioned but which was as strong as either of the others. If one reads through the files of the "American Architect," for instance, of fifty years ago, the name of Eastlake bobs up on almost every page. And here is a curious literary coincidence. Nine people out of ten, if there be that number now interested in this phase of manners and art, believe (and with excellent reason) that Charles Locke Eastlake, R. I. B. A., author of "Hints on Household

Taste" and the inventor and founder of the Eastlake Style, was Sir Charles Lock Eastlake, painter, President of the Royal Academy, *arbiter artisticarum* in the palmy days when the Prince Consort was at his busiest as an uplifter and Gladstone was boring the Queen to extinction by "addressing her as though she were a public meeting" and when that other Prince of Wales was getting rid of his inhibitions and worrying the lives out of his noble mentors. But Sir Charles, a Tory of the Tories, could never have written anything so revolutionary, even if he had not died in 1865, eight years before this book was written.

It was in his book, "Hints on Household Taste," that Eastlake made his plea. It is a bitter arraignment of the earlier Classic Revival and of its successor, the hybrid style of the fifties and sixties. Eastlake was a contemporary of the Victorian Gothic Revival in England, which he apparently supports. He made an eloquent plea for the return to the good old days of honest English craftsmanship. Wood should be worked in forms adapted to its character, with dowels and pegs and chamfers all plainly evident. Iron should be wrought on an anvil, not cast in moulds. Brick should be laid in cunning patterns, and stone should be rugged and primeval. He backed up his theories, which were excellent, with practical designs, which he claimed were adapted, as in fact they were, to these different materials. A very sensible book indeed.

This book of Eastlake's was very popular, but what our architects, craftsmen, and decorators did to his designs, forgetting the traditions of Harrison and Phyfe, was terrible. The great top-heavy walnut bedsteads with that curious incised decoration of discs and broken wheat stalks, the corner what-nots with innumerable stories of shelves containing fascinating collections of great shells and coral and sea urchins, the chamfered and ceiled wainscoting with inserts of florid tiles, the lambrequins and Brussels carpets, the wax flowers "*sous cloche*," the bronze Venus de Milo with a clock in her stomach (we had one in our family)—these are all imps that were housed in the Pandora's Box Eastlake so earnestly and honestly put together. A curious example of a good and sensible man sowing the wind and reaping the whirlwind. He will go down in history with those equally well-meaning immortals who introduced the thistle to Canada and the rabbit to Australia.

This Eastlake style was extremely fashionable, and its disciples were great sticklers for its purity. There is a house in my town which used to be pointed out forty years ago as "pure Eastlake." But most of this Victorian Gothic was not pure, and the mélange of Gothic and Eastlake is often today incorrectly referred to as "Queen Anne"—after the brain child of the fashionable British architect, Norman Shaw, who, with his friends, selected the name themselves. The mode couldn't have been known in this country much before 1878 and, in fact, it is only correctly applied to certain houses that were built contemporary with our Romanesque Revival.

I have before me a photograph of a house built in 1876 by two young architects who afterwards became famous. It is very unpleasant to look at, and a description can hardly leave a kinder impression. The house is built of the rockface white limestone known in the West as Joliet. The entrance is reached through a narrow porch or stoop with high chamfered posts and brackets in the Eastlake manner, supporting a second story porch equally high and equally narrow. This porch has no conceivable use, as it is too high to supply shade and too narrow to afford comfort. It adds a piquant note by reason of its Swiss chalet style. Above it, the building continues in the form of a tower surmounted by a huge gambrel roof. This roof is covered with differently colored and differently shaped slates elaborately laid out to form rows and patterns, and the whole is crowned with a fancy cast iron cresting. One looks over the house in vain to find a piece of wall or any feature that is not writhing in architectural agony. Bays projecting even from the corners; oriels with elaborate chamfered stiles; jig-saw brackets (the apotheosis of the turning-lathe came a little later) and panels of wood in patterns; many, many chimneys, all with buttresses, panels and chimney-pots; high, narrow windows, some filled with diamond panes and some with plain sheets of plate-glass—the whole a pathetic but faithful reflection of the naïve and parvenu attitude towards art of the prosperous citizen who took his wife and children to Martha's Vineyard and Saratoga, who ate canvasback duck and terrapin at Delmonico's, and to whom the Philadelphia Exposition of 1876 was the greatest symposium of the fine and useful arts since the Pan-Athenaic celebrations on the Acropolis.

Consider a public building, one of the best of this period and of this style (we are still contemplating the Victorian Gothic), the old Museum of Fine Arts in Boston. It is distinctly Gothic, all the openings having pointed arches; it is distinctly picturesque and Romantic with gables, dormers, and pinnacles; and it is distinctly Italian, the influence of Ruskin and his "Stones of Venice." We can see the fine Italian hand in the alternate courses of white stone and dark brick, in the slender but short colonettes with their large flowery capitals, in the round terra cotta medallions with projecting heads from the Ospedale Maggiore in Milan, in the arcades which transport us back to the Piazza San Marco in Venice. An English building with Italian detail, and with hardly enough mistakes to make it entirely American!

The Victorian Gothic had a certain picturesqueness that covered a multitude of technical sins. Not so that other model of our mid-century architecture, the French Napoleonic Renaissance. Classic architecture, no matter under what guise or in what age it may appear, has a code of laws that must be observed. The stylobate, column and entablature have certain definite members, and these appear always in a certain order or relationship. Furthermore, the detail requires an amount of sophistication and practice that cannot be learned over night. One may well argue that the previous Greek Revival would have given our Parvenu architects this very training, but it must be remembered that the Greek Revival consisted for the most part in copying and re-copying the Greek orders, and applying them as best might be to the buildings of the day—a very simple exercise. There was absolutely no attempt at and no necessity for originality with the Greek or even the Roman style. The French architecture of the sixties and seventies was a more elusive thing. It was alike in no two buildings—rich and explosive in the hands of Garnier, subtle and demure as practiced by Labrouste. It would have been a rich dish even for the educated Englishman of the time, but for the American who didn't know a console from a cartouche, it resulted in architectural colic.

The French type was just as popular as the Victorian Gothic. Perhaps as a rule the larger houses and buildings were French. The prevailing feature was invariably the mansard roof, made popular and fashionable by the great additions to the Louvre being built by Visconti under Louis

Napoleon. Another unfailing ear-mark was the cupola. The cupola was the cachet of wealth and respectability, the prerogative of the merchant prince. For a college professor or small tradesman to have built a cupola on his humble home would have been, I have no doubt, a sort of lese-majesty! The orders were used, but in a singularly impure form. If the building were commercial in its purpose and of any height, they were piled one upon the other, one for each story. This may have been more logical than the frantic proportioning of the nineteen hundreds, when each building was resolved into base, shaft, and cap; but reason, if it existed, was not the result of thought, but merely the limitation imposed by naïveté and ignorance. The whole façade was crowned by a high cornice, usually of wood or tin, and the inevitable mansard roof. Railway stations, legislative halls, hotels, hospitals, churches, banks, college buildings, art galleries, even factories—where is there one that has stood the test of time, or has originated a type that has endured?

Our architects were much embarrassed by the lack of drawings, books, and photographs of these Parisian models. This necessitated strenuous attempts at originality, a subject upon which contributors to the only architectural publication of the time have a great deal to say. Nevertheless, they drew as much as they could on the three fountainheads. First, the great opera house by Charles Garnier, commenced and completed between 1863 and 1875, was a veritable mine. Examine one of our old-timers dated in the seventies (they are usually dated; we must thank them for that!) and see if you cannot find some decaying garlands and beaded capitals, the originals of which glimmer at this moment in the electric lights of the Avenue de l'Opéra, or hang over the sauntering throngs in the grand foyer, echoing back, perhaps, comments on the singing of Chaliapin or the acting of Marthe Chénal.

The beautiful Bibliothèque Ste. Geneviève on the beloved "rive gauche" was second only to Garnier's great work in its influence on us. The architect was Labrouste, whose peculiar style is sometimes called *Néo-Grec*—an ultra-technical definition which need not disturb us. It was characterized by great restraint, and yet, at the same time, by an equal candor. Lebrouste told the whole truth in his buildings, concealing nothing. What the Eastlake mode was to the Victorian Gothic, the *Néo-Grec* was to the French, and curiously enough, some details in these two ornamental systems were quite similar. We shall find this same Library of Ste. Geneviève serving twenty years later, in more skillful hands, as the model for the Boston Public Library.

In the third place, those features in the work of our architects of this period which cannot be traced with certainty to Garnier or Labrouste may pretty safely be accredited to the work on the new wings of the Louvre—the superimposed orders, the cornices especially and always the mansards.

There were many amusing by-products of these importations. The Brown Stone Front, for instance, which became a furious fad in New York City. Thousands of these high-stooped, mansard-roofed houses were built all alike—like so many peas, if peas had happened to be born brown. The stone is soft and of a not especially attractive shade of brown. Mr. A. C. Bossom states in an article in the "American Architect" that the lower Vanderbilt mansions, one of which was razed in 1925, was designed by Richard M. Hunt to be built in marble or limestone, but so great was the rage for brown stone that the dictator of fashion himself was swept off his feet, and these great houses became the forefront of the dark brown tide sweeping up Fifth Avenue and the dark brown taste that characterized society.

A man who lived behind a brown stone front often did business behind a cast iron front, another by-product of this energetic age. The cast iron front buildings, as their name implies, were brick buildings covered with an architectural skin of cast iron, anchored to the masonry behind. The skin might be wrinkled and furrowed with the five orders of Classical architecture, or it might be freckled and pock-marked with the ornament of Mr. Eastlake, but it was in any event hardly "the skin you love to touch." Inside were the old familiar high ceilings, the dank and dark stairways, the heavy and dismal wooden trim and plaster cornices. The utter unsuitability of the building, it would appear, for business purposes fifty years ago could not have been greater than at present.

The interior decoration and architectural treatment of a building of the seventies, particularly that of a residence, was much the same in the two styles. The Victorian Gothic would run more, perhaps, to the Eastlake, for Gothic detail would very seldom be attempted in the interior furnishings. As we have intimated before, these buildings were very badly planned. The ceilings were excessively high, and so were the windows and the doors. The halls were exceedingly narrow, and so were, more or less necessarily, the stairs that ran up along one side of them. A city house had a high stoop, the kitchen usually in the basement, often the dining-room too. In suburban houses the hall was usually in the center with two rooms on each side, generally alike in size and proportion: parlor and sitting-room on the right, library and dining-room on the left; upstairs four bedrooms in similar positions, cut down a little in size by the introduction of closets. There was a bathroom, often (perhaps I should say always) at the head of the stairs. You remember it, up a step with a ground glass panel ornamented with sand-blasted scrolls in the door? The floors were of soft wood and entirely covered with carpet, usually ingrained with large patterns of highly colored floral motives. Satins were in vogue for window-hangings and portières, which were draped to the jambs and crowned with elaborately festooned lambrequins. The walls were usually covered with wall paper, wall paper resplendent in hue and self-assertive in design—"a great advance," says a writer of the time, "on the old custom of decorating with the painter's brush or covering the walls with tapestry."

. The favorite wood was black walnut, though many a fine old merchant prince would take his awestruck guest into the hall and point out to him the twenty different kinds of wood in that extraordinary piece of cabinet work serving the useful purpose of a staircase. The fireplaces were very characteristic. There was one in each room upstairs and down. They were all of marble, usually of slabs not more than an inch in thickness—a moulded slab a foot wide on top for the shelf; another slab, carved with incised Eastlakian designs and serving as an apron, rested on upright slabs serving as pilasters. The round-headed narrow opening was bordered with a robust cast iron frame, and the back and sides were cast iron as well. Inside was a basket for cannel coal. The flues were invariably too small, and the throat incorrectly constructed.

Eastlake in his invaluable book describes the decoration of the drawing-room minutely. "Paper hangings," he says, "should in no way be allowed to cover the whole span of a wall from skirting to ceiling. A 'dado' or plinth space of plain color, either in paper or distemper, should be left to a height of two or three feet from the floor. This may be separated from the diapered paper above by a light wood moulding, stained or gilded. A second space, or frieze, left just below the ceiling, and filled with arabesque ornament painted in a distemper ground, is always effective." All of this would be crowned by a heavy plaster cornice or cove, and in the middle of the ceiling the invariable heavy and highly ornamental plaster rosette, from the centre of which hung the chandelier with all its brass chains, its scalloped ornament and its sand-blasted, etched-glass globes.

Another by-product of the Victorian Gothic was known as Downing's Cottage Style. Robert Downing, an American, antedated Eastlake as an architectural reformer, and in Chapter IV it was stated that his "style book," containing many designs for "cozy frame cottages," was one of the first influences that undermined the Greek Revival. These were, one might say, little sisters of the rich, poor relations of the Victorian Gothic, but, as is sometimes the case with poor relations, extremely numerous. The family resemblance is strong throughout. Very high sharp-peaked roofs, vertical outside wooden siding, the joints covered with continuous wood battens, and remarkable wooden grilles, cut out with a jig-saw and invariably fastened to the under sides of the gable eaves. Here again as in all other styles of the period the high and narrow motive prevails in windows, doors and porches.

In the realm of church design, the Victorian Gothic naturally had the field to itself but, notwithstanding its monopoly and its opportunity, it acquitted itself badly indeed. This was before the days of the Akron Plan and the rise of the Sunday School. The auditorium was practically the sole problem of church architecture, which makes its failure hardly the less excusable. My early recollections of such a church are vivid. It was built of Milwaukee brick, and was in two high stories. On the corner was a tower with a spire—lean and awkward offspring, perhaps, of some far away English village church. The windows were high, thin and narrow, and the detail, carved in Joliet limestone, was so scant and awkward that even to childish eyes it seemed unbeautiful and repellent. The ground floor contained the Sunday School from the vestibule of which, by steep and narrow steps, the walnut stairway led a winding course to an upstairs vestibule. Here the late comers, crowded together in the narrow space, awaited the end of the long prayer. An odor of damp matting permeated the air. The auditorium, once gained, was very high and very bare. It was entirely without architectural treatment except that the plastered walls leading up to the pointed ceiling were frescoed along the top and along the bottom with what the local decorator considered to be Gothic ornament. He was mistaken. There was a high gallery running partly around the room, supported by attenuated cast iron columns. The chancel in which the gallery culminated, as was proper, had received the greater part of the attention and the expense. It was a pathetic example of the frequent failure of devotion, enthusiasm and sacrifice without knowledge, to create beauty. But why continue with a description which would contain an irresistible temptation to ridicule? For ridicule applied to temples that were built, particularly in the West, in the heroic days of evangelism would be little less than sacrilege. When the fate of the Union was at stake and a new empire was to be consolidated beyond the Mississippi, the people, perhaps, had little time for the fine arts. This old church, built in 1871, was torn down to yield to a modern one.

In this architectural garden of the sixties and seventies there were not all weeds. Here and there a rose lifted its head, all the more lovely, perhaps, for its isolation. The earliest of these—which is so early that it may be more properly considered a vagrant from the Classic Revival garden next door—is Trinity Church, New York. It was built by Richard Upjohn, who along with his works received in Chapter IV hardly as much attention as he deserves. Trinity is excellent English perpendicular Gothic, the style that we find, for instance, in the nave of Winchester or the tower of Canterbury. It was the result of independent study and observation on Upjohn's part and was not in any sense connected with or even a forerunner of the Victorian Gothic, which was an importation of some fifteen years later.

A nearly analogous case is that other fane that lifts its twin towers on upper Fifth Avenue, St. Patrick's Cathedral, of which James Renwick was the architect. Renwick was born in New York in 1818, and was precocious enough to graduate from Columbia when seventeen. He started his professional life as an engineer working on the Croton Aqueduct and the reservoir at 42nd Street and Fifth Avenue. Besides St. Patrick's he built Grace Church, New York, the Smithsonian Institute and the old Corcoran Art Gallery in Washington. Renwick lived until 1895.

Although St. Patrick's came fairly within the confines of the Victorian Gothic movement, there is very little evidence of it in its gray stone walls and its French Gothic detail. Renwick had nothing like the prestige nor the practice of Upjohn, and so perhaps he deserves a fuller measure of credit for his independence of the prevailing mode.

Perhaps in so considerable a building he feared to depart far from the great models of the middle ages, for St. Patrick's is 306 feet in its interior length, 108 feet of clear height in the nave, and with towers 330 feet in height— about equal in measurement, that is, to the church of St. Ouen at Rouen, the great monument of 14th century Gothic to which it apparently owes its inspiration. Renwick, notwithstanding his success with the sobriety of St. Patrick's, soon was drawn into the vortex of the Parvenu modes, and his later works bear all the ear-marks of the times.

The two buildings referred to above were in the period, but not of it. New Old South Church in Boston, built by Cummings and Sears in 1876, however, was a real child of the times, differing only in its manner and appearance from its ill-behaved and decidedly unbeautiful brothers and sisters. The Gothic of this building is entirely Victorian. The architects had obviously absorbed Ruskin, and had not been blind to the work of Sir Gilbert Scott. Color and detail show alike the Italian bias of the great critic and the glitter of the Albert Memorial.

A building very similar in style and of equal excellence in design is Memorial Hall at Harvard University. Hot condemnations emanated from the architectural pundits of the day of the wooden vaulted ceiling and wooden ribs which Ware and Van Brunt, the architects, had dared to span over the great auditorium. The debt of American architecture to William Robert Ware is very considerable. In addition to his buildings, always examples of what an architect of good taste and scholarship can do even with a bad style, he was the first director of the first architectural school in America, the Department of Architecture of the Massachusetts Institute of Technology, established in 1865. Ten years later another Ware, William Rotch, returning from the École des Beaux Arts became, in 1876 the first editor of the first architectural publication in America, "The American Architect." For thirty-one years in this important capacity, he did much to improve taste and skill in the profession.

Three men meet at the crossroads of 1876, Richard Morris Hunt, Henry Hobson Richardson, and Charles Follen McKim. Hunt at the time was forty-eight years old, Richardson thirty-eight, and McKim twenty-five. Each of them was destined to be the hero of his epoch.

Richard M. Hunt was born in Brattleboro, Vermont, in 1828, of a distinguished family. His father was a member of Congress; his brother, William Morris Hunt, the painter. His education was conducted in the "grand manner." One of the first Americans to seek Paris for his training, he studied and received his diploma at the École des Beaux Arts. Afterwards he traveled extensively; then returned to Paris, and entered the office of Lefeul, architect of the Louvre, under whom he designed and superintended the Pavilion de la Bibliothèque. He returned to the United States in 1855 when the architecture of his native land had reached its ultimate nadir. Into this sea of darkness he splashed like a brilliant meteor, and though it submerged him more or less for twenty years, yet he reigned as a sort of architectural viceroy, holding the glories of Europe in fee; a Brahmin of the Brahmins; the companion of the Vanderbilts, the Astors, the Goelets; the President of the American Institute of Architects; the recipient of the gold medal of the Royal Institute of British Architects; Chevalier of the Legion of Honor; and Associate Member of the Institute of France. After forty years of distinguished practice he died in 1895.

Probably many of Hunt's admirers will rise in protest at the statement that the Parvenu epoch was his proper milieu; and even the enthusiastic admission that Hunt was a great architect, and that it was better to reign in Hell than serve, as he did in his later years, in Heaven, would not for them remove the sting. Yet not only Hunt's chronology, but his works themselves, definitely make him the outstanding figure during the life of this period.

Hunt's first commission was the Rossiter House in New York, executed as early as 1855. An examination of the photographs of this mansion (it has been destroyed long since) show a building exactly in the style of Visconti's Louvre with rusticated columns and garlands, all in the carefully studied manner that the young architect had learned under Lefeul. An amusing and eloquent example of the influence of such a building is afforded by the front next door, which copies as closely as it can this brilliant neighbor from Paris. It would seem to me that even Hunt was unable for long to maintain his standards or even his taste, for his next house, Dr. Williamson's in Boston, is a distinct let-down, and has donned with its neighbors the prevailing mansard roof. Hunt soon abandoned even a semblance of the French style he knew so well, and in the Vanderbilt houses in Newport we find him piling on the oriels, bay-windows, crestings, and so forth, with the best of his contemporaries. Nor did he hesitate to keep company with the Victorian Gothic; in fact, two of its largest, though not its best, examples are by his hand—the New York Tribune building and the Presbyterian Hospital, also in the metropolis. It is only in the second half of his career, in the early eighties, that he sought again his forsaken Egeria, and there followed that brilliant series of masterly and magnificent palaces which made America's social aristocracy famous throughout the world. But the epoch in which he finally shone had been pre-empted by Richardson, a greater man than he. Hunt's long practice of forty years carried him through the Romanesque Revival and into the domain of McKim, and his last work, the Administration Building in the Columbian Exhibition, was one of the first monuments of the modern period of eclecticism.

I have mentioned 1876 as marking a parting of the ways. It is the year of the Centennial Exposition in Philadelphia, a year usually regarded as epochal, and the end of the era of bad taste which we have been describing. Certainly the exposition itself was no indication of any such finis. It was rather the beginning of the end than the end itself. I believe the causes of the overthrow of this atrocious régime may be exactly determined; first in the brilliant efforts and examples of Hunt, Richardson and McKim, and secondly by the exhibition at Philadelphia of foreign, particularly oriental, works of art. The visits of foreigners and their frankly expressed condemnation of our art, the spirit of self-examination which fills the pages of the early numbers of "The American Architect," all presaged the coming of better times, and at least the will to do. Where there's a will there's a way, and the way in this case lay through education, but it was another half century before the awakening of 1876 had really leavened the lump.

Who in this forgetful and irreverent age has the faintest idea of the Centennial Exposition of 1876 or the slightest respect for it? Who knows now that there were 249 buildings, great and small, that a narrow-gauge railway encircled the grounds, that the total admissions were 10,164,489, that the largest attendance was on Pennsylvania Day, September 28, when 275,000 people passed the turnstiles? Yet all this was so. I have said before that expositions, when they are international, have a mighty influence on contemporary architecture, and this was one of the great ones. Its legal name was the United States International Exposition. Its site was the beautiful Fairmont Park in Philadelphia, of which it occupied 465 acres.

Two architectural competitions were held to determine the design of the buildings and the disposition of the grounds. As the official report naïvely states, "Owing to the difficulty of harmonizing the various designs submitted, the management discarded them all and selected their own engineers." The use of the word "engineers" is significant. The influence of the engineers must have been immediately evident as the two largest buildings were located end to end, contiguous to the railway tracks, nor was there any but the slightest attention paid to a dignified and beautiful general scheme, or to the architectural arrangement of the buildings, to the end that orderliness, beauty, and convenience might be obtained. That there was or could be, moreover, a great art in itself of Landscape Architecture was hardly suspected in the seventies, and yet many pages are devoted in every report of the Exposition to a description of the beautiful lawns, flower gardens and trees, and the vast amount of filling, fertilizing and drainage, that went into their creation.

The principal buildings were as follows: Main Exhibition Building, Art Gallery, Machinery Hall, Agricultural Building, Horticultural Building, Woman's Pavilion, the United States Government Building, and Judges Hall.

The main Exhibition Building held the foreign and domestic manufacturing and crafts exhibits, and it was of no mean dimensions—1880 feet by 464, with an interior height of 70. The beauty, taste, and skill of the foreign exhibits and the sumptuous manner in which they were displayed, compared with the crudity of our own exhibits for the display of which the government had not appropriated one dollar, brought the blush of shame to the cheek of many a one-hundred per cent patriot, and fired the soul of many a fifty per cent architect and craftsman to do better work.

It is hardly in our province to trace the influence of the art exhibits housed in the permanent gallery known as Memorial Hall. The large building entirely devoted to photography intrigues us. Photography was the wonder of the age, although a writer in the "Atlantic Monthly," commenting on the importance given it in the Exposition, points out that a photograph can never be a work of art, for art requires the direct intervention of the human hand and soul.

An architectural description of the buildings need not be extensive. They were almost all in the Mid-Victorian style. The main buildings were of wrought iron frames, filled in between in the lower portions with brick and above with glass. Memorial Hall was of granite and stone, and favored the French influence in its design. Its style was contemporary French of the hardy mansard variety with which we are familiar. Professional readers may be interested to know that the entire group of buildings cost $3\frac{3}{4}$ cents per cubic foot.

So passed the Centennial. The babies who were trundled through the stifling heat of that particular summer are middle-aged men and women, creators of the extraordinary age in which we live. The brides and grooms who gazed at the wonderful Corliss engine and the Centennial

fountain are old ladies and gentlemen thoroughly ac-
climated to the automobile, the airplane, the cinema. The
creators of the Exposition are gone, builders who builded
better than they knew.

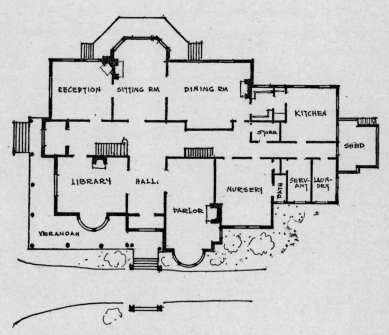

House in Oakland, California. Built in 1876. This house is of wood.
It is a mingled Gothic and Classic style and has a mansard roof and a
cupola.

CHAPTER VII

THE ROMANESQUE REVIVAL 1876–1893

H. H. Richardson and His Great Adventure

SOME day when you are wandering along Main Street, turn your eyes for a few moments from the new Methodist Church, so cleverly done in Gothic, and from the new City Hall, resplendently Colonial in its trim white columns and red brick, and rest them on the corner building across the street. You have noticed it before, but only with a shudder of horror as hopelessly old-fashioned; but note it now more carefully. It is all of brown sandstone, cut rock face. The features of the first story are the huge round arches enclosing with their deep reveals the doors and windows. Above are windows, some round-headed, some square-headed, but all have deep jambs and big expanses of heavy plate glass. There is little or no cornice—only a heavy copper gutter—but the roof is high with copper-covered dormers, and in one corner there is a little tower which vies with the huge chimneys rising here and there. The ornament, especially in the arches, is heavy and barbaric, as is, in fact, the effect of the whole building. Inside, the woodwork is of oak—golden they called it—heavily varnished. There the old building stands, still sturdy and vigorous enough, but clad in the rusty habiliments of more than a generation ago. Yet look at him with respect, ah, lean upon him lightly, for this rusty veteran was once a *beau sabreur* of the most romantic period in

American architecture. He is an exemplar of the Romanesque Revival and once travelled in the train of the greatest of American architects, H. H. Richardson.

The Romanesque Revival is unique in the annals of American art in that it is the first and most important movement that was not a copy or echo of a similar manifestation in Europe. Our Georgian architecture, beautiful and appropriate as it is, was a direct importation from England; our Post-Colonial was largely inspired by a similar movement of a stricter Classicism in France; our Greek Revival, you remember, was brought over in Latrobe's gripsack; and our Victorian Gothic—Eastlake and Mansard style of the Parvenu period—was a feeble and disordered echo of European fashions. The Romanesque Revival, although it used the details of the French Romanesque of southern France to which it went for inspiration, was different in that it was not a copy or an echo or an importation of any similar contemporary fashion in Europe or elsewhere. There was no Romanesque Revival in France or England or anywhere else when Richardson first threw his emblazoned banner to the breeze. No, this was an architectural adventure of our own, and, like most adventures, filled with deeds evil and good, defeats as well as victories, woes as well as joys. But as an aesthetic exploit of the Jack London type it is nothing to be ashamed of: and, read in its pages of gray granite illustrated with dragons and gargoyles, nothing over which to go asleep.

You will remember that in the preceding chapter architectural taste in the United States had reached its nadir, although the Centennial Exposition in 1876 gave promise in faint rainbow hues of better days. Hunt, Richardson, and McKim, we read, were the triumvirate who overthrew the dragon of bad taste, but it is Richardson who was the hero, and whose name is forever linked with the Romanesque Revival.

Henry Hobson Richardson was born in St. James's Parish, Louisiana, September 29th, 1838. We need not go into his ancestry other than to remark that his great-grandfather on his mother's side was the Dr. Priestley who discovered oxygen and did many other things that set his generation agog. Young Henry's early talent for drawing and mathematics, and his other graces also, secured the boon of a college education, and he was matriculated at Harvard University in the class of '59. He seems to have been, like Alberti or Peruzzi, a sort of wonder youth— eager, active, affectionate, generous, excelling in athletics, a fine horseman, an expert with the foils. Blindfolded he could conduct several games of chess simultaneously and his fondness for music made him an adept on the flute. Added to all this, his contemporaries aver that he was "very handsome, tall, slightly and gracefully built, with thick curly dark hair, a warm complexion, very dark and brilliant hazel eyes, and finely-moulded features." The final touch comes in his brother's words that "he was fond of ladies' society," and doubtless they were fond of his. I almost forgot to chronicle that he was regarded as the best-dressed man at Harvard. It is with genuine relief, therefore, that we are informed that he stood only moderately well in his classes!

In 1860, after a year's preparation in Paris, Richardson was admitted to the École des Beaux Arts—the second American to enter the architectural course, R. M. Hunt having preceded him. Here he spent a long time, the happiest years of his life and the saddest, for the terrible Civil War was sweeping over his country and reduced him from affluence to poverty. Here he worked as almost no

American has worked since, and here he sustained an internal injury that remained with him throughout his life and was finally the cause of his death. It would be pleasant to trace his life in Paris and search out the places where he lived. Their names were the same in those far-off days as they are now and just as provocative of memories of laughter and of tears—the Rue Cambon, the Rue de Vaugirard, the Rue Mazarin, the Rue de Luxembourg all gave him domicile.

The war put Richardson in a curious position. He had strongly opposed secession, but nevertheless he rushed back to Boston, the only place he could get to, intending to enlist in the southern cause. Boston was not the best place for this purpose, and, as he refused to take the oath of allegiance to the Union, his friends shipped him back to France as a substitute for clapping him into jail. Nevertheless, Richardson stated that this abortive visit to his native land was one of the most important events of his life. He wrote at the time, "Paris is to a man what college is to a boy—I mean as regards life. I shall never cease to thank Heaven for my short trip to Boston. . . . It gave me an opportunity to compare side by side the habits, customs, lives, of the French and Anglo-Saxons." This is most significant, for in his architecture and in his life Richardson regarded himself ever after as intensely American. In another letter to his fiancée—for he had become engaged while at college to Miss Julia Hayden of Boston—he says, "Paris has no charms for me except my studies. My visit to you—and I thank Heaven for it— put an end to those it might have had."

The pinch of poverty, amounting to privation, soon made it necessary for him to get a job, which he found in the office of the great Labrouste, architect of that extraor-

dinary building, the Library of Ste. Geneviève—a building that has powerfully influenced American architects
from the old, bad Parvenu days down to the time when
it inspired the design for the Boston Public Library, which
today blandly stares Richardson's greatest work in the
face across the cultured expanse of Copley Square. So he
worked day and night, half of his time, as he said, at getting his education and half at earning his bread. In 1865,
the war over, he returned after six and a half years to
America, landing in New York.

Richardson's education and training have been treated
somewhat extensively here because of their great part in
his future success. His brother, confident of the young
man's genius, had given him five years to stand at the head
of his profession. This prophecy, almost literally fulfilled,
saw an unauspicious beginning to so remarkable a career.
Why Richardson opened his office in New York is something of a mystery. His family implored him to return to
New Orleans, his friends wanted him in Boston. He was
even invited to settle in Mexico City and shine as court
architect to the doomed Maximilian.

Ordinarily a young architect begins his career with
several years as a draughtsman in an architect's office, but
Richardson, doubtless feeling that his practical training
with Labrouste had already accomplished this preliminary
stage, decided to begin immediately as a practitioner and
to acquire commissions and attain fame by the competitive route.

There are two methods by which a young architect may
aspire to success. One is the slow but sure way of beginning with a small commission, usually a house, and for a
relative or friend. This building, if good, attracts another,
and so on. The second way is to achieve commissions by

winning competitions—obviously a hazardous undertaking, but with great stakes. Older-established architects almost uniformly oppose competitions. Each, secretly fearful of his ability to win, wants the commission given to him direct. The American Institute of Architects has hedged these contests about with so many restrictions that one wonders whether the rules of the Institute are aimed at protecting its members or at discouraging competitions. But the success of many a young genius would have been long delayed and the world deprived of many a brilliant structure from Brunelleschi's dome to Hood's Tribune Tower had there been no competitions.

Richardson's chance in any sort of architectural competition was excellent. Here he was one of only two men in the country educated at the Beaux Arts, while the rest of his competitors were almost entirely self-educated. The first course in Architecture, that of the Massachusetts Institute of Technology, was not opened until 1866. Added to this unrivalled training he possessed native genius, an enormous capacity for hard work and a willingness to undergo privation if necessary. Finally, his success was assured by the low standard of work that prevailed about him.

But Richardson did not take the easiest way. His entire training and practice in Paris had been in Classical architecture. As he said, he could build a row of Classic buildings from Boston to Philadelphia had he wanted to. The contemporary French version of the Classic style would have been very popular in the United States, especially in New York. Block upon block of pathetic attempts using mansard roofs and debased French detail abounded. Richardson could have done that sort of thing correctly with his eyes shut. He had been steeped in it and it would have been second nature to him. But there is no evidence with perhaps one unimportant exception that he ever used the Classic style after he left Paris. Even in his completion of the Albany State House, a building already half built in Classic form, he insisted on using the Romanesque.

Richardson could not see the genius of America in the garb of Greece or Rome. It is a little difficult for us, perhaps, to understand how he saw it in the garb of twelfth century France. One must remember that Richardson was a Romanticist. He saw his countrymen everywhere about him adopting the Gothic Victorian guise. Perhaps he saw in the Romanesque a style of fundamentals, a form of architecture that began at the beginning of things even with fewer shackles than the Gothic, a style that lay all open to the seed of originality. However, in his first commission, won in competition in 1866, he used the Gothic for his vehicle. It was a large commission—the Church of the Unity in Springfield, Massachusetts. On the strength of it he married.

Shortly afterward he entered partnership with Charles Gambril of New York. This alliance, which gave the name of Gambril and Richardson to the firm, was a very nebulous affair. A partnership it appeared to be in business administration only. In it each member prosecuted his commissions independently. The use of the firm name continued for some twelve or thirteen years and then was dropped without any formal dissolution.

Richardson's next important building was the Brattle Square Church in Boston, won in competition in 1870. When I was a boy at the famous institution of learning around the corner, we used to call it "the church of the holy bean-blowers" on account of the great figures on top of the towers, armed with long golden trumpets. In the

few buildings designed heretofore he had, in a degree, gone
with the tide in employing the Victorian Gothic, but in
Brattle Square he broke with his colleagues and with the
vernacular style. Not only was the building in the round-
arched Romanesque, a style unheard of in America, but
it was of a largeness and simplicity so far removed from
the complication and pettiness of the prevailing Victorian
Gothic that its effect was revolutionary. Other works followed, but the great service of the Brattle Square Church
was that it opened to Richardson the gates of the competition for Trinity.

Trinity Church, Boston, is Richardson's greatest work.
It is probably America's most famous church. It is certainly a milestone in its architecture. When two such great
souls as Richardson and Phillips Brooks joined forces in
perfect accord something tremendous was sure to result. Richardson won the competition for Trinity on an
exterior design very different from the one that now lords
it over Copley Square. It was Romanesque, but abounded
in complications which Richardson afterwards swept away
with his great hands in the completed building. This is
particularly true of the tower. His biographer relates that
the architect, in bed with one of the recurrent attacks of
his chronic malady, was pondering over the design of this
great feature. His friend Olmstead had sent him some
photographs. In turning them over his eye lighted on the
old tower of the Cathedral of Salamanca in Spain. He in-
stantly saw in it the germ of Trinity. The original drawings were discarded, and the beautifully simple and powerful tower we now see took the place of the lesser conception that had won him the prize.

Its great size, its unrivalled location and the nation-wide
fame of its great rector, Phillips Brooks, made the build-

ing of Trinity Church a matter of interest throughout the country. The style of its architecture, French Roman-esque, and the method of its construction called forth many expressions pro and con in the architectural press of the day. In 1877 architectural publications were far more controversial than they are in 1936; today, if we have time to look at the pictures we are doing well. A particular bone of contention in Trinity was the covering of the great granite piers together with all the walls by a skin of lath and plaster, but Richardson's intention from the outset was to have a "color church." His dream was of mosaics such as those that glorify the mighty vaults of Sancta Sophia, the rude walls of the churches in Ravenna, but this, for reasons of cost and perhaps of acoustics, was out of the question. Great fields of plaster gave him his best opportunity for color.

To help him in this most important work he called in the ablest decorator in the country, John LaFarge, and under the hands of this master the great barrel vaults glow with some of the fire of San Marco. The windows became a matter of equal importance since color was the goal, and here again the architect insisted on the employment of the artist, not the artisan. Although there was no precedent for windows of this character, those of Trinity still hold their own among the best in the country. The best of the Trinity windows are by Sir Edwin Burne-Jones executed by William Morris, John LaFarge and Clayton and Bell of London.

LaFarge, like Michael Angelo, working almost without compensation, labored up to the last moment, and spent all of the night of January 31st on the scaffolding. The next day the staging came down, and on February 9th, 1877, the great church, with the eyes of America upon it, was consecrated. The Governor of Massachusetts, the Mayor of Boston, the architect, the artists, the builders, were invited guests. One hundred and seven clergymen walked in solemn procession up its broad aisles chanting the twenty-fourth Psalm, "Lift up your heads, O ye gates, and be ye lift up, ye everlasting doors; and the King of Glory shall come in." No wonder the influence of Trinity was immeasurable, not alone in the beauty of its architectural forms, its scheme of color, its decoration and use of stained glass, but in the beauty of holiness as well.

The phenomenal success of Romanesque Trinity was followed by a shower of important commissions—library buildings for Woburn and North Easton in Massachusetts, Sever Hall for Harvard College, and his magnificent designs for the Protestant Cathedral at Albany which were never consummated. Curiously enough, Richardson built but two churches after Trinity. The principal works of the few remaining years left to him are as follows: the completion of the Capitol at Albany, done in association with Eidletz and Olmstead; libraries at Quincy and at Malden, Massachusetts, and at Burlington, Vermont; City Hall at Albany; Law School, Harvard University; the Ames Building, Boston; the Pittsburgh Court House and Jail; the Marshall Field wholesale store, Chicago; Chamber of Commerce, Cincinnati; various railway stations; and houses for John Hay, B. H. Warder and N. L. Anderson in Washington, and for Franklin McVeagh and J. J. Glessner in Chicago. Of these he admired most the Pittsburgh buildings. He said during its building, "If they have honored me for the pigmy things that I have done, wait till they see Pittsburgh." Richardson was right in this estimate of his work. The Field Building as well was practically faultless, and the Pittsburgh Jail, like the great rocky mass of the Florentine Pitti Palace in Ruskin's words is "brother heart of the mountain."

I should delight to write further of Richardson's pulsing life, of his trip through Europe with Phillips Brooks, of his great atelier and home combined in Brookline; of the great number of students and draughtsmen who flocked about him, worked for him, and went out into the world preaching his gospel. It would be interesting to describe the man—his huge size, his eager manner, his lively tongue. It would be still more edifying if I could write of his ideals for American architecture and of his theories for realizing them—but this is a history of architecture and not a biography.

Richardson died April 27th, 1886. His funeral took place in Trinity Church, his most famous work, and the service was read by Phillips Brooks, his close friend and co-laborer. Only a few weeks before his death he had been elected Honorary and Corresponding Member of the Royal Institute of British Architects, and previously he had become a Fellow of the American Institute of Architects and of the American Academy of Arts and Sciences.

The earmarks of Richardson buildings are, first, a Romantic and picturesque mass, studied for its effectiveness from every angle; second, a rich skin or texture, sometimes of roughly hewn stone, often of brick—achieved by the use of different materials, as, for instance, the yellow-gray granite and red Longmeadow sandstone in Trinity, or by the use of patterns, as the checker-boards of the Harvard Law School, or by the carving, richly and powerfully employed, in all of his buildings, or by various surface treatments of the same material, as the rough and smooth granite of the Field Wholesale Store; and third, the architectural features themselves. These last we have not the space to analyze, but we may note that he was inordinately fond of very high roofs, of clustered windows, of deeply arched doorways. These features were carefully studied to the last degree. His interiors were not less characteristic. Now we paint everything one tone or no tone —an easy task—but those were the days of color. Oak, onyx, marble, brass, leather, mosaic, fresco—all were called upon and all handled in masterly fashion.

Richardson adopted a policy at the outset to which he adhered throughout his career, a policy requiring vast courage but certain to result in preëminence. It was something like this. He refused to be dictated to in regard to the architectural design of his buildings; he never allowed a design to leave his office until prolonged study had demonstrated its perfection; he allowed only the finest of materials and workmanship to enter into its construction; in the carving of stone and wood, in decoration, in leaded glass or any of the decorative arts, he employed only the best talent available. Phillips Brooks, in commenting on Trinity, said, "For the first time in America we see artists, not artisans, collaborating with the architect." Richardson never allowed a contractor to be selected for considerations of price alone, and for this reason was opposed to the selection of the builders by competitive bidding. All of this resulted in costly buildings. Richardson was known as an expensive architect, but he argued that if the result is superlative the price is forgotten; if the result is inferior it is never forgotten nor forgiven.

The reputation which he built up by a policy almost regal and despotic attracted big commissions and rich clients. He lost no time on mean or cheap jobs. He never did a pot boiler. Each building, at least in the enchanted eyes of the time, was a masterpiece. To live in a house by

Richardson was a cachet of wealth and taste; to have your nest egg in one of his banks gave you a feeling of perfect security; to worship in one of his churches made one think one had a pass key to the Golden Gates. But if one could not afford, or had not the temerity, to go to the master himself, one could get someone else to do something like it, and getting other architects "to do something like it" all over the country spelt the birth of a national style, short-lived though it was destined to be. The Romanesque style became the fashion. What more is there to say?

New York, it is true, remained stony soil, and so in a measure did the South, where the evil blight of Reconstruction still cankered commerce and building and the soul. The movement was strongest in the youthful growing cities—Chicago, Cleveland, Cincinnati, St. Louis, even San Francisco—though Boston, the mother ground of the style, still put forth its most beautiful flowers.

Richardson in a sense ignored construction. His purpose was the achievement of beauty through strength. His was not the philosophical mind that could see beauty in the perfect suggestion of construction, and yet it was this opportunity that was offered the Romanesque—an opportunity that romanticism seems to have reached out half hesitantly to grasp when in 1893 the prize was snatched away. Richardson died in 1886, two years after the invention of the skeleton iron frame which made possible the sky-scraper. What he would have done with it we can, of course, only conjecture. This man who once said, "What I want most to design is a grain elevator and the interior of a Mississippi steamboat," would have gone forth joyfully one may be sure to meet so American a problem as the sky-scraper.

It is somewhat curious that America's greatest contribution to the art of building, the skyscraper, should have appeared in the midst of the Romanesque Revival, and that so appearing it should owe little to Richardson. First of all a definition or an understanding is necessary. Skyscraper, as used in these pages, means a high building, the outside and inside walls and floors of which are supported on a skeleton or frame of iron or steel columns and beams. Almost a corollary to the principle of a metal skeleton was that of isolated foundations, which means that for every steel column there was a separate foundation, unconnected with its neighbors. While many examples of isolated foundations can doubtless be found in ancient buildings the principle developed in Chicago * and applied to the skyscraper was a novel one. At first these were "floating foundations," that is, platforms composed of a grillage of iron rods and concrete. Now we sink "caissons" or cylinders of concrete that descend to hard pan or bed rock. Where solid masonry walls are used, as had been done for thousands of years, the wall must be thick at the bottom and thin at the top. The higher the wall, the thicker it must be, and thickest on the first floor where space is most valuable. In skeleton steel construction, however, the walls are no thicker at the bottom than they are at the top, and walls supported at each story by steel beams can start at any point or can be built simultaneously throughout the entire height of the building. The tremendous economic and structural value of such an invention is evident. Buildings could now be of any height provided one could get from the ground to the upper stories, and this provision was taken care of by the simultane-

* "The art of preparing foundations for all kinds of buildings with particular illustration of the 'Method of isolated piers' as followed in Chicago," by Frederick Bauman, 1873. Pub. by J. M. Wing, Chicago.

ous development of the high speed passenger elevator.

Wrought iron structural beams were first imported and used in the United States in 1855, but it was not until 1875 that structural beams were "rolled" in any quantity, though rails had been manufactured many years before. Jones and Laughlin first produced Bessemer Steel I beams in 1889, and Open Hearth beams in 1895. These wrought iron beams were bolted to cast iron columns for the support of floors of various kinds. In all cases previous to 1884 the walls of large buildings were built of solid masonry and supported not only themselves, but their share of the floors as well.

There never has been any serious contradiction of the fact that Chicago is the birthplace of the skyscraper. The embarrassment was considerable, however, as to the legitimacy of two skyscrapers, babies who saw the light about the same time. These were the Home Insurance Building and the Tacoma Building. At the time of the previous printing of this book both of these buildings were standing. Since then, however, both have been destroyed, simultaneously as a matter of fact. This gave the architects of Chicago, who have always been intensely curious in the matter, an opportunity to make what might be called a blood test. Commissions of architects and engineers examined each building and took photographs. What they found is this in a very few words. The Home Insurance Building was begun in May, 1884. The architect was William LeBaron Jenney who had been General Sherman's Major of Engineering during the Civil War. This building was found to have been constructed as follows: On the two street frontages a solid masonry wall extended two stories in height. Above this began a skeleton of cast iron columns, wrought iron floor beams, cast iron lintels. The court walls are of this same skeleton construction their entire

height. The party walls (those abutting on adjacent buildings) are solid masonry their entire height in accordance
with the building ordinances. The metal skeleton, composed
for the most part of cast and wrought iron, was naturally
primitive and experimental though it had stood without a
flaw for forty-four years. The Tacoma Building, Holabird
and Roche, architects, was begun in 1887. It was found that
on the two street fronts skeleton construction more advanced in design extended from grade to cornice. This was
also true of the court walls. The party walls were, as in the
Home Insurance, solid masonry. What the architects had not
known was that there was a solid masonry transverse supporting wall about the center of the building, extending its
entire height. In view of all this evidence, the commission
of architects * that examined the Home Insurance Building
ended their report with the following words: "We have no
hesitation in stating that the Home Insurance Building was
the first high building to utilize as the basic principle of its
design the method known as skeleton construction. . . .
We are also of the opinion that owing to its priority and its
immediate success and renown, the Home Insurance Building was, in fact, the primal influence in the acceptance of
skeleton construction, the true father of the skyscraper."

These revolutionary structures were followed by the
Rand McNally Building by Burnham and Root, of skeleton steel and entirely covered with terra cotta—the first
all terra cotta building in America; and in 1891 by the
Masonic Temple, twenty-two stories in height—the highest building in the world at the time it was built. All of
these buildings are in Chicago, the home of the sky-
scraper, and all are in the Romanesque style. Electrical,
mechanical and sanitary engineering kept pace with the
development of the tall building, and solved the problems
of mounting height and other exigencies of construction.

* Ernest Graham, Alfred Shaw, Richard E. Schmidt, Earl Reed, Andrew Rebori,
T. E. Tallmadge, chairman.

These, in brief, are the startling changes which were injected into the Romanesque era, and they are the causes of the change of scene from Boston and the East to Chicago and the Middle West. As Richardson had dominated architecture in the East, so John W. Root, his most brilliant disciple, held like sway in the West. Root was the junior member of the firm of Burnham and Root. In the succeeding chapter on the World's Columbian Exposition I shall try to appraise the greatness and service of Daniel H. Burnham; but I shall say little of him here save to remark that without him his gay and brilliant partner would have had few of the opportunities which came his way.

John Wellborn Root, like Richardson, was a Southerner, born in Georgia in 1850. Also like Richardson, though at a much more tender age, he was shipped to Europe to avoid the dangers of the Civil War. Root made the trip on a blockade runner, and for the next five or six years studied drawing and music in Liverpool. He entered the University of the City of New York, graduating in the class of '69 as a civil engineer. Like Richardson again, he was in demand in every circle because of his athletic ability, his social graces, his spontaneous and magnetic personality. In New York Root worked for a year in the office of Renwick, the architect of St. Patrick's Cathedral. The great Chicago Fire brought him to Chicago, where in 1872 he entered the offices of Carter, Drake and Wight. It was there that he met Daniel Burnham, a fellow draughtsman, and they straightway became fast friends. In 1873 the firm of Burnham and Root was established. Like Richardson, young Root was a Romanticist, but unlike Richardson he had a flair for invention and engineering.

Here is Louis Sullivan's description of him: "He, Root, was not of the Burnham type, but red-headed, large, bullet-headed, close-cropped, effervescent, witty, small-nosed, alert, debonair, a mind that sparkled, a keen sense of humor—which Burnham lacked—solidly put together, bull-necked, freckled, arms of iron, light blue, sensuous eyes, a facile draughtsman, quick to grasp ideas and quicker to appropriate them, an excellent musician . . . a man of quick-witted, all-around culture which he carried easily and jauntily, and vain to the limit of the skies."

Very early in his career he invented the system of "spread foundations." Chicago is built on mud; below the mud is clay which extends downward some sixty or seventy feet until the old mother rock is reached—the adamantine road over which the glaciers slid a hundred thousand years ago. Today in building a very high structure great caissons, or solid piers of concrete, are sunk down to the rock, but back in the seventies it was the custom to use stone resting in the muddy clay and stepped off to provide the proper area for the support of the building. These foundations were very bulky and tremendously heavy in themselves. Root's scheme was to lay railroad rails crisscrossed, and around and about them to pour concrete. This resulted in a very stiff "floor" "floating" in the mud, of little weight and occupying little room in the basement. These "spread" or floating foundations became almost universal for all large buildings in Chicago up to about 1900, when piling was introduced, later to be supplanted by the caissons. This construction of floating foundations was first used in Chicago in the Montauk Block in 1882. Root was also the first to use the cantilever construction for foundations, too technical to explain in these pages, but of great value in the support of lot line or party walls.

Following the Montauk Block came a long series of

offices, residences, churches, banks, and other buildings among which are, the Monadnock, Insurance Exchange, Rookery, Woman's Temple, Masonic Temple, all in Chicago; the Society for Savings and the Cuyahoga Building in Cleveland; the American Bank Building, Kansas City; the Equitable Building, Atlanta; and the Chronicle and Mills Buildings of San Francisco.

Of these all were Romanesque except the Monadnock, the Rookery and the Woman's Temple. The Monadnock from "turret to foundation stone" has not one inch of ornamentation of any description. It is a huge mass of brown brick, some eighteen stories high. The corners are cut off by a slice which begins with nothing at the bottom and increases to a width of several feet at the top, where the whole wall flares out with the graceful outline of a bell, very similar in effect to an Egyptian pylon. This clever device of cutting off, or "chamfering," the corners produces the optical illusion of a slope or batter in all the walls, the whole effect of which fills the beholder with the sensation of a tremendous lift or soaring of the entire structure. At the time of the Columbian Exposition it was the Monadnock Block that received the most study and praise from the European critics. It is interesting structurally as the last example of a high building using the old solid masonry walls.

The Rookery is an epochal building. In style it appears to be Romanesque, but if you will carefully examine its ornament, which is profuse, you will discover that it is East Indian or Hindoo—a wayward child of Root's seething brain, an architectural *tour de force*. It is not the style, but the plan, of the building that makes it of great importance. It is the first "modern" office-building plan; by which I mean that if it were to be built today it would differ very little in arrangement. The problems of arrangement of light courts, of corridors, of stairs, and the divisions of offices, were here for the first time intelligently solved.

The Woman's Temple was a national monument to the Women's Christian Temperance Union, and the greatest material creation of the Union's great founder, Frances Willard. Some years ago its proud pinnacles and towers went down in a cloud of dust and memories to make way for a great "super-building," a sign of the new era. Old Peter B. Wight, the architect, who brought John Root to Chicago, told me at the age of eighty-eight that he had lived to see every one of his buildings destroyed to make way for a greater construction. The average life of a commercial building at the present time is about thirty-five years. The Temple was not Romanesque in detail, but it was decidedly of the romantic persuasion. A great court opening into the street, flanked by tower-like structures which were crowned by the crenellations and the steep roofs of a sixteenth century French château, made the building one of the most picturesque structures of this age of architectural romance. The culminating touch—a great copper spire or *flêche* which Root designed—was most unfortunately never added.

The best work of Burnham and Root, the high watermark of the western school of the Romanesque Revival, is the old Art Institute, now the Chicago Club. The Chicago Club and the Field Wholesale were two architectural masterpieces, loved as well as admired by the citizens of Chicago—the first for its friendly aspect and gaiety, for the Romanesque can be gay, and Richardson's great work for its titanic force. Their solidity and architectural fame seemed to insure them a great age. Both, unhappily, are gone, the first through a collapse during alterations and the second need-lessly, it would seem, as the site of this work of genius is now occupied as a parking lot.

Richardson's great atelier in Brooklyn, half home and half workshop, was the last of the old order of architec-tural offices. Here the master was teacher as well as archi-tect. Monday nights the entire office force met at dinner with the Falstaffian bulk and wit of the great man at the end of the board and no skull at the feast to say what you might or might not drink. Young men used every influ-ence to get into Richardson's office, where many of them worked for nothing for the sake of the training and the prestige.

With the coming of the sky-scraper and the tremendous engineering problems and responsibilities it entailed, this more or less happy-go-lucky method of conducting an architectural office came to an end. Burnham and Root were the first of the highly organized and efficient archi-tectural organizations that carried on the great building enterprises of the last generation and are carrying them on today—offices that often have two hundred and more draughtsmen and superintendents in their employ, and do as much work in a year as Michael Angelo or Sir Christo-pher Wren did in a lifetime. "Delegate, delegate," said Daniel Burnham, and that necessity spells tragedy to many an architect. Richardson in his smock, surrounded by his boys and drawing with charcoal on a sheet of brown pa-per, discoursing the while on the philosophy of design, is a more appealing picture than many an architect of today offers, who behind his mahogany desk, surrounded by stenographers, signing his name to contracts, discourses the while on first and second mortgage bonds.

It is extremely interesting to watch the course of domestic architecture in the Romanesque Revival. The stone houses and the brick houses were for the most part frankly and entirely Romanesque, but in those days, as now, the greater number of houses were of wood.

To design a wooden house in the Romanesque style was a pretty difficult operation. In the first place, there are no wooden houses left of the many which were undoubtedly erected between 500 and 1200 A. D., and, more important still, Richardson had created few precedents for his countrymen in this material. Nevertheless, the period was extremely prolific in wooden construction. What do we find? In the first place, the old Eastlake ornament of the Philadelphia Exposition and the Parvenu period is gone, to appear no more—no incised ornament of broken wheat stalks and sunken rosettes, no chamfers, no iron crestings, no jig-saw work. Nor do we longer see any of the familiar hall marks of Victorian Gothic—the pointed arches done in wood, the wood crestings—nor the mansard roofs, nor the heavy pseudo-Classic cornices with great wooden brackets. All the high narrowness has vanished, but the picturesqueness remains, augmented with romance.

The plans are irregular and rambling, especially the stairs, which are broad and with many landings; fireplaces are as frequent as of yore, but with wide yawning mouths for cord wood. In general, however, the proportions of rooms with their lower ceilings, the short halls, better kitchens and pantries, more numerous bathrooms, larger closets, marked a distinct advance in practicality over the previous period.

It was in the exteriors that the architect locked horns with the difficulties of the prevailing style. Romanesque is essentially an architecture of stone; even brick is a poor substitute. The deep lowering arches, the rugged carving,

the brutal surfaces, require stone for their expression.
Wood with its lightness is impossible as a vehicle. The
architects of the day very wisely abandoned almost entirely
the attempt to use the letter of the style, but they stren-
uously endeavored to carry out its spirit. The picturesque,
the romantic, the varied, the wayward, became the ideal.
High roofs, huge gables often with English half-timbering,
wide porches and portes-cochère, and corner towers, were
salient features. The tower was usually circular. It was
always capped with a simple conical roof. The porte-
cochère usurped the position of the cupola as the hall
mark of affluent respectability, and the stables that gave
it its *raison d'être* were often almost as elaborate as the
house.

Texture, so vital a requisite in a romantic style and so
easy to attain with stone, was arrived at in various ingenious ways, chief among which, perhaps, was the use
of shingles. These covered not only the roofs, but often
the walls—usually the upper half. The shingles were cut
in various sizes and shapes, and were applied in various
ways to obtain patterns and variety in their appearance.
Siding was the favorite covering for the lower portion of
the building—the first story. This siding was usually very
narrow and often moulded along its exposed edge. Exterior plaster or stucco was just coming into use and we
not infrequently find it in gables between the half-timbers.
Sometimes it was speckled—hardly adorned—with pebbles
or broken glass.

It is in ornamental woodwork, however, that the architect of the eighties put his trust. His slogan was, "Down
with the jig-saw, up with the turning-lathe!" Forty-five
years ago Wisconsin, Michigan, and the northern states
had not been denuded of their white pine and oak. Skilled

labor was cheap. So the "mill work" on a building could be fashioned to the heart's desire with no worry about cost. Balusters, spindles, columns, were all turned and used in profusion outside and in. Grilles filled in the heads of the wide doors, great screens of turned spindles enclosed the stairs, and the porches were veritable *tours de force* of the turning-lathe. Houses such as these are properly called "Queen Anne." I am often asked to define this epithet. Our Queen Anne is really the imported variety of the style invented by Norman Shaw and his coterie in England and must be confined between 1878 and say 1890. That makes it almost exactly contemporary with our Romanesque Revival and their mutual romanticism certainly clasps their hands. The term is incorrectly applied, therefore, to houses in the Parvenu period which are earlier. Often our Queen Anne houses were closely based on the English work, in which case they bore no trace of the Romanesque. More frequently, however, they were a mixture—Queen Anne picturesqueness with Romanesque detail.

It is extremely interesting to turn over the leaves of the "American Architect," say in the year 1885. House after house such as we have described will pass by, then suddenly—a Colonial house bearing the name of McKim, Mead and White or Wilson Eyre, or Peabody, so modern that it startles us; and then, perhaps, we come to a Parvenu offering of some old-timer who looked with disdain fifty years ago on all this modern stuff.

The interiors of houses of this period, with the exception of those by Richardson himself and those by the New York men who held aloof from the Romanesque, were apt to be pretty bad. In the first place it was the age of golden oak. The grilles, spindles, and other turned work of the period, were all in this distressing material. So were the panelled wainscots, the beamed ceilings and the wooden trim of every description. For the benefit of those fortunate ones of the younger generation who have never seen oak mistreated in this fashion be it said that this splendid wood was filled, stained and highly varnished to a bright reddish-yellow hue. This period marks as well the coming of the hard wood floor, also of golden oak.

Fireplaces continued to be bizarre, somewhat after the Queen Anne fashion, with many little mantel shelves and cubby-holes. The facing was invariably in color. Onyx was a prime favorite in replacing the marble of the previous period, and so was tile, usually pictured. A bevelled mirror, or several such, frequently formed part of the ensemble.

Wainscots continued in the vogue, especially in the dining-room. They were usually elaborately panelled. The old plaster cornices with the elaborate rosette in the center of the ceiling disappear, and we find a new ceiling treatment—a wood cornice (golden oak) and wood beams (golden oak). These beams were, of course, false, and, while usually parallel and running straight across the ceiling, were often, on the contrary, broken up into panels and patterns. These beamed ceilings, being something new, were especially fashionable. The decorated frieze terminated by the picture moulding remained in favor, and the walls were covered with wall paper, usually bad, sometimes with stenciled canvas, sometimes with leather.

The carpets of the preceding age had gone out and given place to rugs. Oriental rugs were cheap and plentiful in the eighties, and as beautiful then as they are now. Often the heavy responsibility of redeeming a whole room would fall on a delicate Kermanshah or a robust Bokhara.

The furniture of the day was, as a rule, golden oak,

though there were many hold-overs of black walnut from the preceding style. It was mostly heavy and not beautiful. Where carving occurred, as in the legs of dining-room tables, it was usually Romanesque.

Rooms were often filled with a lot of awful rubbish. I have in mind a particular one: At the door, which divided in half and slid into the wall, stood a small ebonized wood negro boy with a turban and oriental garb, proffering an iron plate for calling-cards. The door-opening was hung with a curtain made of strings of glass beads and short lengths of cane which tinkled and crackled as you passed through. On the floor was a really beautiful oriental rug partly concealed by the skin of a huge Bengal tiger with glass eyes, long teeth and a red tongue. The furniture was various—mostly oak, but with some mahogany and gilt pieces. On the upright piano stood an alabaster model of the Leaning Tower of Pisa and some bisque candlesticks— a shepherd and shepherdess. A cabinet in rococo style arranged across the corner—this was the cat-a-corner age —contained ivory elephants, dried sea-horses, coral, French snuff boxes, a Japanese dagger, an opium pipe. In front of the window stood a high, green marble pedestal, and on it a marble statue of "Innocence." On the walls hung a colored photograph of the Taj Mahal, invariably referred to as the most beautiful building in the world, and in a red plush frame a doorway from the Alhambra in plaster relief, cunningly painted. Over the fireplace was a huge engraving of the "Lion's Bride" in a golden oak frame. The lighting fixtures were cast brass, originally intended for gas but wired for electricity. The window draperies were of pink figured damask, held back with silk ropes— beautiful, perhaps, in themselves, but hardly *en rapport* with the magenta wall paper. The feature of the room which must not be neglected was the circular bay formed by the corner tower. This bay had high windows, the transoms of which were filled with leaded glass in powerful—one might say poisonous—colors. A semi-circular window seat encompassed the bay and oriental silk hangings slyly hinted at a separation from the main room, for this was the cozy corner. A Turkish hanging lamp, a teak wood table inlaid with mother-of-pearl, some scimitars arranged in a pattern on the wall, and a rubber plant, carried out the oriental note with the seductive suggestion of the unprincipled East.

One other form of building which the Romanesque Revival entirely dominated was the evangelical church. The transformation in church architecture, which was complete, was also dual. The change of style of these churches from Victorian Gothic to Romanesque followed, of course, the example of Trinity in Boston—ugly ducklings, many of them, hatched out under the beautiful swan mother,—but there was a corresponding and complete change in planning as well. This was owing to the development of the Sunday School, which now emerged out of the basement, and to the invention, generally ascribed to Bishop Vincent of the Methodist Church, called the "Akron Plan," from its first use in Akron, Ohio.

Very briefly, in this arrangement radial class-rooms in floor and gallery opened into a high and large assembly room. The class-rooms could be opened for general worship or closed off for class study. Usually this arrangement was accommodated in a wing of the main church building somewhat analogous to a transept, so that the great assembly room could, by the operation of ingenious movable partitions, be opened into the auditorium of the church. The church itself, partly owing to this major operation which had been performed upon it, was usually far from beautiful. It took another twenty years for church architecture to return to the simplicity and beauty of the eighteenth century.

Almost every town in the land has one of these Romanesque Revival churches. One of them stood on a nearby corner of my own town, and in part still stands, for it is being wrecked as I write these words, and a description of it will, I think, fit most of them. Its material is red brick and its trimming red sandstone carved with the familiar Romanesque detail. In place of the thin, narrow, pointed arches of the preceding era, the windows and portals are broad and squat, and have round arched heads. A tower with a dome-like cupola has supplanted the thin spire. In general appearance obesity had succeeded emaciation, and floridity, anaemia. The interior was as startlingly unlike its elder brother as the outside. Instead of being long and narrow, it was short, almost square, and the pulpit, organ, and choir—hardly a chancel under the circumstances— were tucked into one corner. The floor was sharply bowled, and the pews were all curved, which was inevitable in a cat-a-cornered church. The windows were picture windows—biblical scenes done with startling realism on a grandiose scale. The woodwork was golden oak, the organ pipes much in evidence and like the walls and ceiling, highly decorated. One wall, however, seemed to be a huge gate or portcullis, and so it was, for by some mysterious means it would rise or fall out of sight, disclosing the whole of the Sunday School, built on the celebrated Akron Plan.

The reader may not unnaturally conclude that the foregoing descriptions closely approach ridicule, hardly conforming to the opening paragraphs of this chapter in which the Romanesque Revival is heralded as the harbinger of an improvement in taste. One must judge an epoch as one judges a man—by its best works, not its worst. It is true, terrible deeds were done in the Romanesque Revival. One cause of its downfall, in fact, was the inability of Richardson's disciples to carry on the taste or artistry of their leader. This was owing to no lack of enthusiasm or sincerity, but solely to a dearth of education in architect and client alike. Taste—critical judgment, discernment—is the most delicate fruit of learning and grows at the top of the tree. It can hardly be acquired in a draughting-room or a parlor and it is not, as is often supposed, the peculiar inheritance of gentle blood. It is the result only of study and critical observation.

As the number of educated architects rapidly increase through the multiplication of architectural schools, we shall observe that the standard of architectural excellence rises at the same rate. The fundamental quality in great works of architecture that we call taste is not born of a *précieux* knowledge of the novel or the smart. The spirit that lies in the rocky heart of Trinity and dwelt in the stony fastness of the Field Store did not take refuge there from a drawing-room or the salon of a dilettante. Such standards of taste remain inviolate and immutable in the ebb and flow of fashion about them. It is this great gift in Richardson that characterizes his era, bad as much of the work was, as a revival of taste. "Know ye not that a little leaven leaveneth the whole lump?"

CHAPTER VIII

THE WORLD'S FAIR, 1893

Its Loveliness Increases. It Will Never Pass into Nothingness.

WHEN we were children and our stock of conversation had run low, we always filled the void by saying, "Let's talk about the World's Fair." We are still talking about the World's Fair, and the lapse of thirty-three years has not dimmed nor has custom staled its infinite variety. There have been other Fairs since, many of them, and while some of these may, in the sophistication of their architecture, in the harmony of their color, or in the beauty of their lighting, have surpassed the famous old "White City" on the shores of Lake Michigan, to none of them has it been vouchsafed to write "Vale" to one epoch and "Ave" to another.

In the preceding chapter we saw how the robust and vigorous Romanesque, marshalled under the aegis of Richardson, a veritable Hannibal, had conquered New England and the West and if the citadels of New York City, like another Rome, manned by Hunt and McKim and their Classic cohorts, held out against the barbarian hosts the supremacy of the Romanesque throughout the rest of the land was none the less complete.

Charles Moore in his life of Daniel H. Burnham, referring to the choice of the Classic style for the Fair, remarks that "the Classic motive was absolutely new to Chicago, no architect in that city having used it up to the time of the Fair." To have been entirely correct he should have added "in the previous forty years," but he had evidently forgotten the Greek Revival. What was true of Chicago in its almost exclusive preference of the Romanesque was equally true of St. Louis and Cleveland, Pittsburgh and Boston. It was this nation-wide style, for better or for worse, that the World's Fair annihilated.

It will be said, and with truth, that there were other causes contributing to the disappearance of the Romanesque. The death of Richardson, the heroic leader himself, in 1886 was disheartening, especially as he left few trained lieutenants and it was written that the most brilliant of these, John W. Root, was to die in 1891, just before the style of the great Exposition was chosen. Again, architectural schools were multiplying and were turning out in increasing numbers youthful Classicists—Classicists, because all the American schools were children of the great mother in Paris, and, as in the École des Beaux Arts, their training of architects was based on exercises exclusively in the Classic style. We have mentioned the architectural course at the Massachusetts Institute of Technology which was founded in 1866. The University of Illinois followed suit in 1870, Cornell University in 1871, Columbia in 1883, and Harvard in 1890. Another factor was the increasing number of Beaux Arts men returning from Paris, that garden of the Hesperides, which the first of the Argives, old William M. Hunt had discovered back in 1850 and from which he had returned with his pockets full of golden apples. These men were all active and skillful protagonists of Classic principles. Then, too, the rise of the brilliant constellation known as McKim, Mead and White, practising mostly in forms of the Renaissance, had begun

to attract attention and emulation. The excessive stupid-
ities and atrocities, furthermore, committed in the name of
the Romanesque by many of her unlettered adherents were
turning the citizenry away from that style. All of these
causes, and others as well, were leading to the debacle.

There is a class of architectural philosophers who hold
that the World's Fair was an artistic calamity, that its
buildings were whited sepulchres, that its Court of Honor
was an arena in which tens of thousands saw daily the
martyrdom of native art, that the golden text in the entablature of the Peristyle, "Ye shall know the truth, and
the truth shall make you free," should have been erased
and in its place written, "Abandon hope, all ye who enter
here." To such as these the Romanesque Revival was the
last heroic sortie of a Romanticism that had been beleag-
ured since the Middle Ages; to them Richardson was a
Roland winding his horn in the deadly valley of Ronce-
valles; while Burnham and his co-conspirators in decree-
ing the Classic style for the Exposition had plunged a Roman sword into the heart of the most promising bid the
American people had ever made for a national expression
in art. I admit I am very sympathetic to this point of view.
It is probably all wrong, but it is appealing. It is fallacious
because, even without this fairy vision by the lake, our
national restlessness would soon have tossed aside like a
worn-out toy or last year's hat, this gift of the Romantic-
ists, and we should have turned inevitably to something
more amusing and more fashionable.

As early as 1889 New York, Washington, St. Louis and
Chicago each had organizations at work to secure the
proposed Exposition which should celebrate the four hun-
dredth anniversary of the discovery of America. It is unnecessary in a history of architecture to trace the political

198 STORY OF ARCHITECTURE IN AMERICA

and legislative steps that finally determined by act of Congress that the World's Fair, or, more correctly, the "World's Columbian Exposition," should be held in Chicago. A national commission, particularly for intercourse with foreign nations, was appointed, and a local corporation was formed for building the Exposition and conducting it thereafter. The first artist officially drawn into the great enterprise was Frederick Law Olmstead, the landscape architect, with his associate, Henry Codman, a brilliant young architect. Olmstead was invited to Chicago to consult with Daniel H. Burnham, the architect who had been an informal advisor of the Chicago contingent from the inception of the enterprise.

Many sites were considered but were eliminated for one reason or another in favor of Jackson Park, facing the lake near the southern boundary of the city—a park in name only, for the land was a succession of wind-swept sand ridges with marshy swales between, harboring the sparse vegetation usual on old sand beaches, and supporting a few pin oaks, favorite roosting-places for the enormous flights of wild pigeons that had darkened the skies of the early settlers not so very many years before. Olmstead accepted this forbidding site with reluctance as he realized the enormous artistic and engineering difficulties that would somehow have to be conquered.

In October, 1890, John W. Root, Burnham's partner, was elected consulting architect and Burnham was made chief of construction. Burnham was further entrenched in his position with powers that made him virtually a czar over the entire artistic and constructional work of the Exposition. He was ideally fitted for this supreme command. But forty-two years of age, the head of an architectural firm that had probably the largest practice in the

United States, he came to the work with a prestige that
was unchallenged and invaluable. Added to this, his figure and personality were those of the chieftain; as his biographer says, "As with MacGregor, where he sat was
the head of the table." I have seen him many, many times
(for I was seven years in his office) come into the draughting-room with the great of the earth in the arts and in
business, but it was he who dominated the scene, he who
occupied the stage's centre. Generous, jovial, companion-
able, as I well knew from personal association, he could be,
I was also aware, hard as granite and inexorable as fate in
carrying out a chosen course.

Burnham and Root, together with Olmstead and Codman and Gottlieb, the engineer, determined tentatively on
the number, sizes and disposition of the principal buildings.
All this was set forth in a large sketch made by Root himself and submitted to the national commission and to the
local corporation. On December first, 1890, it was adopted
as the plan of the Exposition. Nothing was said or indicated in it regarding the style of the buildings, and the
plan covered only the buildings in Jackson Park, for at
this time it was intended that some of the buildings should
be located in the lake front in the centre of the city. The
idea of dividing the Exposition was shortly after abandoned.

In accordance with the recommendations of an important memorial submitted by Burnham and his associates,
five firms of architects were selected to design the principal
buildings. These names undoubtedly represent what the
best thought of the time considered the best architectural
talent in America, consequently, they are of historic
caliber, and here they are: Richard M. Hunt of New York;
McKim, Mead and White of New York; George B. Post

of New York; Peabody and Stearns of Boston; Van Brunt and Howe of Kansas City. In January, 1891, these distinguished gentlemen, together with five Chicago architects, some of whom will be mentioned later, met in Chicago. Burnham was a great believer in the efficacy of dinners to raise money, smooth over difficulties and arouse enthusiasm. After dinner there were, of course, speeches. Mr. Burnham was not a graceful nor a witty speaker but a very forceful and direct one. A number of Burnham's famous dinners were held, usually at Kinsley's, a celebrated restaurant and a not unimportant institution in the upbuilding of Chicago. The Easterners who came perhaps to scoff went home filled with enthusiasm to work. It was his farewell to these guests that cost John Root his life. Gaily and thoughtlessly on a cold winter night he had escorted each guest to his carriage and contracted pneumonia in consequence. Undoubtedly the eventual spectacle lost much of the warmth and romance of this remarkable man. Root had been a great protagonist of the Romanesque. Whether he had expected to build part or all of the buildings in this style is not known; Burnham merely stated in regard to this interesting conjecture, "I cannot, of course, believe that the architecture of the Exposition would have been better had he lived, but it certainly would have been modified and stamped with something of his great individuality." With Root gone, Burnham remained only on the insistence of the directors.

The next step was the apportionment of the various buildings among the architects, the determination of their sizes and locations and the general elevations of the terraces, the definite location of the lagoons and canals, and the height of a uniform cornice-line for the Court of Honor.

At this point in the proceedings, Burnham summoned Augustus Saint-Gaudens to the work. Saint-Gaudens appeared at the February meeting of 1891. It was a dramatic occasion. At it each architect was to be called upon to exhibit for the criticism of his fellows the designs he had made for his portion of the work. Burnham writes of the meeting in racy style. It began in the morning and, characteristically, the host started the proceedings with a breakfast. Presumably it was held in his great Romanesque Library in the Rookery Building, and one can visualize the black waiters from Kinsley's in their white aprons passing around to the heirs and assigns of Phidias, Bramante and Christopher Wren the griddle cakes and coffee, the cigarettes and cigars. Soon they got down to business. Peabody proposed a transverse canal between the buildings; supported by McKim, and carried with enthusiasm. "Next Saint-Gaudens took a hand. He said the east end of the composition should be bound together architecturally. All agreed. He suggested a statue [later to be realized in the great figure of the Republic by Daniel Chester French] backed by thirteen columns, typifying the original states. All hailed this as a bully thing." The meeting was continued. The aged Hunt, crippled by rheumatism, but with his old fire unabated, "sat on the edge of the table and told about his Administration Building with its dominating dome expressing the leadership of the Government. . . . Then came George B. Post. He had a dome four hundred and fifty feet high. When they saw that dome a murmur ran around the group. George turned about saying, 'I don't think I shall advocate that dome. Probably I shall modify the building.'" He did. McKim had a portico extending out over the terrace, which was extremely prominent. He withdrew his portico before the murmur came.

"So the day went on. Luncheon was brought in. Then came the large Chicago committee. The winter afternoon was drawing to an end. The room was as still as death save for the low voice of the speaker commenting on his design. It seemed as if a great magnet held everyone in its grasp." Finally, when the last drawing had been shown, Lyman J. Gage (the president of the Exposition) drew a long breath. Standing against a window and shutting his eyes, he exclaimed, "Gentlemen, this is a dream." Then he smilingly continued, "You have my good wishes. I hope the dream can be realized." It was now that Saint-Gaudens made the remark that is so often quoted. Rising from the corner where he had been silently sitting, he came over to Burnham, took him by both hands, and said, "Look here, old fellow, do you realize that this is the greatest meeting of artists since the fifteenth century?"

When the Classic style was officially adopted for the Exposition we cannot, strange as it may be, exactly say. If the Romanesque was to die, we should have liked to have seen him executed in orderly fashion, fairly tried by a jury of his peers, a verdict rendered and a sentence passed—all set down in the records in proper fashion for the delectation of the historian and the philosopher. Instead it appears that the hoary old offender was quietly done to death with neither fuss nor feathers. Who his executioners were was and is still a secret. Daniel H. Burnham said he didn't know how it happened. Mr. Mead "had a distinct impression that it was the unanimous opinion of the eastern architects that the Classic motive should be used," and this opinion was expressed at their preliminary meeting held in McKim's office in New York City. At the same meeting it was decided to recommend a common height of cornice for all the buildings. This was in Decem-

ber, far back in 1890. Mr. Ernest R. Graham, the Assistant Director of Works, in a letter to me says, "The design
of the buildings facing the Court of Honor was given to
the eastern architects, and their Classic character was the
result of many meetings." At any rate, when the drawings
were presented at the Chicago meeting they were all,
almost without exception, in some phase of the Classic
style.

At this juncture, that is, shortly after the death of John
Root, another luminary blazed forth in the architectural
heavens. He was Charles B. Atwood, a temperamental,
almost an irresponsible, genius from the East. Burnham had picked him out to fill the great vacancy left by
Root in the private practice of the firm. But private interests were soon sacrificed and Atwood was catapulted
into the maelstrom of the Fair. According to Mr. Moore,
Atwood designed more than sixty of the Exposition buildings besides various ornamental features. His great work
was the Palace of the Fine Arts and the Peristyle. Burnham
tells the story:

"I asked him to design an art building, and explained
what was wanted. He was very gentle, with an engaging
manner, and certainly he was a very great artist. His Art
Building in design was the most beautiful building I have
ever seen. I sent a blue-print of the Art building to New
York. The architects took it to the Players Club, whence
they sent the most enthusiastic telegram saying that it was
a triumph of architecture.

"When it came to the Peristyle I sent a letter to the governor of each of the thirteen original States, asking for a
granite column to carry out Saint-Gaudens's suggestion.
I asked Atwood to prepare a drawing for those columns,
but he kept putting me off. One day I told him I could
wait no longer. Then he pulled out a drawer and showed

me a column beautifully drawn. He inquired if I had really made up my mind about the scheme. I asked what he meant, catching from his manner that he was holding back something. He said he felt that the screen as planned would be too thin, that something more solid and better tied together was needed. He was very gentle, but I perceived that he had in mind some scheme, and I asked if he could suggest anything. Thereupon, he took out a drawing of the Peristyle exquisitely rendered. It was as if some one had flung open the Golden Gates before me. I told him there was no question about it. I sent a copy to New York. There was not even a suggestion of a possible alteration. They telegraphed most emphatically that they were glad of the change."

John Root's vision had been an assemblage of buildings full of fire and color. That Burnham had sympathized with this dream is indicated in his appointment of William Prettyman, a close friend of Root, as director of color. Prettyman concluded that a groundwork of ivory picked out with other colors would be the best. In the meantime one of the buildings, that of Mines and Mining, had been practically completed and its color was an immediate problem to be decided. The subject was under discussion. Prettyman was in the East. Someone (Burnham does not remember who) shouted out, "Let's make it all perfectly white." The suggestion was adopted. This led to Prettyman's resignation (one can hardly blame him) and the appointment of Frank Millet, the artist. Mr. Graham wrote to me of this as follows:

" 'The White City,' as it was called, came about in a very interesting way, . . . various color designs for the numerous buildings had been considered for months without coming to any decision, until the time was so short that immediate action had to be taken. It was found that it would be impossible to give the various buildings individual color treatment, and at an evening session at which Mr. Atwood, Mr. Millet and I were present, we hit upon the scheme of white-washing the buildings by means of a squirt gun. This was the first time that such a method was used, and it proved to be economical, time saving, and produced a strikingly attractive, uniform treatment, which resulted in the Exposition becoming known as the 'White City.' "

Francis D. Millet was paid the largest salary of any one of the staff—$15,000 a year—and was perhaps its most picturesque member. He had had an eventful career—as drummer-boy in the Civil War and later as war correspondent of the London and American newspapers—and was a man whose genius for friendship made him a welcome guest in the assemblages of men. He was one of those mysterious princes whom we all envy, who go everywhere and know everybody. After the Fair was completed he remained and became director of publicity. The triumphal processions of the Sultan of Jalo and the sanguinary battles in the Midway were none too reliable inventions of Millet to coax the visitor inside the gates during the dark days of the panic of '93. He waved his hand from the deck of the sinking Titanic in final farewell to a joyous life. The life of Millet and his associates in their barracks in Jackson Park during the strenuous days of construction are the most picturesque in the Exposition annals. Within that battered caravanserai, whose portals made alternate night and day, artist after artist in no pomp at all abode his little hour and went his way. Old Omar himself would have beautifully fitted into the picture. It is not the great and dignified figures of the master architects with their cutaway coats and white collars that appeal to us as much as those livelier, younger chaps with dirty smocks and no collars. They brought the *vie de Bohème,* the *botteghe* of Florence, and the porticoes of Phidias to Jackson Park. I am indebted to an old guide book for the roster. Maynard with his Pompeiian decorations; Edwin Blashfield, "gentlest of knights of brush and pen"; Kenyon Cox; C. Y. Turner "with the visage of Shakespeare and a wit as lively"; Gari Melchers with the aroma of Paris and the salons and with his cross of *Légion d'Honneur* that the great Chevannes had pinned upon his breast; Carrol Beckwith; Dodge; McEwen; Reinhart; Walter Thirlaw; Alden Weir; Simmons; and Robert Reid—these were the painters, as lusty a band of young Pans and Apollos as you'd find in the annals of Olympus.

To this Parnassian festival came also the sculptors. It was the first time in American history that Painting and Sculpture had stood hand in hand with the protecting arms of Architecture about them both. Saint-Gaudens, of course, was the giant, the recognized fountain-head of authority and inspiration; he acted almost entirely as a consultant, his only actual work being in association with his pupil, Mary Lawrence, on the statue of Columbus. Daniel C. French, whose great statue of the Republic framed by Atwood's peristyle dominated the eastern end of the Court of Honor, was there, Frederick MacMonnies, whose great creation was the Columbian Fountain with its lovely maidens and sea horses—a fountain which should be restored in marble; Herman McNeil, Philip Martiny, Edward C. Potter, Bela Pratt; Edwin Kemys, whose American animals guarded the bridges over the lagoons; Lorado Taft, who represented Chicago in this glittering galaxy; Paul Bartlett, John J. Boyle—all these and many others completed the band.

Every morning the entire group was obliged to make a complete tour of the grounds under the guidance of Mr. Ernest Graham, the energetic assistant director of works. This was Burnham's insurance that the ensemble would never be lost sight of in the work of any one of the artists. On Sunday Theodore Thomas, that giant in the realm of music, came out with his orchestra and soothed the savage breast with strains of Beethoven and Bach—another idea of Burnham's, who recognized in the order and rhythm of music its close kinship with architecture. With this phalanx in the foremost rank the fight against time proceeded until the great Exposition triumphantly opened its gates on May 1st, 1893.

The Exposition as completed, with its banners fluttering in the breeze, its fountains splashing in the sunshine, its lagoons troubled by the course of the launches and gondolas which crashed into a million fragments the fairy visions reflected on their breasts, its emerald lawns jewelled with flowers and birds, and its tremendous and many palaces with their regal equipment of terraces, bridges and esplanades all bathed in sunshine against the azure setting of the lake, furnished a spectacle unequalled in the history of the world for the magnificence of its beauty. Imperial Rome in the third century might have approached but surely did not surpass it. Such was the conviction of my boyhood, and thirty-five years of increasing sophistication, which have included most of the architectural spectacles of the generation, have not dimmed the splendor of that picture nor changed in my mind the school-boy's verdict.

Only the great buildings need be mentioned. Architecturally, the palm went to Atwood with his Palace of Fine Arts, the only building on the grounds built with any

claim to permanence, and now after a generation of neglect and ruin happily in the course of restoration. It is pure
Greek Classic, in the Ionic order except for its low dome,
and even that looks as though it had been dropped into
position on its beautiful shoulders by the hands of Callicrates himself. The south portico is especially interesting.
Atwood borrowed it complete from a Prix de Rome design of the time, and when Bénard, its creator, saw his
drawing in its consummation he remarked that he had had
no idea how great an architect he was! All Atwood's other
work—the great peristyle that took the place of Saint-
Gauden's thirteen columns, and the terminal station with
its ingenious and beautiful façade that scarcely anyone in
the expectant throng paused to look back upon and admire—was of superlative quality.

The Administration Building by Hunt was the next in
popular esteem, and it majestically and regally occupied
its post of honor at the end of the great court and opposite
the golden figure of the Republic. Technically, I think
it suffered in comparison with its two beautiful compan-
ions, the Agricultural Building by McKim, Mead and
White, and Machinery Hall by Peabody and Stearns. The
first was pure Roman. The cadence of its façade of three
bays, separated and terminated by pylons flanking symmetrically a great porticoed central pavilion and crowned
with a low dome on which was poised the ethereal Diana
of Saint-Gaudens, made a façade of the greatest beauty
and distinction. The ceilings and walls of its porticoes were
decorated by Maynard, the great sculptural groups of Martiny's Horoscopes terminated the pavilions. The building
was a perfect symposium of the careful proportioning of
McKim and the decorative instinct of Stanford White.

The note struck by Peabody in Machinery Hall has

echoed the longest. It has reappeared in expositions again
and again when the other sweeter strains have long since
died away. The building was frankly a jewelled box, a
fantastical screen, to protect or conceal the real building
within. This was exposition architecture *de rigueur*. No
theories of form expressing function for Peabody! What
he wanted was a joyous stage set, and at that he has never
been beaten. The style, I should say, was French in disposition, particularly in its colonnades which remind one of the
Place de la Concorde and Perrault's east end of the Louvre,
and Spanish in decoration. The twin towers, the domes
over the corner pavilions, the silhouette—the entire ensemble had a dash and vim that fire the blood even in
faded photographs or blurred memories. It was an admirable building.

The great Manufactures and Liberal Arts Building, the
largest building in the world, was dignified and satisfactory, its corner and central pavilions being adaptations of
the well-worn triumphal arch motive. Uninspired as it
was, it was vastly superior to either the Electricity Building, a naïve and awkward essay in Roman architecture,
or the Mines and Mining Building, which was something
still worse. These two buildings were eloquent proofs of
the inadequacy of hands and minds trained in the Romanesque school of the Middle West in handling, without
some practice at least, the Classic problem. Fortunately,
two opportunities were given the Westerners to show what
they could do in a style of their own choosing: the Fisheries Building and the Transportation Building. The Fisheries
was not intended to be a building of great importance, but
it ended by being one of the outstanding successes of the
Fair. It was the swan song of the Romanesque, a song so
full of charm, of humor, of pathos, that it must have

wrung a plaster tear along with the smiles from the brilliant pagan throng sitting in triumphant splendor around the Court of Honor. Henry Ives Cobb's reputation as an architect will largely rest on the frogs, the lobsters and the sea-horses that he or some one working with him so cunningly wove into the ornament of this enchanting edifice.

The other sport from the parent stock, the other black sheep in the merino flock, was the Transportation Building of Adler and Sullivan. The young Irishman of this team, with his black beard and his flashing eyes and his eloquent tongue, got a special dispensation to break two principal canons of the creed, namely, that the Classic style should be followed, and that the buildings should be white. More will be said of this epochal building in another chapter, but here it may be said that it was the antithesis of, say, Machinery Hall—not a beautiful papier-maché simulacrum with canvas leaves and paper blossoms, but a real tub of genuine azaleas rolled onto the stage. It gloried in the fact that it would die with the first frost, that it was stucco and not marble, that it was only a shed the purpose of which was to furnish cover for an exhibition of locomotives and Pullman cars. Sullivan claimed it was of no style whatever, "merely the harmonious expression of harmonious and clear thinking." Curiously enough, its frank expression of its humble purpose, helped along by its brilliant color and golden portal, was as popular with the laity as with the critics; in fact, to the intelligentsia from over-seas it was the only really American building. We shall hear of this again.

Of the other almost countless buildings, which scarcely need mention in so short an essay, some were bad, such as the United States Government Building, and some were very bad, such as the Illinois State Building; but for the most part they were excellent. What they lacked in beauty was usually made up in interest and variety.

The turnstiles of this greatest of all expositions clicked for the last time nearly a half century ago. Fire and the wrecker have long since humbled its proud forms into the dust from which they had so miraculously sprung. Thousands of automobiles roar through the ways that once echoed to the hoofs of old Dobbin and the march of the Columbian guards. The voices of bespectacled dons in the halls of a great university on the Midway have drowned out the cries of the Bedouin camel drivers and the sinful strains of the Streets of Cairo. Moving picture theatres light the skies that once threw back the effulgence of the dome of the Administration Building. The gaunt and decayed carcass of the Palace of Fine Arts awaits the trump of its resurrection, while in its shadows irreverent and enfranchised members of the younger generation fracture the Victorian canons.

"The old order changeth, yielding place to new." This new order, which has been our *milieu* and whose last days we are now watching—if, indeed, they have not already passed—was the result architecturally, at least, of the great Exposition. The Exposition found our country in the rough arms of the Romanesque, albeit those arms were slowly but surely loosening their grasp. The end of the Exposition saw her freed from her barbaric captor, and the monster himself dead, and, what is more, buried deep, while already our fickle Andromeda was casting arch glances in the direction of her Classic hero.

The best commentary on the change is to be found in the architectural press of the time. From 1880 to as late as 1894 at least two-thirds of the illustrations of American contemporary architecture are in the prevailing Romanesque, or some nearly related picturesque style. At the close of the Fair an immediate change is observed, and from then on various forms of the Classic mode prevail. In brief, the spectacle of the exhibition had been so overwhelmingly beautiful that layman and professional alike returned home convinced of the superiority of the art of Greece and Rome.

It would be difficult to point out so definite an artistic revolution in the realms of painting and sculpture, but a great revival of taste is undeniable. Never before had the vast majority of those who gazed at the lunettes of Blashfield or the panels of Maynard seen a mural painting or realized its possibility in conjunction with a proper architectural setting. Sculpture, rare enough now, Heaven knows! was entirely unknown as a complement to architecture before the Exposition brought that brilliant crowd of young sculptors to populate the buildings and grounds with beasts and birds, gods and goddesses, angels and archangels. Considering the splendid success of the sculpture of the Fair, it is hard to understand why, with the unquestioning acceptance of its architecture, a greater revival in the use of sculpture did not take place. The reason probably is that building is a necessity while sculpture is a luxury, and the years immediately following the closing of the Exposition gates were not those in which people inordinately indulged in luxuries of any sort.

But of the profound change in architectural taste and performance there can be no question. The Exposition found the country Romantic, and left it Classic, and with the change in ideals came a vastly increased interest in the arts. The architectural schools automatically assumed a new importance and usefulness. Before the Fair the average architect had learned or attempted to learn his profession in the draughting-room. The draughting departments of Richardson, Hunt, and Burnham and Root, were in a real sense schools where young men offered their services, often without remuneration, in order to learn the art of architecture at the fountain head. However inspirational and poetic this system might have been, it could not fail to be superficial and incomplete, and could not for long compete with the four years' training necessary for a degree given by the great architectural schools. The demand for the college-trained man in architecture became the more insistent on account of the highly technical demands of Classic design—an elaborate technique that did not exist in the picturesque and free-and-easy Romanesque.

But more important than all this, the World's Fair, if it did not itself bring them forth, at least assisted at the birth of new types which were to supersede for almost every kind of building the old forms and visages. The description of these new architectural types will be the major duty of a succeeding chapter.

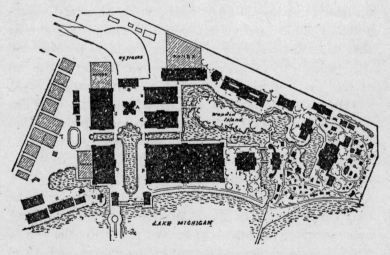

Plan of the World's Columbian Exhibition of 1893.

Principal Buildings.

A. Administration	H. Mining	O. Fisheries
B. Railroad Terminal	I. Transportation	P. U. S. Government
C. Machinery	J. Choral Hall	Q. State Buildings
D. Agriculture	K. Horticulture	R. Foreign Buildings
E. Peristyle	L. Women's Building	S. Forestry, etc.
F. Manufactures	M. Illinois Building	T. Live Stock
G. Electricity	N. Fine Arts	U. Convent La Rabida.

CHAPTER IX

LOUIS SULLIVAN, PARENT AND PROPHET

THE great, ordered, Classic palaces in the Court of Honor at the World's Columbian Exposition swept the mass of the American people off its feet and the Romanesque Revival into limbo. But it was quite another building that evoked the admiration of the visiting foreigners and aroused the interest of the intellectuals. This was the Transportation Building. Its architecture was based on no precedent; its material pretended not to be other than it was; its function was manifest in its form; its architect was Louis Sullivan.

To a few enthusiastic young architects, to a handful of dreamers, to a sprinkling of poets, philosophers and visionaries, its golden arch was a veritable rainbow promising that our artistic slavery to Europe would soon cease, and that beneath its coruscating arc would be found the pot of gold that had been sought so long—an American Style. The search for this pot of gold makes one of the most entertaining and tragic romances in art—an expedition into the unknown that well-nigh ruined the Argonauts who undertook it and which returned them, years later, battered, apparently defeated and without their prize.

When these two paragraphs were written in 1927 under the chapter heading of "Louis Sullivan and the Lost Cause," Sullivan was being made the hero of a tragedy, the plot of which was his failure and that of his disciples to establish an "American Style" in architecture.

It may be said parenthetically that the idea of an "American Style" was not born in 1893. We find it mentioned, discussed and prophesied long before in the pages of the architectural magazines. As far back as 1879 in the "American Architect" an article appeared entitled "Originality in American Architecture; Combatting the Prevailing Demand for an American Style." I never thought that Sullivan relished the efforts of his disciples and admirers in forcing him to take the "lead" in the drama. I often talked to him long ago about the possibility of an "American Style" and his reply was to the effect that we younger architects should hew to the line of his principles and if the chips, in falling, formed an American Style well and good, but as for any self-conscious effort he was against it. No wonder the crusade in our eyes was a failure. We failed to see in the mind of our leader an objective far beyond the trophy of an "American Style."

A tremendous change, however, has occurred in the last five years in regard to Sullivan's proper position in the history of architecture. More and more he is regarded as the true father of the vast architectural phenomenon known as the "New Architecture" or better, I think, as the "International Style." And if it can be shown that the Transportation Building is the true progenitor of the Century of Progress, for instance, or that Sullivan's philosophy of Functionalism is the basis of the work of LeCorbusier, Gropius, Lescaze, and the other Internationalists of today, then his bulk becomes in truth colossal and he may well take his seat among the very mighty and see on either hand the creators of new orders—Callicrates, Isodorus, the builder of Chartres, and Brunelleschi. There is no space here to demonstrate either possibility but the genealogy of secessionist, now become functional, architecture roughly sketched may prove suggestive, even convincing: the Transportation Building by Louis Sullivan, 1893, the "Chicago School," 1894–1910; L'Art Nouveau in Europe, 1898; Secessionism under Wagner, Hoffman, etc. in Germany and the North countries, 1910; publication of the works of Frank Lloyd Wright in Germany, 1912; LeCorbusier, Gropius, and the other "Young Pioneers," 1914; Saarinen's second prize design for the Tribune Building, 1922; the Century of Progress, 1933. The question, however, of Sullivan's claim to immortal fame is only one of degree and whether the new architecture is with us for aye or a day and whether it is begotten solely of him or not the conclusion is the same in either case; Sullivan belongs to the ages.

Now let us get back to our story. Sullivan and his followers fought the Eclecticism that followed the World's Fair tooth and nail but it was a losing fight. The Eclectics defended, when they took the trouble, their right to pick here and choose there from the treasury of other lands and other times with very good arguments. They said that the blood of the men who built the French cathedrals, the German abbeys, the Italian palaces, and the English manor houses flowed in their veins as well and they saw no reason for not enjoying such a princely heritage when and where it pleased them, and, by the beard of Phidias, they intended to do it and they did. Besides, to them architectural style was a language. A pointed arch told the observer to bow his head, a half timber gable filled his mind with domestic bliss, an Italian loggia called to him to twang his lute and be gay! And by the use of these elements a building told its story in a language that the world understood. No, neither the profession nor the laity had any patience with the voice crying in the wilderness, "Prepare ye the way of a new architecture." But let us listen to the voice for it still rings forth.

In the Transportation Building, the Wainwright Building of St. Louis, built in this early time, and in his writings, Sullivan elucidated a great law—the "idea" expressed in his autobiography—that the form should express the function. If the purpose of the Transportation Building was to house Stephenson's Rocket and Pullman's cars, the building should look like that, not like a magnificent palace or a Roman bath. Sullivan went farther. He said, in effect, "The building must tell the truth about its construction and material. Instead of the magnificent shams of the Court of Honor which pretend to be of marble but are in reality built of plaster, my building shall tell the world that it is plaster, and glory in the fact." So he painted its plain sides with colors and figures in much the same way that Richardson painted the plaster vaults of Trinity; and when he used ornament, as he did profusely in the golden arch, it was as he described it "of the surface—not on it," a kind of ornament that in no way suggested carving, but rather the mould and liquid plaster.

The third element Sullivan introduced into this remarkable building—a third corollary he attached to his law and which became in the eyes of his followers more important than the law itself—was complete originality. Nothing of ancient, mediaeval or Renaissance Europe, nor, in fact, of any of our own previous styles—for they in a sense were European—should enter into the building. The ornament and the lines must be original, indigenous, of "pure design." Originality, however, has nothing to do with the relations between form and function, and this corollary proved to be a tail heavier than the kite and at first turned a magnificent flight into a disastrous crash. But it had been a great adventure.

Louis Sullivan, in his "Autobiography of an Idea" the

finished copy of which was placed in those wonderful hands of his when he lay dying, says that he was born in Boston on September 3rd, 1856. He died April 14, 1924. He was born, as he remarks, of a "mongrel breed," mostly Irish, but with a strong strain through his grand-parents of German and of French. Brought up in prosperous circumstances in Puritan New England, his genius seemed independent of his environment, and fed on itself for nutriment.

He went to the Massachusetts Institute of Technology —another great architect who laid the foundations of his success in a splendid education. These were the early days of "Tech," which had been founded in 1866, and Louis came under the tutelage of Professor William R. Ware, of Ware and Van Brunt, architects, and head of the department of Architecture. Ware, you remember, was the architect of Memorial Hall at Harvard, one of the half-dozen or so good buildings of the Parvenu Period. His assistant was Eugène Letang, *diplomé de l'École des Beaux Arts*. I remember that, though he had long since passed from the earthly scene, in my student days the flavor of the romantic and bearded Letang still hung about the ateliers—the first faint lure of Paris and *la vie de Bohême*.

After a year at "Tech" he apparently grew weary of the discipline and routine, for he says "he felt the need and the lack of a red-blooded explanation, of a valiant idea that should bring life to arouse this cemetery of orders and of styles." He began to dream of the fountain head, the École des Beaux Arts, so he went to New York and bearded the lion in his den, old Richard M. Hunt himself. Hunt told him of life in Paris and his work with the great Frenchman, Lefeul, on the Louvre. On he went to

Philadelphia. There he entered the office of Furness and Hewitt, practitioners of "Gothic in pantalettes," as Louis describes the Victorian type. From the windows of their offices he watched the run on the banks that followed the Jay Cooke failure and the panic of '73.

The panic ended his job, and he departed for Chicago —Chicago, sprawling out of the mud and the ashes of the great fire. He loved it all, "a crude extravaganza, an intoxicating rawness, a sense of big things to be done." Louis entered the office of Major William LeBaron Jenney. Jenney is the man who anticipated the Tacoma Building by extensive use of skeleton iron construction in the Home Insurance Building. Louis says he soon found out that the Major was not really in his heart an architect at all, but by nature and in toto a *bon vivant*, a *gourmet*; yet he was a grand figure in the days after the fire. Here Louis' philosophy and architecture kept equal pace with his restlessness and his ambition, and in 1874 we find him bound for Paris.

In Paris he performed the extraordinary feat of passing his examinations for the École des Beaux Arts after only six weeks' preparation. He celebrated by taking a trip to Italy—a trip, as he says, to verify Taine's comparison of the Sistine Chapel ceiling with the Last Judgment. As he says, here in the Chapel of Sixtus "he communed in silence with the superman. Here he felt and saw a great free spirit. Here he came face to face with his first great adventure. The first mighty man of Courage. The first man with a great Voice. The first whose speech was Elemental. The first whose will would not be denied. The first to cry Yea! in thunder tones." Sullivan overwhelmed by the genius of Angelo is interesting. He was certainly not influenced by his work. It must have been the touching that he felt, shoulder to shoulder, of courage and power and loneliness. In the haze of that vast symphony he saw "the primal power of Life at work."

On his return to Paris Louis became a *nouveau* in the Atelier Vaudremer. M. Vaudremer was an *ancien* of the Villa Medici, as the winners of the Grand Prix de Rome are called. Apparently the *vie de Bohême* and the *camaraderie* of the atelier appealed as little to the black-haired Irish-American, who spoke French like a native, as it had to Richardson only ten years before. Work was the thing, and soon, owing to his restlessness and his introspective philosophy, we find him chafing at the bit of scholasticism. The school became as a tinkling cymbal. "He felt that beneath the law of the school lay a law which it ignored unsuspectingly or with fixed intention—the law which he had seen set forth in the stillness of the Sistine, which he saw everywhere in the open of life."

The next year found him back in Chicago—Chicago in the doldrums of the panic of '73—but he was a brilliant and amazingly swift draughtsman, and he was soon employed. Sullivan, like Root, a natural mathematician, developed at this period a fine flair for engineering. The great Eads Bridge, crouching for its mighty leap across the Mississippi, fired his imagination and inspired him more than the greatest of the puny buildings in Chicago.

In 1880 he became a partner in an old established firm, and in another year the partnership became known as Adler and Sullivan. The new firm rapidly surged to the front and challenged the supremacy of Burnham and Root —Adler the ballast, Sullivan the sails; Adler the wheel horse, Sullivan the prancing leader.

For his work before the Fair—and it comprised many large commissions—Sullivan claims the same independence and the same philosophy that made the Transportation Building epochal. There is certainly no evidence of any such philosophy in such of these buildings as are standing today—possibly in the commercial structures, a thinning of piers and a widening of windows, and a certain originality of ornament, but its flavor in the seventies is of the prevailing mode, Eastlake, Queen Anne, and the Frenchman Labrouste. Sullivan's work of this period does not equal in beauty and it does not surpass in originality the contemporary work of John Root.

In the eighties Sullivan became a convert along with the rest to the Romanesque Revival, though he never would admit it. His Auditorium Building in Chicago stands, as far as the exterior is concerned, as one of the greatest examples of this style, yet there is no suggestion in the form of this building of its primary function in the housing of a vast auditorium. In fact, its great tower, which makes of the building a veritable Palazzo Vecchio, seems to preclude the possibility of a huge hall lying beyond.

The Auditorium Building reeks with personalities. Within its granite portals have come the great of the land and of all lands. The most brilliant of the song-birds of opera have fluttered and carolled within this stony cage; rulers, statesmen, captains of industry as visitors to the great exposition or the opera have here been entertained. To the lover of architecture it is an absorbing artistic document. Into it went Louis Sullivan, one of the crowd, a practitioner of the vernacular, understood and beloved by everyone; out of it came Sullivan, the mystic, an apostle of a new creed, unto the public a stumbling-block and unto his profession foolishness.

It took several years to build the Auditorium Building. As in other buildings, the plans having been made and the specifications written, the construction was well under way before it was necessary to work out the details for decorative or ornamental portions, especially those of the great auditorium itself, and it was in this interval that the metamorphosis of Sullivan occurred. The great Romanesque granite façade might have been by Richardson or Root, but come within, examine the carvings on the maple finish of what was once the bar and is now one again, go into the huge auditorium, look up at the misty ceiling with its rhythmic recessional of mighty arches, study the golden grilles on either side of the proscenium—in short, wherever there is ornamentation you will observe that this is no longer Romanesque, but something quite different. Where the Romanesque was material, this is ethereal; where the old was of common and brutal forms this new is of fairy-land—the germ and the beginning of life, the tender shoots pushing their way up through the softening sod, the twining tendrils and the bursting bud. "O soft melodious Springtime, first-born of life and love," wrote Sullivan on the wall. Through this vernal symphony runs another motive, geometrical and cold—frost patterns on the pane, snow crystals on a black sleeve, dew glistening on forsaken webs. "A great life has passed into the tomb, and there awaits the requiem of winter's snows."

This is not rhetoric or fine writing. Sullivan actually attempted a plastic symbolization of such thoughts, and as he read them into his design we, if we are sympathetic and discerning, can read them out. It is therefore in the Auditorium Building that Sullivan broke with conformity and became a knight errant on his own, a Galahad. No more Romanesque came from his hand after that building. This does not mean that he was hostile to the Romanesque as it was being practised in his time; merely that, on the wings of genius, he rose above it. Indeed, he apparently saw hope for American architecture in the Romanesque, for he bitterly attacked the Classicism of the World's Fair. He speaks of the "virus of the World's Fair," "the virus of a culture snobbish and alien to the land," "the damage wrought by the World's Fair will last for half a century from its date," and in a last word of bitterness unusual for him he writes, "For architecture, be it known, is dead. Let us therefore dance lightly on its grave, strewing roses as we glide," and, apparently in reference to the gathering of the American Institute of Architects before the Grecian Lincoln Memorial in Washington and the presentation of a medal to Henry Bacon, its architect, "Indeed let us gather in procession, in the night, in the rain, and make soulful, fluent, epicene orations to the living dead we neuters eulogize."

The first fruit of the new dispensation developed in the Auditorium was the Wainwright Building in St. Louis, built in 1890. Sullivan told me himself that it was the first building in which he had incorporated all his architectural principles. In it he thought the form of every part expressed the function of that part. The form also expressed the construction, the steel columns being indicated by the vertical piers that rise clear to the cornice. The ornament was entirely original, and, he believed, wholly American. This building was followed chronologically by the Transportation Building at the Fair, the Schiller Theatre—as it was called when built—a striking composition of great renown at the time, the Stock Exchange Building—a great store building on State Street—all in Chicago; the Condict Building, New York City; the Prudential Building in Buffalo and the Gage Building in Chicago.

This Gage Building still stands in my opinion as one of the best expressions of the skeleton steel commercial skyscraper. In masonry buildings the heaviest mouldings are at the bottom, indicating strength. A skeleton building is only a little stronger, if at all, at the bottom than at the top, and, since this is the case, the base, being nearest the eye, should have the most delicate ornamentation. Therefore in the Gage Building the first story, occupied by shops, is clothed by a shimmering skin of exquisitely modelled cast iron. The vertical shafts, extending clear to the cornice, are merely the narrowest of terra cotta protection for the steel; the windows, consequently, have the maximum of glass exposure. The spandrels or spaces above the top of one row of windows and below the sill of the next are of terra cotta or iron elaborately ornamented. The cornice is slight and of simple though unusual form. All the ornament is Sullivan's own.

The Gage Building marks the high point of Louis Sullivan's material achievement. The death of Dankmer Adler, his partner, the constant and swelling tide of New York Classicism of the Beaux Arts variety, and the nonconforming sort of life that Sullivan himself led, together with an arrogance that brooked no interference or compromise, gradually lost him the great commissions that had previously been his. Without complaint he turned to the little things. No longer permitted to be an Angelo, he would be a Vermeer; no longer a mighty forester, he would plant a little garden. These little things of Sullivan rank among his greatest works. The Getty tomb in Graceland cemetery, Chicago, approaches so closely to perfection that one gasps at his temerity. The series of small banks, of which that at Owatonna is the best known, are rich and gorgeous blooms that waste—we trust not—their sweetness on the desert air of Minnesota and the prairie states. Sullivan devised many practical novelties for these buildings, and in their construction introduced and made popular "tapestry" brick, which was made to his order.

The last works that he engaged in were the writing of his "Autobiography of an Idea," a book which spreads before the world his philosophy of life, and the preparation of a series of plates illustrating in full his philosophy of ornament. The originals of these plates, published by the Press of the American Institute of Architects, belong to the Art Institute of Chicago, and are, as far as I know, the most remarkable and beautiful pencil drawings of an architectural character in America. Considered as drawings alone they are examples of a virtuosity that has never been excelled. The designs are of two kinds "organic," based in vegetable forms, and "inorganic", based on geometrical forms. Their meaning in a word is this: "The germ is the seat of power." Add to it "a will to live," and, directed by the genius of man, it will grow and flower through simple forms to the most complicated and involved structures. This theory is developed in the organic plates, culminated in his masterful drawing, "Impromptu" —a lovely and amazing fantasy, an exposition, to my mind, not so much of any inherent desire on the part of the germ as of an exuberant genius on the part of the artist. In the series of inorganic plates simple Euclidian forms are elaborated; these culminate after a geometrical metamorphosis in a beautiful design entitled "the Awakening of the Pentagon."

While these drawings were nearing completion he had begun his book. Discounting the exaltation of the ego therein, the ambiguity, and the arrogance of the assumption that thoughts there stated had never been set forth before, we still have a remarkable document. It looks forward to the ultimate emergence of man "as Free Spirit, as Creator, as container of illimitable powers for the joy and peace of mankind." Sullivan lived this philosophy of a religionless hope, in which man was to find his salvation and triumph in himself alone. Financial reverses, the loss of prestige, and, worse still, the apparent overthrow of his teachings in the waves of Classicism that followed the Fair, evoked from him no bitterness and no complaint. They merely meant the postponement of that happy day which his faith and logic showed him to be inevitable, and which, after all, he had never really expected to see.

Pointing out the mistakes of prophets is a weakness of scribblers, so it is with hesitation that I beg leave to indicate what in my belief were the mistakes of Sullivan. While he made no claim to the founding of an "American style," an expression which he never used as far as I know, he did regard his method of design as a plastic expression of democracy, as "Leaves of Grass" done into stone and iron and plaster,—of the people, by the people and for the people. As a matter of fact, his system of ornament was aristocracy itself. Like those who understand Einstein, there were scarcely fifteen men in the country who could draw or model his ornament. The system that underlies his designs, though it may be the last word in logic, is as baffling and difficult to trace as those intricate labyrinths that underlie the lacelike arabesques of the Alhambra.

His second great fallacy, without which we would have had no Sullivan the decorator, is his refusal to regard architecture in its stylistic aspects as a language—a language which, with other tongues, saw its beginning in the dawn of our culture; a language which the architect must speak if he is to be understood in this practical world. In a building, the plan and construction are the thought; the ornamental details are the words. It is the laws Louis Sullivan laid down governing this "thought" in a building that have made him a prophet. Form follows Function. Here, like the creator of the ceiling of the Sistine, "he is the first mighty man of Courage. The first man with a great voice. The first whose speech was elemental. The first whose will would not be denied. The first to cry Yea! in thunder tones."

To found a school is the priceless prerogative of the prophet, and, though the altars may be broken and the disciples of whom the world was not worthy martyred in the amphitheatres of Philistinism, it is impossible to destroy the influence of his thought. Sullivan's style has passed on and lives only as a haunting architectural memory, but his thought is growing in importance and momentum, and will dominate the architectural expression of the nascent era.

It is to Sullivan, the teacher, and to his disciples that we must now turn. In the late nineties and the first few years of the new century his teaching and example permeated the philosophy and execution of the architectural draughtsmen and younger architects of Chicago. The Chicago Architectural Club became a forum for the discussion of the new gospel, and its atelier the proving grounds for the new style. Feeling ran high between the advocates of Classicism and those of Rationalism, between the Beaux Arts and the "Bizarre." Sullivan gave a series of addresses to these youngsters which were collected and published from time to time in the architectural journals as "Kindergarten Chats." They spread the law of form and function, the theory of "pure design" and "indigenous ornament" to other centers. Mr. Claud F. Bragdon, of Buffalo, the architectural necromancer of fourth dimensional design, and Harvey Ellis of Minneapolis, the young Keats of the T-square, professed the faith, but in the main the battle raged in the Windy City, the East observing the fray with amused tolerance.

The most brilliant of Sullivan's disciples was Frank Lloyd Wright of Oak Park, Illinois. Mr. Wright was educated at the University of Wisconsin as an engineer. He is as original in detail as Sullivan, and superior to him in composition, in both plan and elevation. His purpose is in part the expression of the supremacy of the machine. "The machine is the normal tool of our civilization. Give it work that it can do well." Hence he abolishes carving and mouldings and handicraft. Broad bands take the place of cornices, and "built in" furniture supplants the products of Grand Rapids. He endeavors always to bring out the inherent natural quality of the material, and it was he who introduced the use of softly stained wood, often rough, of rough plaster, rough brick often with joints deeply raked, leaded glass of extremely interesting and original design, stone broken and crude in its forms. In the prairie country, where most of his work is done, he made a successful attempt to harmonize the building with the terrain. "The prairie," he says, "has a beauty peculiarly its own, and we should recognize and accentuate this natural beauty, its quiet level. Hence gentle, sloping roofs, low proportions, quiet sky-lines, suppressed heavy-set chimneys and sheltering over-hangs, low terraces and outreaching walls, sequestering private gardens."

Wright is a past master in planning. Many of his plans, like those for the Imperial Hotel in Tokyo, even when entirely divorced from their practical significance, are exquisite pictures in themselves. These plans show his ideas of the simplification of functions. The fewer the rooms and divisions, the better. The all-one-room first floor, with different functions indicated by screens or other architectural devices, was his ideal. Here he had been anticipated by John Randolph of Roanoke, who, you remember, divided his house into rooms by the simple expedient of painting their outlines on the floor with white paint.

One further aspect of his art should receive attention—namely, his debt to the Japanese—though he remarked to me, "You are all wrong; I'm not indebted to the Japanese—the Japanese are indebted to me." From them he seems to have received inspiration and encouragement to reduce the requirements for a house—as, for instance, the number of rooms—to the simplest terms, and to eliminate as far as possible such appurtenances as movable furniture and pictures. From the Japanese, too, he apparently learned to make doors and windows an integral part of the design, not floating on its surfaces. And from them also he must have learned that intimate liaison between art and nature which makes his work sink into and be lost in the embrace of rock and shrub and tree.

Mr. Wright has to his credit a long list of extremely interesting and often beautiful buildings of varied purpose. I cannot think of one that is dull or labored. A student of his work would divide it into a first, a second, and a third manner, but that is beyond the limits of our present space. The Midway Garden in Chicago is generally regarded as his best; closely following are the Imperial Hotel in Tokyo; Unity Church, Oak Park; the Larkin Building, Buffalo; and numerous houses such as the Fricke, Winslow and Coonley residences in Oak Park, which, incidentally, illustrate his succeeding manners and the later Millard house in Pasadena.

Like Sullivan, too, Wright is a prolific writer and propagandist. Some of his essays, such as "In the Cause of Architecture," are excellent examples of forceful English. His book of his own work published in Germany, 1912, is an accepted milestone in the advance of the new architecture.

Now in these later mellow years, Wright, as the high priest of Taliesen, has almost been relegated to the position of an old master. As one who took the mantle of Sullivan as it fell from him and smote the waters so that they parted hither and thither, he is venerated by the modernists the world over. This may not be all to his liking as Wright is a born martyr, though, after all, this may be his greatest martyrdom to find everybody agreeing with him, and Taliesen may prove his most enduring monument—his martyr's palm.

Here in the heart of Wisconsin, beautifully located and beautifully built, is a group of buildings dedicated "to developing a well correlated creative human being capable of effective concentration upon the circumstances in which he lives." Here architecture, music, other arts and the various crafts are taught or, better perhaps, lived. Six honor men direct the efforts of seventy apprentices in manual as well as mental creation. Taliesen, under the direction of Wright, has recently produced "Broadacres," a plan for a decentralized and "architecturally reintegrated" community. The world honors Frank Lloyd Wright and smiles indulgently at his quaint belief that he invented architecture.

I have avowedly endeavored to mention only those among Sullivan's followers whose work has been decisive, not listing the scores who have done excellent work but whose total effort was not pivotal. Yet to pass by the little band who formed the "Chicago School" and who fought and sacrificed for the truth, as they saw it, would be too

much to ask of one of their comrades in arms. Myron
Hunt, Robert Spencer, Dwight Perkins, George Elmslie,
George Dean, Hugh Garden, George Maher, Birch Long,
Vernon Watson, William Drummond and many others
—were too lusty and jovial a crew to be known by
posterity as a band of reformers, but posterity will not
forget as valiant architects! Those who have not gone into
the greater beyond are seeing today the triumph of their
early principles. So complete was the solidarity of this group
and so single their aim that the style actually produced a
limited grammar (of proportion) and a vocabulary (of
detail) of its own and in fact enjoyed an extensive vogue in
the western states.

The most striking element in the exterior of a building
by one of the Chicago School was its horizontality and
lowness. In a house, for instance, a strongly marked base,
the sills and heads of all windows continuous and on the
same line, a wide projecting cornice with a flat soffit and
a low roof, usually hipped, emphasized the horizontality.
Porches projected from corners and garages were connected by low walls, so that there was a composition of
parallel and descending roof-lines spreading out the house
more and more on the ground. All materials were used
with equal favor. Wood was usually rough as it came from
the saw, and the stucco was often stained. Doors were low,
and the windows, invariably casements, often leaded in a
cobweb-like manner and usually disposed in groups. The
chimneys were low and very broad, even if they served
but the kitchen stove. A closer inspection reveals the aus-
tere abnegation of all the sinful graces and curves of the
seductive Renaissance or the equally evil and superstitious
Gothic. For the aforesaid curved mouldings and other
Classic attributes of the devil, ingenious and often beauti-

ful combinations of bands and flat surfaces at different angles were piously substituted.

The interiors of these houses were equally characteristic. Plans of the sort described as typical of Frank Lloyd Wright's work prevailed. Be it said here that if these independents did nothing else they at least revolutionized the planning of the small house. There was no such thing as a sensible and scientific plan for a small house thirty years ago. Most of the conveniences that make for economical housekeeping and convenient living which we take for granted today date from that period. The interior of the house presented open vistas and low ceilings. The same horizontality was augmented here by the "continuous trim," a level band of wood running about the room and connecting in one straight line the tops of all the windows and doors. The fireplace was usually very broad and low, often of "Roman" brick (I do not know how that happened!) and devoid of ornament except for occasional tile inserts. Oak was the favorite material for trim, usually in a grayish-brown finish and waxed—never varnished or painted. The walls were of sand-finished plaster, stained again. Wall paper was anathema. Rugs, Navajo or one-toned, partially covered the hard-wood floors.

Such a rigorous interior required furniture, lighting fixtures and even pictures in the same style, and this was one of the difficulties. In such a room mahogany furniture, crystal chandeliers, and oil paintings in gilt frames made a combination too horrible to contemplate, yet that was usually its destiny. The story is told of Wright that he actually requested the chatelaine of one of the houses he had built to have her gowns cut in lines and made of materials, (samples of which he herewith enclosed) harmonious with her house. Few people building houses can afford to discard wedding presents and the accumulations of successive anniversaries and Christmases; and even should they be able to, these objects, unlovely as they may be, often have beautiful associations, which put something into the home beyond the provisions of architecture. In a house, the style of which is flavored by the past, furniture and other things, unless they are unmistakably bad in themselves, are usually in harmony regardless of their age or style. Hence these curdled and undigested interiors with period furniture and ancient art placed in a Sullivanesque environment were a great factor in the undoing of the reform.

The failure of this style to rise beyond a merely local movement or to exist beyond the generation may be ascribed to several factors—it never became fashionable; not enough people of consequence adopted it to give it authority with the general herd; and it challenged, attacked and locked horns with the Beaux Arts, the great architectural school in Paris, when that school was at the height of its influence in America. This meant the hostility of all the East, particularly of New York, where most of the Paris men were working. It also meant the hostility of the architectural schools in America, where Beaux Arts methods of teaching universally prevailed. It failed to produce any transcendently beautiful or very important piece of work—no Trinity Church to pipe an irresistible strain for children to follow. It had the message, it had the enthusiasm, it had the leaders; but the "breaks" were all against it.

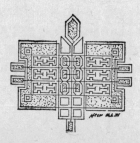

CHAPTER X

ECLECTICISM 1893–1917

In Which the World is the Store House and Taste the Door Keeper

WHETHER because of the travail in producing the great Fair or because of the panic of '93, Chicago, when the captains and the kings departed and the gates to the White City were closed, lay exhausted and inert. Her brief architectural supremacy of ten years in the latter half of the Romanesque Revival was at an end, and the supreme reward of the Fair—a new era in architecture—was politely purloined by those suave gentlemen from New York, her distinguished guests, who dined at her board and carried off her silver spoons in their pockets! Henceforth or for another twenty years at least, New York was to be the fountain head of architectural modes, the *arbiter elegantiarum* in matters of style and taste.

What had happened was something like this. Away back in the Parvenu period of the fifties and sixties we had our first indications of architectural eclecticism, or choice in styles. This was a significant phenomenon, for up to that day throughout the history of civilization only one style had been used at a time. The eclecticism of the sixties, however, was a very limited affair—choosing only between the French Mansard Roof style and the Victorian Gothic with its variant, the Eastlake. The Romanesque Revival, which followed, seemed to be a return to the ancient "one style at a time" method. But New York, it must be remembered, never opened her gates to the Romanesque, waiting, as we shall see, for the opportunity when by a brilliant sortie on the enfeebled conqueror she could put him to flight and regain her supremacy. That opportunity came in 1893.

The chief factor underlying the development of this new period was the vast increase in education in the last decade or two of the nineteenth century. For the architect this education was of two kinds, on the one hand there was a tremendous increase in the number of men from the schools, both our own schools at home and those abroad. Between 1885 and 1895 men returning from the Beaux Arts increased tremendously while young men studying architecture in American schools in the same period were legion. Since 1893 important schools of architecture have been founded in many universities, such as Harvard, Pennsylvania, Carnegie at Pittsburgh, Armour Institute in Chicago, and state universities such as Ohio, Michigan, and Minnesota. These had been preceded by architectural schools, you will remember, at M. I. T., Columbia, and Illinois. In addition, the Society of Beaux Arts Architects, founded in 1894, by their establishment of ateliers in various cities and by their extension courses in competitive design, have greatly added to the knowledge of design and skill in draughtsmanship.

Conversely, office education, so important a factor in the seventies and eighties, ceased to have any weight after '93. The architect who began as an office boy and learned his "trade" in an architect's office was one with Nineveh and Tyre. For the public, also, education was leavening the lump. Its great architectural school was the World's Fair, but there were other agencies. European travel was one. The publication of an increasing number of magazines on home building, house furnishing and gardening, another. To these the proper meed of praise has never been given. What was the result of all this education? For the public it meant an acquaintance with the historic styles of architecture and a love for them, and for the architect it meant the ability to design and build in almost any manner.

Of this new movement in which architects were college bred and technically equipped and the public sufficiently sophisticated to know one renaissance from another, Charles Follen McKim, senior member of the firm of McKim, Mead and White, of New York City, was the acknowledged leader. The Agricultural Building, that stately and rhythmic edifice that stretched along the southern side of the Court of Honor, was one of the great buildings of the Fair. In architectural judgment it probably ranked second only to Atwood's Palace of Fine Arts. It came directly from the hands of McKim, yet it was not this building, brilliant as it was, that won for its author the leadership of the new régime.

For this we must go back to Boston and to Copley Square. On the east side of that beautiful breathing-space, you will remember, looms the gigantic hulk of old Romanesque Trinity, while on the west side reposes in polite tranquillity the Italian Renaissance palace known as the Boston Public Library. The drama of this situation should appeal even to the least imaginative: the supreme work of Richardson facing the first great work of the man who vanquished him. For nearly twenty years the mighty Romanesque barbarian had marched roughshod over the country, driving the timid Colonial, the proud Roman, the ascetic Gothic to cover with hardly a struggle. But now his day had come. There stands his suave and smiling conqueror, a young David beside the fallen Goliath but calm and serene in his hour of triumph. The Boston Public Library was the first important expression of the wave of Classicism that emanated from the Fair. It is also the first important public work of McKim, Mead and White. I mention the work before the man because on it McKim mounted to the seat of authority which he was not to relinquish for a quarter of a century.

Charles Follen McKim was born in 1847. This made him twenty-three years younger than Hunt and thirteen years younger than Richardson. He was born of a stern abolitionist and reformer, and a beautiful Quakeress. Neither had any outstanding artistic talents, and, in fact, the boy had no inkling of his hidden genius until after he had gone to college. In McKim we find again the curious inclination to be an engineer, and it was to prepare for the mining engineering course at the Lawrence Scientific School at Harvard that he went to Cambridge in 1866.

According to authorities, Russell Sturgis, architect, encyclopedist and critic, was responsible for McKim's giving up engineering and devoting his life to architecture. McKim started his education at what is ordinarily considered the top, for we find him in 1867 knocking vigorously on the doors of the École des Beaux Arts. Whether the enthusiasm of the biographer, or some undiscovered relationship between good looks and architecture or perhaps McKim's well known penchant for following precedent is responsible, I do not know; but we find that he, like Hunt, Richardson and Root, was "slender, graceful, and distinguished." McKim remained two years in Paris, when he returned to America and entered the office of H. H. Richardson. Here, in what was the best architectural school in the country, he spent three years; then he opened a modest office in New York with Mead and Bigelow, the partnership continuing until 1879 when Stanford White, a fellow pupil of McKim's in Richardson's office, joined the firm in Bigelow's place.

It is a notable thing, and speaks well for the individuality of the firm, that from the very first none of the partners showed the slightest indication of following in the footsteps of Richardson. None of the enthusiastic devotion and acquiescence of John Root here. Unless the Louis Tiffany house in New York can be considered such, St. Peter's Church, Morristown, is the only important example of a Romanesque building by McKim. McKim had an orderly mind and the Greeks' love of beauty: besides which he had a quiet persistence that accomplished wonders. Never must beauty, dignity or taste be sacrificed on the altar of power, originality, or any other ugly thing. This does not mean that in eschewing the Romanesque McKim kept his tunic entirely free from some of the purple stains of the romanticism that surrounded him. Some of his country houses at Narragansett Pier and Newport, with their shaggy manes and weather-beaten faces, are romantic to the core, though in the detail he carefully adheres to Georgian precedent. His old adviser, Russell Sturgis, even went so far as to say that these picturesque indiscretions were his best work, but we shall not agree with him. Undoubtedly McKim and his partners deliberately determined on the consistent use of Classic architecture or some of its Renaissance derivatives for all their buildings. Perhaps a trip made by the four of them, McKim, Mead, White and Bigelow, through New England in the early days of their practice had something to do with it.

They had other policies, too. They would use only the finest building materials and accept only the best workmanship; they would call upon painting and sculpture, through their greatest exponents, to adorn a building; and, the point of most interest to the layman, they would occasionally choose some famous historic edifice as a model and adapt it to American needs. Of this last policy the first completed example was—since the famous building has in the past year been torn down—the tower of Madison Square Garden in New York, 1891, which owed its form to the Giralda in Seville. Another was the Boston Public Library, 1895, obviously inspired by the Bibliothéque Ste. Geneviève in Paris. In the Herald Square Building, 1894, in New York, we see the familiar lines of the Palazzo Consiglio at Verona; in the New York State Building at the World's Fair, the Villa Medicis in Rome; and in the Tiffany Building, 1906, the features of the Vendramini Palace in Venice. There was no taint of plagiarism in these adaptations for there was no necessity for it, and patent rights have long since expired on Classic works of art. I have never heard any explanation given. Apparently this larceny was committed in a spirit of fun as Shakespeare might rifle Boccaccio's treasure or as Beethoven might raise to Olympus a simple German *lied*.

The commission for the Public Library in Boston was given McKim, Mead and White in 1887. The building was not completed, however, until 1895. Two or three times a day as a student for four years, except during the vacations, I passed its serene façade. There seemed to my impressionable years a very aura of good taste surrounding it in which I took a daily spiritual bath. Beside the carefully studied proportions of the building itself, there were the beautiful shields and medallions by Saint-Gaudens over the main entrance, the trade-marks of the old printers by Mora between the arched windows, and within the noble frescoes by Chavannes and the murals by Edwin A. Abbey. This was before Sargent had painted his cryptic decorations in the upper halls.

In those days they told an amusing story of the building of the Library which I have taken great pains not to verify. Around the frieze of the building runs a list of names of the great in art and science through the ages. These are mixed up with little regard to either chronology or geography. A bright boy on his way to the Boston Latin School discovered that if you began at the upper left hand corner and took the initial letter of each name, the result spelled out the names of the architects, "McKim, Mead and White." So great was the uproar in the Back Bay that the frieze was torn down and rebuilt at the architects' expense. What happened to the ingenious draughtsman in their office who designed this granite acrostic the chronicle does not state.

I owe another debt to the Library. When I was an undergraduate, the bronze statue of the Bacchante by MacMonnies, who did the beautiful Fountain of Time at the World's Fair, had been erected in the center of the lovely courtyard. Great was the scandal and outcry aroused by this harmless and ingenuous young woman. The papers were full of protests that the "pure serene" of the Library was no place for one of her temperament and point of view. I wrote in my sketchbook an apostrophe to the maiden, some of the lines of which still stick in my memory:

What was it, fair Bacchante, tell us, pray,
Claret, gin fizzes, or absinthe frappé,

Amontillado, or a wine more old,
Covered with cobwebs, dust, and ancient mold?
Or was it some rare vintage of the Gods
We mortal clods can never hope to taste?
Her laughing lips are silent. Like the Sphinx
She guards the secret of just what she drinks.

The interrogation got me no answer, but the effusion resulted in a berth on the college paper.

McKim's firm, by carefully avoiding the picturesque
and sticking closely to some phase of Classic architecture,
consistently maintained the decided lead gained by the
Library. A brilliant series of clubhouses followed, culminating in the magnificent University Club on Fifth Avenue, New York, completed in 1900—faintly reminiscent
of the fifteenth century Ricardi Palace in Florence—undoubtedly the finest clubhouse in the world and the prototype for the many clubs which followed it. Of his numerous residences, the Villard houses, built in 1885, probably
exerted the most chastening influence.

The buildings for Columbia University, 1893, were
equally notable, and the library with its magnificent approach was at the time regarded as one of the dozen
most beautiful buildings in America. Its great Roman
bulk rises from the plan of an equal-armed cross, the
crossing roofed with a low dome on a high attic, and the
entrance announced by an imposing decastyle (ten-col-
umned) portico in the Ionic order.

McKim's work on the University of Virginia was not
so much an architectural opportunity as a sacred trust.
This historic and beautiful building, you remember, was
the greatest work of Thomas Jefferson and one of the most
important monuments of the Post-Colonial. In 1897 it
was seriously damaged by fire. In remodelling it McKim

and Stanford White removed an intervening floor, giving it the clear rotunda that Jefferson had intended, but which he had been prevented from carrying out by the necessity for many rooms.

Another commission of the same character was the restoration and extension of the White House in Washington in 1903. This, you will remember, is also a choice example of the Post-Colonial. Originally built by Hoban, it had suffered many alterations under various administrations, and, in addition to living quarters for the President's family, it housed the executive offices as well—a situation which finally became unbearable. Under Roosevelt's administration McKim, with full appreciation and sympathy for Hoban's original work, added the wings for the offices and removed many of the architectural accretions, restoring the state dining-room, in particular, to the dignity which belonged to it.

The restoration, or rather remodelling, of two other buildings added to the luster of the firm. One was the Bank of Montreal. Here the old portico was left unscathed, and a splendid banking room worthy of Ancient Rome was added and blended into it. A similar major operation which restored the patient to perfect health was performed on the old Greek Revival Custom House of New York City. Now it is the National City Bank with an interior perhaps the noblest of its kind in the country, and the old historic façade is preserved for posterity.

McKim could descend from the grandiose to the exquisite without desecrating in the slightest degree his sense of scale or fitness—witness the beautiful Johnson Gates in the Colonial style at Harvard, and, best of all, the J. Pierpont Morgan Library, New York, built in 1906. This little building, the plaything of a man to whom cost meant nothing, was a challenge to McKim that he did not hesitate to take up, for in this building there could be no alibi; if a mistake occurred, be the blood on the architect's head. As far as I can see, it is practically faultless, although if the two small windows on either side of the entrance had been omitted, I believe the design would have been improved, but other than that the building is as perfect a one as we human beings can hope to effect. The style is the Italian Renaissance of the period of Peruzzi.

The last work McKim personally engaged upon, and the greatest ever achieved by his firm, is the Pennsylvania Terminal Station in New York City, built between 1906 and 1910. I have said something about insufficient tribute being paid in the consummation of a building to the owner, the party of the first part, the father of the building. Had there been no Alexander J. Cassatt, there had been no Pennsylvania Terminal, at least in its present magnificent form. We will hear of him again and of his munificence to Washington and its Park Commission.

Mr. Cassatt acquired two city blocks—between Seventh and Eighth Avenues, and from Thirty-first to Thirty-third Streets—in the heart of the metropolis. He then drove tunnels below the North River, which came up out of the ground on this land he had purchased. The opportunity to build over this tremendous abyss the largest railroad station and the most magnificent in the world was given by Cassatt to McKim and his partners without competition or reservation. The ingenuity and the engineering skill that solved and overcame the problems and difficulties of access to what is, in fact, the terminus of two railroads (as the Long Island Road had been purchased and must be accommodated) need not be discussed here.

The station as built consists of a kernel or cella in the center of the area surrounded by a magnificent screen of pavilions and Doric colonnades enclosing the whole extent of the property. This central portion contains as its heart the general waiting-room. It is 280 feet long, 100 feet wide, and 145 feet high. For its motive McKim went to the tepidarium, or warm room, of the Imperial Baths of Caracalla in Rome. Eight gigantic Corinthian columns with their entablatures support a vast groined and coffered ceiling. The curtain walls between are decorated with a lesser order in the Ionic style, and in their upper portion pierced with huge clerestory windows. The simplicity of the scheme, its vast dimensions, the beauty of the detail, and the magnificence of the materials result in the noblest room in America.

Hardly second in interest is the concourse. Rome has no say here, and American engineering rules undisputed. In dimensions only a little smaller than the waiting-room, the concourse is all of steel and glass. The steel columns and girders are given graceful forms—an opportunity seldom taken advantage of in America, though Baltard in the Church of St. Augustin in Paris fifty years before showed us the possibilities of metal architecture.

Charles F. McKim's life, like his architecture, was carefully ordered and disposed. One might say it was arranged, as we architects have it, "on axis." On one side was his private life and practice, and on the other his service to the state. This public service may be divided into four major activities: as architect only second to Burnham at the World's Fair; as president of the American Institute of Architects; as founder and first president of the American Academy at Rome; and as a member of the Park Commission of the District of Columbia. His work at the

World's Fair has already been described in the chapter on that subject.

Directly after the end of the Fair he threw himself into the establishment of the American Academy in Rome. Mr. Granger, his biographer, wisely suggests that it was the sight of architects, painters and sculptors working together at the great Exposition which gave him the idea. At any rate, his plans for the Academy provided for those three arts, and to them music has been added since. McKim had always been very much interested in architectural education. He had already founded three scholarships, the Julia Amory Appleton Fellowship in Architecture at Harvard in memory of his wife, and a travelling scholarship at Columbia. It is the great ambition of every graduate student in architecture to win a travelling scholarship, and great is the prestige, the joy and the good that redounds to the victor. In those days there were three famous scholarships that took the winners to Europe. Now there are many more. They were the McKim Fellowship of Columbia, the Rotch Travelling Scholarship of Boston, and the Stewardson Memorial Scholarship of the University of Pennsylvania. The presence of the scholars in Europe with no place to lay their heads or set up their drawing boards gave McKim his opportunity for a beginning. He took quarters in the Palazzo Torlonia in Rome, hired a director, and enlisted as pupils the winners of the three scholarships. In 1905 this school was incorporated as the American Academy in Rome by a special act of Congress, and the bill was signed by Theodore Roosevelt. Its present beautiful quarters on the Janiculum Hill in Rome were designed by W. M. Kimball, now the senior partner since 1914 after the death of McKim, as a model for Italian architects to follow in designing Roman villas;

nor have I space to more than mention its distinguished supporters—Burnham, La Farge, Saint-Gaudens, J. Pierpont Morgan, Senator McMillan, nor some of its graduates—J. V. B. Magonigle, John Russell Pope, Paul Manship. By the will of McKim the Academy in Rome will eventually obtain his entire fortune of a quarter of a million of dollars. If I have said so much about the Academy, it is because I want to drive home the importance in the Eclectic period of European scholarship and the principle of European study. The keynote of Eclecticism is taste, and taste is discrimination, and the sense of discrimination can best be obtained by cosmopolitan contacts.

And finally we might mention his services on the Park Commission of the District of Columbia. He was not chairman of the Commission; he was not, as far as I know, its leading spirit, but the time for a brief account of this Commission belongs in this Eclectic period of which we have chosen him as the symbol.

The location of the capital of the new republic on the banks of the Potomac had been a political compromise, effected at the end of the Revolutionary War between claimants for New York, Philadelphia and other cities. It was one of the first and most difficult duties of President Washington to fix the exact location and after that develop a plan for the new city. Washington appointed Major L'Enfant, a young French engineer, to coöperate with him in selecting a site, and, that being accomplished, to devise a city plan. To this work, as we may well suppose, Washington's Secretary of State, Thomas Jefferson, lent his good judgment and enthusiastic support, supplying plans which he had obtained abroad of Paris, Amsterdam, Strassburg, Turin, Milan, and other cities. L'Enfant's Gallic temperament led to his dismissal in 1792, but not

until he had made a design for a city which for breadth
of conception, architectural insight and practicability is
scarcely short of the miraculous. With a prophetic vision
which aroused the guffaws of the nation he made plans
for a city of two hundred and fifty thousand people. Andrew Elliot, his assistant, with the constant support of the
President and Thomas Jefferson, proceeded faithfully to
carry out, the plan of the French engineer. The feature
of L'Enfant's plan, aside from his broad avenues which
radiated from circles said to have been inspired by Buona-
parte's use of the boulevards of Paris for his artillery on
the Thirteenth Vendémiaire, was a great mall with the
Capitol at one end and a monument to Washington at the
other. But as the years passed, little or reckless men succeeded the great, and things happened to the plan. In the
Greek Revival the Treasury Building was built across the
axis of Pennsylvania Avenue, shutting off the White
House, and along in the Parvenu Age the ugly State, War
and Navy Building farther boxed in the work of Hoban.
Railroads crossed the mall, and ugly buildings began to dot
its fair surface.

In 1900 the powerful American Institute of Architects
held its annual convention in Washington at the same time
that Congress was in session. The principal subject for discussion before the convention was the architectural development of the City of Washington. Speeches by members were regarded as news, and made the first page of
the Washington dailies. These attracted the attention of
Senator McMillan, who conferred with officers of the Institute, of which Robert S. Peabody was president. McMillan was convinced, and through his efforts a park commission was appointed by the Senate. This commission was
composed of Daniel H. Burnham, architect and master of

men; Charles F. McKim, architect and master of taste; Augustus Saint-Gaudens, sculptor and the first artist in the nation; Frederick Law Olmstead, Jr., landscape architect, inheritor of the prestige and ability of his distinguished father. These gentlemen, the mighty of the land, threw themselves without compensation into the formidable task of making a plan for the development of the capital of the United States.

They made their final report, illustrated with elaborate drawings and models, in 1902. It was seen that the commission had adhered to the plan of L'Enfant, extending it and elaborating it to conform to the greater city. The principal feature of the plan was the mall, a great kite-shaped parkway extending from the Capitol to the Potomac, two and two-thirds miles long. The stately Capitol should crown one end, the proposed Lincoln Memorial, the other. The axis of the mall should be interrupted in two places only—at the foot of Capitol Hill by a monument to Grant, and on the axis of the White House by the Washington Monument. On either side of the mall should be built the great buildings of the Republic, while its open spaces would be planted with trees, shrubs, and flowers.

The plan was received with enthusiasm, but there were grave difficulties. The Pennsylvania Railroad happened to have its station in the center of the mall, and its tenure of this location had just been assured to it in perpetuity by an act of Congress. I have heard Mr. Burnham tell how he asked Mr. Cassatt, the president, as a public-spirited citizen to "get out." When Cassatt was persuaded that the presence of the railroad meant the ruin of the plan, he tore up his tracks, tore down the old station, and got out; and he did more—he built a magnificent new station north of the Capitol, a worthy portal to the first city of the land. This whole transaction illustrates the real greatness of spirit of these men—men who gave years of their time without compensation for an ideal of beauty, and a railroad that spent unnecessary millions lest it might prevent that ideal from being realized.

I do not know that McKim's presidency of the American Institute was particularly notable. He was principally interested during this time in getting the government to incorporate his favorite child, the American Academy in Rome. In this connection he gave a famous dinner at Washington, and to insure a full attendance he ran a special train at his own expense from New York. These were the days of great dinners. You remember how useful Mr. Burnham found them in launching the project of the World's Fair. It might help in recreating a savory atmosphere if I quote from Glen Brown, the historian of the Institute, the names of some of Mr. McKim's guests— Theodore Roosevelt, John Hay, Ambassador Jusserand, Joseph Cannon, Elihu Root, Cardinal Gibbons, John La Farge, Augustus Saint-Gaudens, J. Pierpont Morgan, Henry James, Thomas Nelson Page, Charles Dana Gibson, Alexander J. Cassatt, General Chaffee, and sixty others. At the end of the repast a loving-cup was passed around, and at the end of its journey was found to contain just a half million dollars for Mr. McKim's project. McKim also purchased and raised the initial payment for the Octagon, a fine Post-Colonial house in Washington, now the permanent home of the Institute.

The American Institute of Architects is a large body of men, practicing architects for the most part, composed of Fellows and Members. There are, as I write, 307 of the former and 2754 of the latter. The Institute does not "fix prices," as many believe; in fact, its few mandates apply only to the ethics of the profession, which are in short, a combination, of the golden rule and the usages common between gentlemen. It ordinarily engages in some particular work each year, such as architectural education, the restoration of historic monuments, and so forth. It publishes a journal and maintains a publishing department. Undoubtedly the most important work it has accomplished has been that described above on the plan of Washington. Upjohn, Walter, Hunt, Burnham, McKim, Gilbert have directed its destinies, and its members are proud of their affiliation. It cannot be said that the Institute in any discernible way has affected the course of architectural style in America. Only indirectly, but not the less powerfully, by raising the standard of architectural practice and by fostering architectural education, has it taken a full share in our architectural progress.

Let us now say farewell to McKim, a man whom the Institute delighted to honor. Beside making him twice its president, it presented to him posthumously its gold medal for distinguished services to the profession, and has dedicated as a memorial to him its permanent home, the Octagon.

I have used McKim in this short account almost as a symbol. He was surrounded, as we all know, by a cloud of witnesses to the glories of Classic architecture, of whom his own partners were among the most brilliant. Stanford White's strong decorative sense showed to its best advantage against the calm background of his partners' work. The Madison Square Tower, the Century Club, the Gorham Building, the Farragut and Sherman statues in which he collaborated with Saint-Gaudens, are some of the many works in which his peculiar genius can be identified. White, more than any other, established the fashion—a fashion fortunately limited to the very rich, and therefore to the very few—of importing complete whole ceilings, fireplaces, columns, and so forth, from European buildings. In a sense White was as influential in the domain of architectural decoration as was his illustrious partner in the broader field of pure architecture.

The first efforts of Eclecticism were a bit naïve and tentative. This is particularly true of residences. The "Colonial" was usually selected as the style to emulate. In those days archaeology had not taught us the nuances between Early American, Georgian, Adam and Post-Colonial, and to the architect of the time "Colonial" meant almost anything with white columns, a cornice and green blinds. So the houses of the period are utterly lacking in the spirit of their models, and they have a curious air of being diminutive state buildings at a World's Fair. Dow, I believe, called them "popinjay Colonial."

Another architectural offering at the triumph of Classicism was the work done under the influence of the École des Beaux Arts. The young men back from Paris and their faithful imitators, filled with the pride of their triumph and a fine scorn of American effort, along the years at the turn of the century built a number of buildings that were ugly then and are today as dead as the Victorian Gothic. In style they were French of the Louis XV and XVI periods as revamped by the facile Gauls of the École. The hall mark of this affliction was the cartouche. The building might have any purpose, the material might be anything, but "toujours le cartouche." They line Fifth Avenue and Broadway today, and their crude imitations still cry their wares, though with cracking voice, on many a Main Street throughout the prairie states. Examples of this style existed in the Senator Clark house, the New York

Yacht Club, the Singer Building, the St. Regis Hotel, all of New York—and scores of others throughout the land of which the most insistent are the Naval Academy buildings at Annapolis.

The attitude of the men from Paris at this particular period was very different from that of those grand old "ancients," Hunt, Richardson, and McKim, who in humility and seriousness of spirit realized that school-days were over, and that the responsibility of directing architectural thought in America was a serious one.

The first problem that cried for immediate solution by Classicist or Gothicist, or whatsoever the eclectic architect might be, was the sky-scraper; and the total result (if we except the scanty work of Sullivan) of thirty years of strenuous effort was almost complete failure. Civil engineers had run up to unbelievable heights skeletons of steel; mechanical engineers, electrical engineers, sanitary engineers, had leaped forward to meet the challenge with new methods and devices; but the architect, alone, doggedly and blindly refused to see in this wonderful new thing a glorious opportunity. He feared the engineers while bearing gifts. To him the problem of the sky-scraper was only the old masonry problem embarrassingly stretched up into the sky higher than temple or cathedral, and to its solution he dragged out the old formulas of Vitruvius, Vignola and the schools. As a draughtsman years ago I stood with one of the most celebrated architects of the country before the drawing of a building some eighteen stories high. The building was to be of skeleton steel construction, with every modern engineering appliance. Its design showed granite columns in the first two stories pretending to support sixteen stories of stone culminating two hundred feet in the air in a huge Classic terra cotta cornice. He looked approvingly at the design and said, "Young man, we can't improve on the Romans."

The formulas by which these buildings were designed were based on the assumption that for proper proportion a building must have a base, shaft and cap. So it should, in general, if it is a masonry or static building and is of modest size. But a sky-scraper is not masonry; it is not even static. It is elastic; it is alive; it is even moving. It has no base, and it has no cap. It is all shaft—an upraised blade that should have run through the heart the musty dogmas of Classic design. They say that the first auto-mobile made had a whipsocket, and certainly these sky-scrapers of the past generation had not only the whip-sockets, but whiffle-trees and wagon-top besides.

In the sky-scraper, unfortunately, the base which was the ground story, was occupied usually by shops which re-quired the maximum amount of glass and the minimum amount of pier, while the architect according to the rules which for two thousand years had been unquestioned should demand at this portion the minimum amount of glass and the maximum amount of pier. In the resulting contest with the owner, a compromise was usually reached satisfactory to neither and disastrous to the building. This base usually ran through two stories, so the third floor was treated as a different feature—an attic to the base, a kind of transition to the shaft. The shaft then followed for the greater number of the stories. This was usually the best part of the building, though even here every effort was made to simulate solid masonry. Vertical lines were elimin-ated and horizontal effects obtained by the use of deep channels between the stone or terra cotta blocks. Often horizontal bands encircled the building. The upper two stories and attic were left for the cap. Often here a row of attached columns or pilasters formed a grandiose termination which in its festive appearance seemed to indicate for this portion of the design the harboring of a great banquet hall or *salle des fêtes*. The crowning folly—hardly a glory —was the cornice which, like a huge lid, closed down on this gigantic box as though to prevent the escape of even hope itself.

This cornice was as big a puzzle to the enchained architect as the base. If it were proportioned to the entire height of the building it would have to be some fifteen feet or more in height and project an equal distance—obviously impossible. On the other hand, if the distracted designer proportioned it to the upper order, then it would be so small that it could hardly be seen from the street. The result was another compromise, but even at that an embarrassing one, for this huge affair, often dizzily projecting six feet or more over a sidewalk crowded with humanity hundreds of feet below, had to be supported by an elaborate system of steel beams and angles bracketed out from the building, and each separate stone or piece of terra cotta hung by iron hooks and rods. The incongruity, the expense, and even the danger of such a construction should have been obvious, yet it took nearly thirty years for us to abolish this ancient whipsocket, and when it came so suddenly how simple, obvious and beautiful it was.

The influence of the World's Fair, the Beaux Arts, and our own schools was all on the side of Classic architecture. A good working knowledge of Gothic was comparatively rare. Hence the first, and for a long time the usual, essays in sky-scraper designs were made in some one of the Roman or Renaissance styles. This was most unfortunate for in the Gothic cathedral lie many analogies to the skyscraper. In the first place, the cathedral is not static. It does not depend, as does the Parthenon, for instance, on the strength, which means size, of its walls and piers to sustain a vertical load. It depends on equilibrium, the playing of one thrust against another. So does the steel frame building, which relies on the tensile strength of the steel, the wind bracing, and the security of the connections. In the cathedral as in the sky-scraper all the loads are concentrated on isolated points of support; the wall has lost its function of load-bearing and becomes a mere curtain. Most obviously of all, the whole motif of a cathedral is perpendicularity. Its theoretical height, as in the sky-scraper, is unlimited. It ever reached as high as it possibly could. There are no rules of proportion that regulate its height in relation to its breadth. One would never say of a cathedral, "It's too high," nor would one ever be justified in saying the same of a sky-scraper. The impossibility, therefore, of using Classic architecture where height is a factor in the equation of proportion is obvious.

The final analogy and argument lay in this vexed matter of cornice. Classic design requires strong horizontal accents or features. The strongest of these is usually the cornice, which occurs ordinarily at the top edge of the building. We have seen the difficulties, artistic and practical, of applying this feature to the sky-scraper, but the Gothic style makes no use of the cornice in this sense. Its buttresses and piers are its cornices, for they give the shadows which determine the character of a building.

It is extremely unfortunate, therefore, that our architects of the nineties did not look, if they had to look somewhere, to the Gothic cathedral instead of to the Roman palace for their answer to the riddle of the sky-scraper. The Reliance Building, Chicago, built in 1895, and the

Fisher Building, built about 1897, both by D. H. Burnham and Company, are among the earliest of the Gothic
sky-scrapers. Both are eminently successful.

The great example of the triumph of the perpendicular
over the horizontal motive in the very high building lies
in the Woolworth Tower by Cass Gilbert in New York
City. I cannot resist the temptation of describing my own
sensation when I first glimpsed it shortly after its completion. I had just returned from abroad, where I had discovered a peculiar test for works of art. Take a sudden
look; if nothing happens, you are beholding a work of
talent, perhaps even of great talent; but if a distinct
physical thrill runs up and down your spinal column you
are in the presence of a work of genius. I made this
interesting discovery, on which I have no patent and which
I hereby commend to Berenson, Porter and other critics,
in walking through the basilica of St. Peter-in-Chains in
Rome. I turned around the corner into the transept, and
found myself of a sudden face to face with the Moses
of Michael Angelo. I not only got the thrill, but, as I
remember it, my hair stood on end as well. "What if he
should stand up!" I tried the test at the Sistine Chapel.
It worked, but nothing happened in the presence of the
monument to Victor Emmanuel. My last and conclusive
test was before the glorious façade of Amiens, to me the
most beautiful in the world. When I arrived in New York
I had forgotten about my discovery, but I was anxious
to see the new and famous tower, so I wended my way
thither in a taxicab. The driver stopped across the street,
and I stepped out. I gazed up and up at that unbelievable
façade, and then the thrill which I thought sacred to the
presence of Amiens and Angelo swept over me. To me
there was no other argument necessary—the Woolworth

Tower was a work of genius. Undoubtedly it is one of the great monuments of the world. On the opposite side of the square stands the supreme expression of the Classicist's principles in the design of the sky-scraper, the Municipal Building by McKim, Mead and White. I looked from one to the other of these two giants, and my mind went back to Copley Square in Boston where fifteen years before grim Trinity and the debonair Library had fought out the same battle.

The result in this case is just as easy to prognosticate. The type of design which denies and conceals the construction, which ignores function in its formal expression, and which applies a style of architecture appropriate only to buildings in which the horizontal element is the predominant one, will in ten years be as old-fashioned as Trinity Church.

In the domain of the sky-scraper, the Woolworth Tower closed the period of Eclecticism, so badly begun, with enough brilliance to partially redeem it.

Next to that of McKim, the most powerful influence in the aesthetics of Eclectic architecture came from Ralph Adams Cram and Bertram Grosvenor Goodhue. For many years these two men worked together in the firm of Cram, Goodhue and Ferguson, but ten years previous to Mr. Goodhue's death in 1924 the firm was dissolved. Mr. Cram is still living. Curiously their influence was dual and about equally divided. Its general effect was to revive the use of Gothic architecture and to revolutionize its technique. As their application of the Gothic style was very largely to the building of churches, the whole domain of ecclesiastical architecture outside of the Roman Church was drawn into the current, and church building, in general indirectly, perhaps, but none the less surely, has been revolutionized through the influence of these two architects.

This influence I have said was dual. Ralph Adams Cram, Doctor of Laws, Doctor of Literature, Fellow of the American Institute of Architects, Fellow of the Royal Geographical Society, and so forth, has exerted his share through two channels—his work and his word. I believe most of the buildings erected during the life of their partnership owe their general plan and spirit to Cram. This plan and spirit were mediaeval as far as Cram could make them. He would have gone farther if he had been able. If the learned doctor could have his way he would have us living in walled towns, vassals of some baron or bishop, and we would be dragging the stones to the rising cathedral, yoked to wooden carts, chanting the *Dies Irae*. But medicine strong as this, diluted with a little sober sense, was necessary to purge the church of the hideous and false ideas of architectural art and architectural planning that almost universally obtained in the closing years of the nineteenth century.

This Cram did in speech and in writing. His book, "Church Architecture," 1901, in which, incidentally, he ignores the fact that there are edifices for religious service outside the Protestant Episcopal communion, exerted a great influence. The cat-a-cornered auditoriums, bowled floors, and frescoed walls read their doom between his scathing lines and beheld it in his eloquent example. "The Gothic Quest," 1907, and "The Substance of Gothic," delivered as lectures before the Lowell Institute in 1916, beckon us back into a mediaevalism where few of us would follow, and none, I am sure, would care to stay unless we agreed with our distinguished guide that "feudalism is the nearest recorded approach to the Christian Commonwealth," and that the thirteenth century, "the perfect union of art, philosophy, and religion," was the best. We would have to blind ourselves, as Mr. Cram has done, to the bigotry, persecution, famine, pestilence, and abysmal ignorance of all outside the hierarchy. But perhaps you can do it. Nevertheless, Cram in his architectural ceremonials, thundering forth anathemas and interdicts on carpenter-architects and purblind building-committees, like some crusading Innocent, did what no other man could do in effecting a reformation—a word, by the way, for which I beg his pardon.

Goodhue's influence was entirely architectural. To him beauty was truth, truth beauty. He was an architect's architect, the god of designers, the darling of the draughting-room—an architect who in some mysterious way had time not only to design and make exquisite drawings of great buildings, but to devise all of their detail from the topmost cresting of the flowering spire to the illuminating of the triptych over the altar, and in addition to make water colors of Persian ruins and dream cities, book-plates, illustrations, and even type. Young architects thought what an ideal life it would be to work only in a world of soaring vaults, of flaming tracery; "and intimately live" with exquisite fabrics, beautiful glass, wrought metals, carving, intarsia, silver and gold; to hold bishops and wardens in their spell while they told them all about credence tables and piscinas, gradines and riddle posts. But it wasn't all beer and skittles even for Goodhue. Undoubtedly the load he carried crushed him before his day.

As in the case of McKim, Mead and White, the work of Cram, Goodhue and Ferguson was superlative from the very beginning. This is an essential quality for the work of him who aspires to be a prophet. There must be the element of surprise, and no time may be lost—no familiarity and soft speaking to breed contempt. He must swim into the ken of an astonished and needy world. We have already considered the ecclesiastical art of the latter decades of the nineteenth century and we know that with few exceptions it was execrable. The bad Gothic of the sixties and seventies had been eclipsed by the worse Romanesque of the eighties and nineties. Anglican and Evangelical alike awaited a new gospel of beauty, and so when these two knights, their lances in rest, with the cry of "Dieu le veult" on their lips, charged the cohorts of ugliness and sham, a paean of thanksgiving for deliverance ascended from every parish.

One of the earliest works of the firm was All Saints Church, Brookline, Massachusetts, 1895, which is not altogether Gothic but of excellent taste. Then followed a brilliant list of buildings for the most part, but not wholly, ecclesiastical, and for the most part, but not wholly, Gothic, such as Trinity Church in Havana, 1905, which is in the fantastic style of Chirriguera, eighteenth century Spanish. Goodhue took an impish delight in taking an exotic style such as this, and then doing something better than the masters of the style themselves had done—beating them at their own game. There were also St. Stephen's, Cohasset, 1900; West Point Academy, 1904; St. Thomas's, New York, 1906; Calvary, Pittsburgh, 1907; Sage Memorial, Far Rockaway, 1901; First Baptist Church, Pittsburgh, 1909; Rice Institute, Houston, Texas; Euclid Avenue Presbyterian Church, Cleveland; and Fourth Presbyterian Church, Chicago, 1912, and St. Andrew's Chapel, Chicago. All these were done before the dissolution of the partnership in 1914, but in each of them the influence of either Cram or Goodhue is easily seen to predominate. The buildings before 1905, and particularly the splendid buildings for the Academy at West Point, show the perfect union of the austerity of Cram and the exuberance of Goodhue. At this time one roof sheltered both. The buildings that followed were done either in the Boston office, directed by Cram, or in the New York office over which Goodhue held sway, and the difference is easily discernible. Of them I should say that Calvary Church, Pittsburgh, was most typically Cram and St. Thomas's most typically Goodhue. After the dissolution in 1914—a rupture regretted by the entire profession—each continued to practice separately.

Bertram Grosvenor Goodhue was born in Pomfret, Connecticut, April 28, 1869. His ancestry on both sides was of the best American stock. His mother sketched and painted, and mother and small son had two adjoining studios sacred to themselves and their dreams in the attic of the old house. Other than this, the youth, unlike Hunt, Richardson, McKim, or even Sullivan, had no architectural or even artistic training, and of school work only the most desultory. That he early fell under the influence of those wan but powerful artists, the Pre-Raphaelites, seems certain. Their ideals of sheer beauty became Goodhue's for the rest of his life. From men like Burne-Jones he got also his love of mediaeval art; in fact, Goodhue might well have qualified as a member of the Brotherhood.

At the age of nine he determined to be an architect, and when still very young went to New York, where he entered the office of Renwick, the architect of St. Patrick's Cathedral. Here he stayed for seven and a half years, living the typical draughtsman's life, working night after night on all sorts of drawings and designs, arguing and drinking beer in a cloud of smoke at the Sketch Club, and spending Sunday afternoons at the Metropolitan Museum.

In those days he was described as "very slight and boyish-looking, with very blonde hair, vivid blue eyes, and very red cheeks."

About 1882 he entered the office in Boston of Cram and Wentworth, and in a year or two became a partner. After many years of intimate work with Cram, during which Wentworth had died and had been succeeded by Ferguson, and the work and reputation of the firm had increased apace, they won the competition for the new buildings at West Point. This was in 1903. In order to handle such a large commission a new office was opened in New York with Goodhue in charge. After this the two offices and the two friends drifted farther and farther apart until 1914, when the partnership was finally dissolved.

The work done independently by Goodhue after the dissolution includes a number of houses in California; the Church of St. Vincent Ferrier, New York; St. Bartholomew's Church, New York; the chapel for the University of Chicago; the Public Library Building, Los Angeles; the National Academy of Science, Washington; and, last of all, the great capitol building at Lincoln, Nebraska. This last, together with the Library at Los Angeles and the competitive drawings for the Tribune Tower and the Kansas City War Memorial, are not Gothic, nor are they Classic. They are purely creative, and I think Goodhue believed them to be truly American.

As I read Goodhue in his works and in his words, he had in his earlier years no fixed principles of art, that is, in a philosophic or moral sense. He talked and wrote about them, but philosophically he was a weather-cock, and most of what he said he did not mean. Beauty alone in any form was his queen and his mistress—his divine Egeria

in whose service his leaping mind and his nimble fingers
were never idle. Had Goodhue died ten years sooner, a
close analogy would have existed between himself and the
poet Keats. His youth, his exuberance, his mastery of every
form of expression, and above all his fanatic devotion to
beauty would make him brother soul to that seraphic trav-
eler in the realms of gold. St. Thomas's would be his Endy-
mion; the Chapel of the Intercession his Ode to a Grecian
Urn; and little St. Andrew's Chapel his sonnet on Chap-
man's Homer.

But his later work developed certain Shelleyan characteristics. An unexpected prophetic outlook came with
age and experience, indications that Goodhue, the blind
worshipper of beauty, had become Goodhue, the revolutionary and prophet. Whether he had abandoned the
Gothic style, which he had blown into life thirty years
before, because he had rung all its changes and because it
held nothing more for him technically, or whether he believed that a new era should be clothed with a new gar-
ment and that the genius of America demanded a more
vital expression, I do not know. Indeed it makes little
difference. But this is true—the capitol building at Lincoln might well have become, had Goodhue lived, a mighty
baton of leadership, a battle-cry in another crusade for the
long-sought American Style. Goodhue, with his great prestige and his tremendous personal following, might have
done what Sullivan failed to do, and what Richardson did
in a partial way and for a limited length of time. Whether
such a movement, lead by Goodhue, with men like Saarinen and Raymond Hood as his lieutenants, could have
succeeded is another speculation, but that his death at the
beginning of such a campaign is an immeasurable blow
there can be no question.

Other than these two forces—McKim for the Classic-ists, Cram and Goodhue for the Mediaevalists—there were no outstanding influences in the Eclectic period. Even Cass Gilbert and these others of his caliber, with his Wool-worth Tower and his Minnesota capitol, did not bend architecture to his own will nor found a school.

About 1881 or thereabouts the intelligentsia and the uplifters began to chatter about the arts and crafts. Wil-liam Morris, poet, artist, manufacturer and socialist of England, is the father of the Arts and Crafts movement, but its ancestry is more ancient for Morris, like a Saul of Tarsus, saw the light in Ruskin's "Stones of Venice" and Ruskin, in his turn, had sat at the feet of Carlyle. The golden text of the movement is, "Art is the expres-sion of man's pleasure in labor," or, as Morris more hu-manly commented on it, "If I were to work ten hours a day at work I despised and hated, I should, I hope, spend my leisure in political agitation, but I fear in drinking." Hence the practical purpose of the movement was to make the work of men's hands more beautiful.

The Crusade saw its actual birth in the furnishing of Morris's rooms, shared with Burne-Jones and Rossetti, in Red Lion Square, London, and in the building and fur-nishing of his famous Red House outside the city. In des-pair at the furnishings offered in the shops, he designed and made, or had made, every article of decorative value that went into the building—the furnishings, the hang-ings, the wall papers, and even the china and the rugs. The huge panelled pieces were painted by Burne-Jones and Rossetti; even the garden took on a new form of beauty never seen before. This was from 1857 to 1859.

The story is fascinating but far too long to recount.

Morris formed a great factory in which were executed by a company of artists mural paintings, stained glass, wall papers, metal work, furniture, embroidery, stamped leather, and later, through the Kelmscot Press, book-binding and fine printing. His influence spread throughout the land. In 1888 the Arts and Crafts Exhibition Society was formed in London with Walter Crane, Ashbee, Cobden-Sanderson and the Morrises prominent in its roster. This is the society which was the parent of most of the American organizations, and after it we need trace the movement in England no farther.

The Arts and Crafts theory was exactly the dish for the palate of the studios, the tea-rooms, and the rostra of the social settlements and community houses—a pinch of reform, a spoonful of socialism and aesthetics to taste, and over it all the flavor of Toynbee Hall and of England's intellectuals made it a highly delectable entrée. The idea lying back of the Arts and Crafts movement was worthy and interesting, and its history in America would be treated here with greater respect had it not been such an out-of-hand importation from England, and had it received proper respect from its own promoters. If we could point today to a single great industrial art school or any considerable revolution in taste or accomplishment, or if we made our papers and textiles at home, as the result of the Arts and Crafts movement, we would recognize it as an important factor in the advance of art in the country, but, as I interpret the improvement in the applied arts since 1891, architecture led the way and the industrial arts that made any progress followed in its train. As it stands, the Arts and Crafts movement left us Elbert Hubbard and the Roycrofters, a host of "uplift" societies (most of which are defunct now), thousands of "lytle shoppes," mission furniture, art jewelry, pyrography. Its effect was not in sum total deleterious (Bertram Goodhue seems to have been a disciple), but the idea that the workman, if happy in his work, could produce art resulted in amateur craftsmen substituting smiles for training and smocks for overalls. Good intentions often took the place of finished technique, and the "loving touch of the tool" for the sterner grasp of usefulness. Architecture teaches that taste and discrimination can be obtained only by education; arts and crafts tell us that it can be conjured up by a formula or a shibboleth.

It is probable that the World's Fair, that turned us right-about-face in our artistic march, had much to do with the limited success of the Arts and Crafts program. The Romanesque Revival was a far fairer field for its manœuvres. The Classic and Colonial, which became the order of the day after 1893, had little use for originality or undrilled art of any description. The Arts and Crafts are still with us, but they are so merged into the ranks that the old battle cries and passwords have been lost—if the cause itself has not.

The remainder of the story of architecture in the quarter century between the World's Fair and the World War, if it were at all complete, would comprise a volume in itself. It would have to recount the labors of hundreds of trained architects and describe a multitude of buildings. In general, however, the picture would show a rapid improvement in the technique of the art in which, as the name of the period would indicate, almost every style was used. It would also show the evolution of a large number of types. This evolution began in many cases before 1893, but it is true in general that the Eclectic period was the most productive we have ever experienced, not only in volume, but in developed and standardized forms of buildings that are distinctly national.

The greatest gift of Eclecticism after all was this development of types which amounted to almost a standardization,—types of buildings that were peculiarly American, not only in purpose and in the use of native materials, but in concept and in a certain breadth of treatment as well. If the detail was reminiscent of Paris or Rome, let us not worry over-much. Style is not the life-blood of architecture; more often it is but the jester's cap and bells, the motley for the crowd. To appreciate the vast material accomplishment of thirty years of Eclecticism, merely consider the finest buildings in America just prior to the Fair of '93. How few they are! From Richardson's hand Trinity in Boston, the Court House in Pittsburgh, the Albany City Hall, some libraries, and the Harvard Law School; from the hands of others the Boston Art Museum, Memorial Hall at Harvard, St. Patrick's Cathedral, The Auditorium in Chicago, Madison Square Garden, Ponce de Léon Hotel, Lennox Library, a few Vanderbilt houses, and the Tacoma Building in Chicago. There is not a great railroad station among them—except perhaps the station in St. Louis— nor college group, nor bank, nor many another type that has since been developed. At the risk of seeming categorical I shall list these types each under its own title, a faint sketch of the vast wealth that the thirty fat years of peace, plenty and eclecticism brought us.

HOUSES

I have spoken of the "Popinjay" Colonial that followed immediately on the heels of the Fair. It shared its popularity with a rather thin and hard adaptation of the Elizabethan half-timber work. At the end of a decade the more sophisticated Italian style appeared, and by 1920 houses had all improved to a point beyond which it seemed impossible to go much further. Sense and sensibility in architecture, decoration and landscape gardening, were required and delivered. There is nothing heroic about this savor of the beautiful in houses, but the desire on the part of the architect and his client for discrimination in the selection of the beautiful and fit is one of the choice products of Eclecticism. In fact, it appeared that the house, like the bicycle, had been about perfected—what with our attached garages, our steel window sash, our oil burners, our electric ice boxes. Whether or not it was a machine for living didn't worry us much in the twenties. At one point, surely, the houses of the eclectic period in its culmination reached the peak and that is in the amenities of charm, taste and beauty in architecture. To mention but a very few, the work of Charles Platt, John Russell Pope, Delano and Aldrich in the East, of Howard Shaw and David Adler in the Middle West, and of Willis Polk, George W. Smith, Bertram Goodhue on the Pacific coast will remain models of good architecture for the future practitioner regardless of Prefabrication and Internationalism. In fact, Eclecticism is still the prevailing policy in domestic architecture.* As time and knowledge advanced the villas of the Val d'Arno, the chateaux of the Loire, the haciendas of Spain, the contemporary English work of Lutyens and others and, last of all, our own Colonial architecture, which we finally studied and understood, were tapped and drawn on. With equal tempo the engineering side of domestic architecture had advanced. Electric wiring, hot water heating, vastly improved plumbing, weather proofing were perfected by enterprising manufacturers. Taste, the sense of absolute pitch, the flower on the topmost bough, is still the goal in large measure of our domestic architecture.

---

* In a questionnaire to architects of the "Architectural Forum" in May, 1935, sixty-two percent of the answers named Colonial as the preferred style for a house.

No Roman described the Coliseum in the first century because everybody knew all about it, nor am I going to describe the house of today. Perhaps you have noticed its geographical uniformity. If you were set down in the midst of any American town, it would be unwise to attempt to get your bearings by examination of the modern houses about you. You might be in Jacksonville, Florida, or in Appleton, Wisconsin. The reason is easy to see. The elaborate villa on the prairies of Illinois and in the foot hills of the Adirondacks both look to Bedford, Indiana, for their building stone. The slate that covers their roofs comes in both cases from the quarries of Vermont. Their oaken floors, trim, and exterior woodwork come from the forests of the South, the face brick probably from Ohio; and there are certainly no local characteristics in plaster, paint, or glass. How different in France, for example! As you bowl along every little house that flanks the roadside has a dull red roof, but when you are whisked over the hills into the next valley all the houses have gray roofs— not a red one in sight. There local materials are always used, but with us the product of every state is laid at our feet. This uniformity of character is very evident to the visitor from across the water, and although the architectural trappings flaunted before his eyes may have been filched from his own homeland, he hardly recognizes them in their setting of American material.

To this uniformity there are two salient exceptions— the sudden now historic burst of architectural activity in Florida, and the slower and more dignified development in California. In both cases the Spanish type appropriately has been followed.

In Florida, paradoxically, the multitude of Spanish villas and bungalows smacks of Hollywood and the moving picture set—plenty of imagination and energy, but of the kind provoked by high fever. Nevertheless, the energy of the ecstatic realtor and the dollars of the restless migrants have produced a local school that for a certain magnificence is unequalled in the country.

We must approach the work of a group of men on the Pacific Coast with much more respect. Led by the late Willis Polk, whose water temple at Sunol, California, is one of the loveliest things in architecture, certain architects banded together in a common high ideal of beauty and fitness have evolved a style so personal and so Californian that we sometimes fear it is hardly American. Men like Reginald Johnson, Myron Hunt, Louis Mulgardt, Francis Underhill, George Washington Smith, the Greenes who invented the Californian bungalow, and many others formed the group. Curiously enough, the first impetus to this Californian renaissance in domestic work came from that Ariel of architecture, Bertram Goodhue, in the unbelievably beautiful Gillespie Villa at Santa Barbara, designed in 1902. This villa, perhaps, and the Spanish missions, too, furnished the cue from which has been produced the brilliant series of houses that have caused the palm for the best domestic architecture in America to be transferred from the Atlantic to the Pacific coast. We are building today better homes for the American citizen than we have ever done before. They are not all good, as they were in Colonial days—many of them are still very bad; but improved taste in the people and extended education in the architect is refining the vintage and precipitating the dross.

CHURCHES

Church design has been entirely revolutionized from two aspects—on the aesthetic side through the examples and teaching of Cram and of Goodhue, who have firmly entrenched the Gothic style in ecclesiastical building, and on the practical side through the departmentalizing of the Sunday School and the development of the social activities of the church. The old "Akron Plan" of the eighties and nineties had entirely disappeared by 1910, given place to a parish house as commodious as the church, with a great assembly hall, large kitchens and social rooms, and with various departments each equipped with its own assembly rooms and classrooms.

Boards of architecture of the various denominations now give technical advice free of charge to congregations and building committees, and there are many good ecclesiastical architects.

The Episcopalians always, and the Evangelical churches usually, choose the Gothic for their architectural expression. Of hundreds of examples, St. Luke's Evanston, John Sutcliff architect, in its Cistercian simplicity is one of the most beautiful. The Colonial is not used as often as might be, though it is particularly fitting as a setting for the Congregationalists with their meeting-house tradition. The Christian Scientists usually select pure Classic in its Greek or Roman phase; the Roman Catholics, the Gothic or Italian Baroque; the Hebrews, some form of Byzantine or oriental style of architecture for their synagogues. This is all as it should be. But here is a little professional confidence: while the Evangelical churches, including the Episcopalians, submit their architects to no test of religious affiliation, the Catholics and the Christian Scientists seldom go beyond their own fold for professional advice, and— is it necessary to add?—the results of this self-imposed limitation are often only too evident.

In the last ten or fifteen years there has been a strong

drift away from the note of modernity and efficiency so insistent in the nineties for the church building itself. Building committees now are inclined to say, "Let the parish house be modern and scientific to the last degree, but we want the church mediaeval." This aesthetic undertow has drowned out even the long-established arrangement of the chancel in denominational churches. Since the days when Jonathan Edwards hurled his denunciations on the Sabbath-breaker, the accepted arrangement for a denominational church has been a pulpit on a platform, usually in its center; behind the platform a high screen; and behind the screen another platform for a choir or quartet with an organ in the vicinity. The communion table was almost invariably placed on the floor of the auditorium at the foot of the pulpit. Variations of course occurred, made necessary by various rituals—a baptistery for immersion must have a prominent place in a Baptist church; the Methodists must have an altar-rail in front of the communion table; the Presbyterians must have seats for the elders below the pulpit,—but the scheme has remained through many generations practically unchanged. Now murmurs are being heard; dissatisfaction in some quarters is openly expressed. Vogt in his "Art and Religion" openly attacks the time-honored arrangement, and many young ministers are turning their eyes longingly to the altars and choir stalls of the Anglicans. In fact, the Anglican chancel, so familiar in Episcopal churches, has now become the accepted form. It is a tribute to the ministry of beauty in religion. Wayward and laughing art may become a "nun breathless with adoration," and a church which willfully or carelessly declines the gentle aid that art can lend fights a battle against almost hopeless odds.

SCHOOLHOUSES

The building of grade schools, and particularly of high schools, has experienced a revolution hardly less marked than that of the churches. The old box type, four or five stories in height, has given place to buildings low and spread out in plan, often occupying great areas, thoroughly fire-proofed and ventilated. As in the Sunday School, a great assembly room is the heart and often the lungs of the establishment. A gymnasium and frequently a swimming tank, together with rooms for vocational training, are now a part of a modern school, which, to be entirely up to date, should be located in a wide open space with trees, bushes and flowers and a spacious athletic field.

Credit should be given men like William B. Ittner of St. Louis and Dwight H. Perkins of Chicago, who have taken the ugly, unscientific, and often dangerous school building of the nineties and made out of it the beautiful and efficient public school of today.

UNIVERSITIES

It was a long, long time before the splendid example of Thomas Jefferson's University of Virginia was emulated in the planning of any other American collegiate group. Up to the time of the World's Fair, buildings in the stylistic vernacular of their own particular period had been scattered hit or miss over the swarded campus. Here, again, the example of the Fair, in beauty and economy of ordered arrangement, was brought home to college presidents and their boards of trustees. A great series of college plans, beginning with the international competition for the University of California, occupied the architects of the country in the first decade of the twentieth century.

Though there were some exceptions, by general consent each college chose—for we are in the period of Eclecticism, you remember—either the Gothic or the Classic in some form to be its style thenceforth. Of the colleges in the Classic style, Columbia heads the list. There is also Greek M. I. T. and Beaux Arts Annapolis, and free-Classic Carnegie. Williams is Georgian, and so are Harvard, William and Mary, and the University of Virginia. Houston is the one example of Romanesque, if it can be so called. The Gothic style was given its first impetus by the beautiful work of Cope and Stewardson at Princeton, and Gothic has been adopted by Yale, West Point, Bryn Mawr, St. Louis, the Universities of Chicago and Pennsylvania and Northwestern University. Each has buildings worthy of mention, but I shall name only five: the brilliant and suggestive Museum of the University of Pennsylvania by Frank Miles Day, Cope and Stewardson, and Wilson Eyre; the equally original Michigan Union, University of Michigan, by Pond and Pond; the craggy and broken Gothic dormitories of Day and Klauder at Princeton; the vast chapel of the University of Chicago that has risen from the ground, beckoned upwards by the spirit hands of Bertram Goodhue; and, loveliest of all, the Harkness Memorial at Yale University.

This last, a series of dormitories arranged about quadrangles and courts and dominated by a gorgeous tower, is without doubt the most beautiful, as it is the most extensive (and expensive) of any university group. With an unlimited supply of money and the best examples of two worlds to emulate, the architect, James Gamble Rogers, has made the best of a golden opportunity. The old world universities are the result of slow accretions; colleges grew like barnacles about the mother ship of learning. Rogers waves his T-square, and creates a five-hundred-year-old group in five years. This "made to order" age, obtained by the most skillful use of materials, offers the only cause of criticism, and that is disarmed by the thought that beauty needs no right of sanctuary.

Across the road from Harkness is Dwight, the unlovely dormitory of the Y. M. C. A. students. An old college mate of mine, Charles E. A. Winslow, professor of Biology at Yale, writer, orator, scientist, and wit, on being asked why the freshmen lived in the magnificent new dormitory and not in its shabby neighbor, is reported to have replied, "They live in Harkness and not Dwight, because their ways are evil."

Perhaps that is also the reason why the young collegians rejoice in the revived glories of the amphitheatre. The tremendous structures built to accommodate the red-cheeked and vociferous younger generation on the occasions of the great football games and other athletic events are a new and vital note in American architecture. In size these rival, as they resemble, the amphitheatres the indulgent Roman emperors built for their unruly children in the days of real sport, eighteen hundred years ago. No attempt here to ape old age,—no archaeology in these vast piles of reinforced concrete; but fill them with fifty thousand of the hope of our manhood and the prettiest of our girls, with cheeks glowing in the November air and eyes shining with the joy of life, and what spectacle in old Rome could have been as fine!

APARTMENTS AND HOTELS

No greater development has occurred in any type of structure than that in the apartment, the apartment hotel, and the hotel itself. This is, obviously enough, due to the crowding of family and transient life into the cities, to the servant problem, and to the increasing complexities of modern life which require the elimination of every waste motion and waste moment. The old dumb-bell flats with their large rooms, long corridors and dark and dingy light-courts, have disappeared. Compact units with rooms often too small, but well lighted and possessing every convenience of things that appear and disappear, have taken their place. The vast apartment hotel, composed of multitudes of little suites and containing luxurious community rooms for every purpose from dining to swimming, is a new type that appeared during the eclectic period.

Hotels, too, have undergone fundamental changes. You could have driven a coach and four through the corridors of the old Palmer House in Chicago and its rooms were apparently constructed for a race of giants—but giants who had to get along without the use of clothes closets or contiguous bathrooms. The Blackstone Hotel, Chicago, built in 1910, while inferior in size and far younger in years than such famous caravanseries as the Waldorf or the Plaza in New York, or the Bellevue-Stratford in Philadelphia, was the first of the growing list of hotels which combined Lucullian luxury with every convenience that the world's busiest people require. It, again, created a type. The Shelton Hotel in New York, if it did not create a type, at least created an architectural sensation. In 1925 the doors of the new Stevens Hotel in Chicago were opened for the assembled throngs. This beautiful monster has three thousand outside bedrooms and three thousand private bathrooms. It is still the world's largest hotel.

RAILWAY STATIONS

Here, again, there has been the establishment, especially for terminals, of a distinct American type of plan employing usually some severe form of Classic architecture. Before the World's Fair the railway stations of this country were a disgrace; many of them still are, but since that momentous event important and imposing stations have been erected. One of the earliest was at Columbus, Ohio, by D. H. Burnham and Company in 1896; others later were built in Pittsburgh, Utica, and Rochester, Minneapolis, Kansas City, and Detroit, while the great new terminals in New York, Washington, and Chicago are not only civic gateways, but have almost become national monuments. Each is some form of the plan which has in McKim's masterpiece for the Pennsylvania Railroad in New York City its noblest expression.

The problem of the suburban station has not received a solution more advanced and certainly not more beautiful than that offered by Richardson forty-five years ago, nor have the problems of the underground and the elevated, and, more important still, of the interurban been more fortunate. All of them are far behind the attractive examples offered by France, Germany, and England.

BANKS

The establishment of a new and distinct type was particularly evident in banks. The classic Roman style with its suggestion of eternal stability was a universal favorite. The all-bank building, where it was once thought that a building used for the sole purpose of money changing would attract the wily depositor, has given place to the office building bank, with the bank in the first two or three stories with twenty or thirty stories of offices above. These not only hold the bank down securely, but furnish a steady supply for its coffers. This change is most eloquently illustrated in the recent destruction of the beautiful one-story bank built in 1900 for the Illinois Trust Company in Chicago, and the erection on its site of the mammoth Illinois Merchants twenty stories in height. It would be a hopeless task to list the notable banks of the last generation. Some have already been mentioned. I shall name but one more, an especially beautiful example—strangely enough, Byzantine in style—the Bowery Savings Bank in New York, the architects of which are York and Sawyer. Go into it and look about you.

CLUBS

The old club, known for its exclusiveness, dark and silent, where one could sit dead for several days in one's favorite chair before being molested, was a well-developed feature in American life before the Fair. It has been, however, successfully rejuvenated. Now clubs tower twenty stories and more in the air. In some respects there is little to differentiate them from the apartment hotel, and there are clubs of every purpose—university clubs; athletic clubs—with gymnasiums, should one want to be alone); doctors' clubs; lawyers' clubs; Bohemian clubs. The real addition to clubdom in the period is, however, the golf club.

Golf, before the Fair, if not unknown, was at least little played in America; now it is a serious matter where we shall get our corn and tomatoes if golf courses continue to cover the land. Golf clubhouses are everything from supreme simplicity to the last work in sumptuousness. Some form of English half-timber is the favorite treatment, and most of them are charming and picturesque.

In addition to all these, types have been established in Y. M. C. A. buildings, in hospitals, and particularly in our libraries, which, largely through the efforts of the American Library Association and the generosity a generation ago of Andrew Carnegie, have been perfected to such a point that they lead the world.

STORES

Great magazines or stores, as we call them, are an important part of our national existence, and for these we have developed an architectural type along with the rest —a very uninteresting and unattractive type, it seems to me. It consists of a huge box, plain and uninviting in its exterior and absolutely without interest in plan—a succession of stories, sometimes with a light-court, and interrupted only by the necessary structural columns, stairways and banks of elevators. The various functions of these buildings are provided for merely by the arrangement in aisles of show-cases and counters which may be in one place today and elsewhere tomorrow. The only thing the department store with its great opportunity has added to architectural advance is the show-window, which has encouraged the plate glass manufacturers in their technique of rolling extraordinarily large panes and the window decorators in filling them with exhibits that bring joy to the American woman and woe to her husband.

Exceptions to the play-safe banality of the great mercantile establishments are very few. Perhaps the most notable is the all-glass-and-steel-fronted Hollidie Building,

San Francisco, from the magic fingers of that curious and lovable genius, the late Willis Polk. Many interesting and delightful shop fronts, however, have been designed and built along the golden pavements of Fifth Avenue and other marts of the fashionable. These are of all styles, often Adam or French, even decorated with Italian *sgraffito*.

EXHIBITIONS

If the World's Fair of 1893 ushered in the period of Eclecticism, then the Century of Progress in 1933 celebrated its demise by entirely ignoring it. What of the other exhibitions that came between? There have been eight important ones since 1893. In 1898 the Trans-Mississippi exhibition at Omaha, and the "Cotton States" exhibition at New Orleans; in 1901 the Pan-American at Buffalo; in 1904, the Louisiana Purchase in St. Louis; in 1915, the Panama-Pacific in San Francisco and San Diego; and in 1926, the Sesqui-centennial in Philadelphia.

All of these gave opportunity to American architects, painters, sculptors, and landscape men. None of them has exerted any noticeable effect on contemporary architecture other than to stimulate effort and imagination among the architects and artists, especially in a decorative way. Three of them have been notable architecturally—the Pan-American, for its first and lavish use of color, and its frankly festive and ephemeral character; and the two exhibitions on the Pacific Coast.

The exhibition in San Francisco was the larger and finer. It was strikingly original in the use of great walled courts, and in its lighting. Who can forget the glory of the jewelled tower flashing with the iridescence of a hundred thousand prisms as they fluttered like aspen leaves in the flooded light? It was an advance on the Pan-American of 1901 at Buffalo in its color treatment arranged by that architect-painter-wizard, Jules Guérin.

The companion fair at San Diego was inferior to San Francisco in every particular but one—the California Building by Bertram Goodhue. Here Goodhue in a few odd moments produced the best example of Chirriguer-esque architecture in the world.

These expositions had always loomed big in my mind for flood lighting and the use of color. In studying the photographs and in reviving my personal memories of each, I have come to the tardy realization that they were far more significant than that.

The exhibition at San Francisco, in particular, was the last expression on the grand scale of that great expression in architecture which permeated the entire Renaissance from Brunelleschi's Dome down to the Great War: and of the basic principle that "beauty is its own excuse for being." It was in very truth the swan song of the Renaissance. The San Francisco Fair was, in effect, a symphony of beauty. Every architect evoked from the instruments at his service every last note of beauty that he could produce. Beauty of mass, of proportion, of detail—beauty of color, beauty of form in sculpture, beauty of illumination, and the beauty of every kind of nature from flower to towering palm. This apotheosis of the beautiful leads us inevitably to the pleasant sins of the Fair—sins, that is, in the eyes of the modern Puritans. Perhaps, after all, there was only one and that is, shall we say, a lack of veracity—the everlasting sin of the Renaissance. Every element of the Fair, from its plaster travertine walls to its triumphal arches, pretended, or at least appeared, to be built of permanent materials to last unto Eternity.

In the Century of Progress 1933 we shall see for the first time the wave of Puritanism in architecture that offers itself in atonement for the sins of the Renaissance.

REËNFORCED CONCRETE

Little has been said in this volume of construction for the reason that our interest has been chiefly aesthetic. But there is one form of construction, at least, which can no longer be ignored, and that is reënforced concrete.

Up to about 1500 there were, and had been for two thousand years, only two basic forms of construction: the post and lintel as used, for instance, in the Parthenon, and the arch with its derivatives, the vault and dome as used, we will say, in St. Peter's in Rome. Along towards the end of the fifteenth century the true truss, composed of members some of which are in compression and some in tension, was invented. That was the third. And now in our era we have added a fourth—reënforced concrete.

Reënforced concrete is made by pouring concrete around and about a grillage of small iron or steel bars. Concrete is usually made of Portland cement mixed with sand, gravel and water. Cement was first used in America in the construction of the Erie Canal in 1817, and in 1870 less than ten thousand barrels a year were manufactured in the United States. In 1926 over one hundred and fifty millions of barrels were produced! Mr. E. R. Graham tells me that to his knowledge no reënforced concrete was used in the World's Fair, yet the principle had been known long before, and a house with walls and floors and a mansard roof had been erected of reënforced concrete back in the Parvenu days of 1873.

Up to the Fair, therefore, concrete had very seldom been

used for any portion of a building which requires tensile strength, like the floors, but, with the advent of steel reenforcing floors as well as walls were constructed of this material. And anyone who sees on every side the elaborate "form" work of wood, with its forest of props, receiving the liquid mixture as it pours out of a prehensile steel spout from some point apparently in the sky, must realize the large importance of reënforced concrete in the domain of building. In Dallas, Texas, there has been constructed entirely of reënforced concrete an office-building nineteen stories in height—the record, I believe, for this material, but it is an important if inconspicuous factor in almost every building of steel or other types of construction. Reenforced concrete has become perhaps the most typical material for the new architecture.

Concrete, like every other new material since the days when the primitive Greeks imitated tree trunks in their fluted stone columns, began its career architecturally by imitating other material, stone being the favorite model. Atrocities in rockfaced concrete blocks are familiar and repellent to us all, but the time is rapidly approaching when architectural forms suitable for this material—forms which can easily be cast or impressed—will be the vogue.

MOTION-PICTURE THEATRES

An Englishman once viciously remarked that the mission of America was to vulgarize the world. One is prompted to pass the thought along with the observation that the mission of the moving-picture theatre is to vulgarize America.

Here was a brand-new clean-cut problem, to wit, the housing of great audiences whose sole purpose in being present was to see pictures in motion on a screen approximately twenty feet square. On account of the magnificent size of the picture it is no disadvantage—in fact, the reverse—to be distant from the screen, but it is a decided disadvantage to be seated where one's view of the screen is at an angle that approaches the acute. The earliest picture-houses recognized this, and they were for the most part long, narrow rooms with ceilings of moderate height. As the room was normally darkened, the architectural decoration was simple.

The popularity of the pictures and the competition of rival houses soon led to the introduction of cheap music and tawdry vaudeville. When song and dance artists and music of a kind were introduced the picture-theatre ceased its evolution along logical lines and reverted to the legitimate theatre or vaudeville house type with cavernous galleries and a huge stage. Now moving pictures are as scarce in one of these buildings as drugs in a drug store. Worse still, architecture was seized upon and dragged into the arena to make the Roman holiday complete, for it was discovered that architecture, if sufficiently tortured, could be made to yell as loud as the electric signs or the jazz band. In one of them, imprisoned in a bedizened wall, is a piece of white marble—a fragment of the Theatre of Dionysus, which once in its setting of olives and laurel on the slope of the Acropolis reflected the violet shadows of the Pan-Athenaic procession and echoed to the golden pentameters of Sophocles.

Certainly we are justified in putting down a black mark against the eclectic period for its treatment of the moving picture theatre. There were, of course, outstanding exceptions, especially when, on rare occasions, the work was placed in the hands of talented architects—such as the East-man Theatre in Rochester, New York, in which McKim,

Mead and White were consultants. Usually, however, the main work was done by self-styled picture house specialists and then turned over for completion to the other self-styled specialist of decoration and furnishings.

I quote from a trade journal describing some of the new picture houses of the day—"Forty-six thousand feet of brilliant Spanish treatment," "the architectural treatment of the auditorium is beyond description with its intricacies of oriental magnificence," "the proscenium arch in which is portrayed the figure of Aphrodite rising from the sea and being viewed from either side by the Wise Men and other characters of this world famous legend"! (The exclamation mark is mine.)

The moving picture theatre has found its salvation in the architecture of "today and tomorrow," but no such fortunate fate awaits its moribund parent, the legitimate theatre, whose future lies neglected in the lap of the gods.

FACTORIES

In the development of the factory the story is a different one. The enormous buildings required, particularly for the manufacture of automobiles, make the construction primarily an engineering enterprise. For years beauty was not considered in any way essential and could not be introduced if it entailed any large addition in expense. Reënforced concrete is the material par excellence for such construction. The architect, therefore, when he got his chance was bound by those very restrictions which often result in the best work. Useless cornices were thrown overboard; so were architectural columns, pediments and towers; so were all historical styles in general, for each has a hungry family of attributes which would have to be provided for. The result in the best instances is about as good as anything we have done. I will mention out of hundreds only two examples, the Ford engineering laboratories by Albert Kahn at Dearborn, Michigan, and the army supply base in Brooklyn by Cass Gilbert.

As it stands today, factory design is more free from the trammels of architectural precedent than any other domain of building, and its future is full of promise.

ART MUSEUMS

Most art museum directors agree that the ideal museum is yet to be built. Perhaps it has awaited the "New Architecture" for its consummation. Certainly in the proposed addition to the Art Institute in Chicago revolutionary ideas of display and lighting will be employed. The following museums are all products of the Eclectic period. Famous for size and prestige are the Metropolitan of New York, the Museum of Fine Arts in Boston, the Art Institute of Chicago, the Pennsylvania Museum of Art in Philadelphia and the museums at Toledo and Detroit. In addition to Boston, Detroit and Philadelphia, the Fogg Museum at Harvard and the museums in Cleveland and Minneapolis are notable for their adaptation to their purpose.

Other museums of other sorts crowd about, but it is impossible to describe them except to comment that while the Field Museum on Chicago's lake front succeeded in repeating some of the architectural features of its famous predecessor, the old Palace of Fine Arts of the World's Fair of '93, it failed in capturing an iota of its inspiration, and that the most extraordinary museum in America is one Henry Ford has built in Dearborn, Michigan. In this unbelievable structure one sees the culture of bygone America reproduced full size—an entire barber shop of the 'eighties, a smithy of Longfellow's time, and instead of a single kerosene lamp or warming pan you can see a thousand.

CITY PLANNING

We may not enter the gardens where "waves the cypress in the palace walk and winks the gold fin in the porphyry font" for landscape gardening, even when it is called landscape architecture, is beyond the ken of this volume. But of its big brother, city planning, a word must be said.

While every town had its common, very few in the earliest days had anything that could de dignified with the name of a city plan. The first to claim the honor, is, I believe, Annapolis, which was settled in 1649. Another was New Orleans with its great Place des Armes, dominated by the Cathedral, and its Cabildo, shielding from view the Vieux Carré, regularly laid out behind it. But the most famous of all was, of course, the city of Washington.

The old plan of L'Enfant and President Washington has already been referred to, and so has the new plan of Burnham and McKim. Le Nôtre, the famous garden architect of Louis XIV and the creator of Versailles, was the grandfather at least of the Washington Plan. His shadow fell across the terraces and fountains of the Court of Honor in '93, and still, like a gigantic gnomon, today points to the passage of style and time in the stately plans of garden and city.

It certainly cannot be said that we have developed anything like an American school of style or method in our city plans. In the first place, these plans uniformly ignore the skyscraper. The magnificent drawings of the Chicago Plan show Parisian buildings of ten or twelve stories with uniform cornices, balconies and mansard roofs. The new order had not appeared and we were in 1909 in the height of our Beaux Arts servility but the absurdity is none the less amazing. Boulevards are still laid out for the victoria and the hansom cab, and long lines of shade trees are shown where only stone and human lungs can live in the atmosphere of smoke and gas. City planners so far have done little to solve the vital problem of city life—congestion both from the skyscraper and from the automobile. Instead we have played with axes and *ronds points,* and have fooled ourselves into thinking that the days of Baron Haussmann and the Third Empire are still with us.

The city plan of the future must solve the problem of congestion. Perhaps the skyscrapers will rise, as suggested in an illustration of this volume, from the centre of open spaces; perhaps the traffic will flow in subterranean and superterranean streets; perhaps the aeroplane with its requirements for landing and starting will require open spaces and annihilate distance to such an extent that the skyscraper will be as profitable and indispensable in the outskirts of the town as in the centre. Undoubtedly separated grades at heavily traveled street intersections will be common with subways for pedestrians under the most crowded thoroughfares, while great arteries will lead from the heart, which is the city, to the veins and capillaries of suburban and country communication. Frank Lloyd Wright says the skyscraper is doomed and that the city, exploding with the pent-up forces of motor cars, electricity, and standardized production, will fly into the open spaces, all of which he beautifully and plausibly anticipates and provides for in his communal countryside Utopia, "Broadacres." LeCorbusier, on the other hand, wants us all to live in skyscrapers in a strange city called La Ville Radieuse. Certainly not at the present time has any city plan that fits and expresses the American scene been devised, although Park Avenue, New York, with its mammoth buildings built on "air rights" over the New York Central, approaches such a solution.

Of the several grandiose plans for rebuilding American cities none has been completely realized. The most important of these are the Plan of Chicago by the Chicago Plan Commission given to the public July 4th, 1909, of which D. H. Burnham and E. H. Bennett were the authors; the San Francisco Plan, finished just before the earthquake and fire (the Plan was entirely ignored in the rebuilding though the civic centre has since been put through in a different location); the Park Commission's Plan of the City of Washington; the Plan of Manila by Burnham and Pierce Anderson, submitted in 1905; and the Zoning Laws of the City of New York.

These last have had more influence on the physical development of the American city than all the other uncompleted projects put together. They were put into effect in 1916. In general, the city was divided into "use" districts, and the height and area of buildings determined for each district and in relationship to the width of the streets. The effect of this epochal zoning law was nation-wide, not only in making popular this kind of beneficent legislation, but in determining architectural forms themselves. For the working out of certain provisions of the New York law for high buildings on narrow streets called into life the step-off building, the beauty of whose pyramidal and cliff-like masses has often resulted in the use of these forms whether the law required it or not.

In Chicago the zoning law, differing somewhat from that of New York, allows any building to be built perpendicularly to a height of two hundred and fifty feet; above that it may ascend to an unlimited height provided such extension does not exceed twenty-five percent of the ground area. If New York with its terraces is realizing its reputation as a modern Babylon, Chicago with its towers will be a revived San Gimignano. The American city plan, as it stands today, is in the same position as the skyscraper of twenty years ago: an unsolved problem. That it will be solved is inevitable. Its solution will be one of the great achievements of the new era. The city planners have been confused and baffled by the kaleidoscopic changes in the American scene, but their aims have been large and their principles fixed in the splendid words of their leader, now gone, Daniel H. Burnham:

"Make no little plans; they have no magic to stir men's blood, and probably themselves will not be realized. Make big plans; aim high in hope and work, remembering that a noble, logical diagram once recorded will never die, but long after we are gone will be a living thing, asserting itself with ever growing insistency. Remember that our sons and grandsons are going to do things that would stagger us. Let your watchword be order and your beacon, beauty."

CHAPTER XI

TODAY AND TOMORROW

In Which We Stand Upon a Peak

WE are yet in the early morning of today but we must look back still farther, a little matter of fourteen years, to see the rising sun awakening the new skyscraper, the first born in the Today of our architecture.

On June 10th, 1922, the "Chicago Daily Tribune" announced an international competition for a high building to house its newspaper and to contain rentable offices. The prizes were generous, and the conditions imposed superlative beauty as well as utility. Two hundred and sixty designs were received, and twenty-three countries were represented in the competition.

The importance of this competition lies in the fact, not that a Chicago newspaper thereby obtained for its building a beautiful design, which it has faithfully carried out, but that among the other two hundred and fifty-nine designs, good, indifferent, bad and very bad, lay a pearl of great price. While the jury of award gave it the second place and a prize of $20,000, and while all the critics and commentators hailed it as a work of genius, not one of us was wise enough to see in it the achievement for which we had searched so long—the solution of the problem of the skyscraper. In one respect we were like Columbus, who, in discovering a new world, thought he had but run across a particularly beautiful part of the old. However, it is in the last few years of the many that have passed since the competition that the profound influence of this building that was never built has become evident; that these half-dozen sheets of white paper on which Eliel Saarinen had so painstakingly and lovingly depicted his dream-building are more potent in the present and the future of American architecture than any creation of stone and steel in the land. The "Tribune Competition" has become architectural history.

In Saarinen's extraordinary conception, architecture, long bound with the chains of precedent and bent double with the load of commercial expediency, bursts its bonds and stands up as a free man. It is as though some titanic seed, planted deep in the earth, had suddenly sprung from the mold into the light in a shimmering bloom of stone and steel. It is the best design since Amiens! As Louis Sullivan described it, "It is a voice resonant and rich, ringing amidst the wealth and joy of life. In utterance sublime and melodious, it prophesies a time to come and not so far away when we shall escape the bondage and the mania of fixed ideas. It goes freely in advance, and, with the steel frame as a thesis, displays a high science of design such as the world up to this day had neither known nor surmised. . . . Rising from the earth . . . it ascends in beauty lofty and serene, until its lovely crest seems at one with the sky."

The design as a whole consists of a pyramidal and telescopic mass, with strongly marked vertical elements, and with the surface slightly enriched with ornament and carved figures. The extraordinary sense of exaltation is obtained not more from the vertical elements than from the entire absence of the usual horizontal lids or clamps known as cornices, for without these heavy prison bars the building escapes, as it were, in joyous freedom into the sky.

Saarinen was fortunate in presenting his design at the critical moment. The New York zoning law of 1916 had, in order to comply with the conditions, forced architects in that city to adopt for very high buildings or for buildings in narrow streets an offset type of construction which resulted in a building that looked more or less like a pile of building-blocks. The virtue in this necessity was not long hidden. A building became a fascinating study of cubic shapes. Unprecedented new forms were called into being. Old and lifelong habits regarding cornices, columns, and their ilk, were forgotten in the presence of this new puzzle-toy, inhibitions concerning self-expression and originality were cast off, and long suppressed architectural desires received their consummation.

Other cities—almost all, whether they needed them or not—copied New York in her zoning ordinances and her step-off solutions. By 1922 the cornice had almost gone. Form, belatedly obeying the ukase of Louis Sullivan, was more and more truly expressing function. Gilbert, Goodhue, Corbett, Hood, had nearly guessed the answer, but chaos and uncertainty still reigned. A clarion call was needed, a voice to speak out loud and bold—and the man who sounded that note was not one of our blood, but a Finn.

Eliel Saarinen of Helsingfors, Finland, was a prominent architect of the Old World before he started his career in the New. He belonged to the European secessionist school of design—a lineal descendant changed in feature but not in blood from Sullivan's Transportation Building.

Undoubtedly the Finlander made his remarkable drawings in a modern, well-lighted, steamheated office, assisted by able draughtsmen, but I like to picture him tracing those fairylike outlines on some icy eyrie by the flashing lights of the Aurora Borealis, or in a glacial grotto with myriad elves about him all busily engaged in making the thousands of curious little lines which give his drawings a most uncanny feeling of enchanted inspiration and of superhuman assistance.

The "Tribune Competition" drawings went on a tour throughout the country. They were published in book form, and the prize-winning drawings were published over and over again in architectural and lay publications. Everywhere, from the *diplomé de L'École des Beaux Arts* to the product of the correspondence school who was graduated in the post office, from the high-brow of the intelligentsia to the low-brow of the ignoransia, the design of Saarinen met with acclaim. The Brahmins praised it on account of its philosophical content; hoi-polloi, because of its beauty.

The principle back of the Saarinen system lies, I should say, in the expression of upward growth against a composi-tion of rectangular masses. This effect is produced in the first instance by the elimination of all cornices and other horizontal accents, and by the insistence on vertical elements in the shape of piers which begin at the base and continue upward until they pierce the sky-line; in the second, by step-offs or set-backs, which, aside from complying with the law, give a pyramidal effect to the building, and allow the greatest subtlety in the arrangement of the masses. The modern skyscraper is essentially a study in form, whereas the skyscraper of yesterday was a study of surface and academic proportion. This insistence on form links it more or less to modern painting, particularly that of the cubist category. The complete expression of its skeleton of steel is perhaps no longer insisted on, as it is assumed that everyone now knows of it, and no longer

needs to be told. If this be true, as some one has oddly remarked, Sullivan has become an "Old Master."

The design of Saarinen was received without reservation;
but far more significant than lip service rendered to it
was the sudden change that began to overspread the face
of the skyscraper throughout the land. The first was the
American Radiator Building in New York by Raymond
Hood, who, with Howells, had won that momentous
"Tribune" competition with a beautiful Beauvais-like
Gothic design. The Radiator Building created nation-wide
comment on account of its remarkable use of color—black
and gold; but more significant by far is its use of the principles of skyscraper design set forth by Saarinen. It is an
historic edifice for it is the first of the group of skyscrapers, already large, that inaugurate the architecture of today.

As the period between the American Radiator Building
and the Depression is the most prolific in the birth of skyscrapers in our country it is obviously out of the question
to list more than a very few. Remember these are all designed according to the Saarinen formula. In New York,
the Telephone Building, thirty-three stories, the Roerich
Museum, and in the super skyscraper class, the Chrysler by
William Van Alen, McGraw-Hill, New York Life, the
Chanin, the Daily News, and the highest in the world, the
Empire State by Shreve, Lamb and Harmon, 1,250 feet to
the top of the mast.

In Chicago, the Merchandise Mart by Graham, Anderson, Probst and White, the Civic Opera and the Pittsfield
Building by the same architects; and by Holabird and Root,
333 North Michigan, the Palmolive, the Board of Trade,
and the Chicago Daily News. In Detroit, the Fisher Building by Albert Kahn and the Penobscot Building. In St. Louis,
the Southwestern Bell Telephone Building and in San

Francisco, the Pacific Telephone. The Depression found the cities already over-built with skyscrapers and a timid return of a reluctant prosperity shows little enthusiasm over renewed construction of very high buildings. It has even been seriously proposed, as we have a shortage of housing and a surplus of office space, that the newly-weds move into the skyscrapers! However, when the pointer in the occupancy index creeps up to the proper percentage the renter, the excavator, and the riveter will appear by magic. The skyscraper's head is bloody but unbowed and its place in our national art is still unshaken.

It is futile and to my notion aesthetically wrong to condemn or oppose the skyscraper. Old Icarus would not have looked more enviously at Lindbergh's silvery plane than would the builders of Amiens and Beauvais, could they stand on Fifth Avenue, and follow with astonished eyes the ascending shafts of Rockefeller Center to a height that makes their own towering cathedrals seem puny and infantile. The skyscraper is far and away the most important architectural achievement of America, her great gift to the art of building. In its train has come the most brilliant era of structural engineering that the world has ever known. From the bottom of the lowest caisson, where one hundred feet below the surface the pneumatic drills have ground to a level the bones of mother earth, to the top of the highest pinnacle, where the staccato notes of the steel riveter drown out the hum of aeroplanes, the vast pile of the skyscraper is fraught with the best construction efforts of the American mind. The engineers, civil, electrical, mechanical, sanitary, have vied with each other in perfecting the application of their science, and the same emulation has existed among the trades—the masons, the carpenters, the plasterers, the glaziers, the painters; the setters of marble, of ornamental iron, of mosaic, and back of them the manufacturers of brick; the quarry men who hew the stone; the great mills that saw the lumber and fabricate the cabinet work; the kilns that bake the terra cotta; the furnaces that roll the steel. These with a myriad others form a vast army whose labors now constitute, next to agriculture, our greatest industry—an army that builds and does not destroy; an army whose march along the crowded ways of life is marked by monuments of stone and steel pulsating with human life, not by mute crosses in the poppy fields.

Scorn not the skyscraper! Its eyes gaze down from immeasurable heights on a welter of humanity and machinery. Its shining flanks are dappled with shadows of aeroplanes that "laugh as they pass in thunder," while "sublime on their towers" the mysterious antennae "join cape to cape over a torrent sea."

The Great Depression of 1930–35, for even these hard dates may some day be forgotten, struck not only the super-skyscraper but the modest affair of ten to twenty stories a staggering blow. It had been long known that stories over fifty should be marked off as advertising. But in the dark days even the validity of the skyscraper idea began to be questioned and many modern buildings no longer capable of earning fixed charges were torn down.* This craze for extraction on the first sign of an ache threatened to turn some of our best financial districts into toothless jaws but the cavities were nicely smoothed off and we got parking areas even if we didn't get parks.

The skyscraper was especially vulnerable, not only on account of its great cost and the luxury features of stories

* In Chicago in 1927 there were 12,025 building permits for a total of $352,-936,400—in 1932 there were 467 permits for a total of $3,824,500.

above the clouds but because all of our cities were over-built in office buildings. It is, therefore, remarkable that the greatest super-skyscraper of all time should have been built during the Depression, and that is Rockefeller Center, New York. This unbelievable building, built beyond the human scale, too much for one man to conceive and con-summate, was the work of an association of architects—Raymond Hood, Harvey Corbett and Benjamin H. Morris —and if someone should write a "Story of Engineering in America" its engineers would occupy a noble eminence. Of the architects, however, Raymond Hood must stand as the symbol. We have already heard of him as designer with Howells of the Tribune Tower and as architect for the first consummation of the Saarinen formula in the Amer-ican Radiator Building in New York. Hood died in the saddle at the height of his career in 1934.

His life, his character, his work was a shout and a blare of trumpets. He was the knight, the apostle, the victim of those extraordinary years in our architectural history that lie between 1922 and 1930. In those eight years the archi-tecture of the skyscraper was revolutionized and Hood was raised on their soaring forms from obscurity to fame. He was not more the creator than the creature of them. What McKim was to the realm of taste, Goodhue to ro-mance, Burnham to order and big business, Sullivan to prophecy, Saarinen to inspiration, Hood was to the meta-morphosis of the skyscraper. Certainly he wrote the first page with his American Radiator Building and he closed the chapter (though we hope for more) with Rockefeller Center.

There are many other men who rank close to Hood, I am aware, in the development of the new architecture.

Perhaps it was Hood's personality, reflected so acutely by this period of architecture, that makes him the symbol of an era, unexampled alike for its brevity and brilliance. Hood was a flame of vigor, imagination, daring. His enthusiasm and eloquence coaxed clients into paths that they never would have trodden in their saner moments. Hood led them to the peaks, though by strange and perilous routes. Adventurously, he never pursued the same path twice himself. There is, therefore, no earmark by which you can identify a Hood skyscraper as you can a Cram church or a Platt residence. All you can say is, "the building is extraordinary, the author might be Hood."

Quite as essential, from the point of view of the client, was his ability to complete the job often in record-breaking time. From his own statement, the American Radiator Building in New York was completed within thirteen months from the day he got the job; the steel was halfway up before the top stories were completely designed! Aside from his temperament, his mastery of the technique of architecture explains much of his fearlessness as well as his waywardness. With unusual talent combined with unsurpassed technical training (a graduate of both the Massachusetts Institute of Technology and the École des Beaux Arts) the thing called architecture was not so much a tool as a plaything in his hands. He knew exactly how far he could go and he always played the limit. His practice was a joy ride, in which everybody got a thrill, including the clients. John Norton, the painter, once said, "no work of art deserves to live if it does not embody a fresh idea"— hence, it must of necessity be experimental. Beauty is not its own excuse for being and the repetition of sure-fire solutions means the degradation of architecture. Hence, the greatness of Picasso; hence, the power of Hood. Every one of Hood's buildings embodies a new idea. It meant courage and it meant labor.

Hood was born in Pawtucket, March 29th, 1881. His father was a well-to-do box manufacturer. First he went to Brown University, where he stayed two years, and then to M. I. T., graduating in architecture in 1903. He worked a while with Cram, Goodhue and Ferguson and then to Paris where he was diplomé in 1911. He returned to America at the mature age of thirty, too late to begin (we used to think), and was for a time associated with Hornbostle in Pittsburgh. At the end of a lean and discouraging period of independent practice, in which at times he contemplated leaving his profession, he was invited by John Mead Howells to join him in the competition for the Tribune Tower. As the world knows, they won first prize.

In the eight crowded and precious years that remained Hood designed the following important structures: American Radiator Building, Beaux Arts Apartments, Daily News Building, The Rockefeller Center, McGraw-Hill Building—all in New York, and the Temple of the Scottish Rites, Scranton, Pennsylvania, and the multi-colored house of General Patterson, somewhere along the Hudson. A number of churches and lesser buildings are scattered. His strong hand is present in the Century of Progress Exhibition in Chicago. He it was who, leaping off an ocean liner (it had landed) with a roll of sketches under his arm, rushed to the meeting of the architectural commission of the Fair and persuaded them to adopt an asymmetrical general plan. He also designed the extraordinary Electrical Group.

He was, of course, greatly in demand in all sorts of activities—on the International Jury for the Memorial to Co-

lumbus in San Domingo, Trustee of the Beaux Art Institute of Design, President of the Architectural League of
New York, Honorary Alumnus of the American Academy
in Rome, Chevalier Order of the Crown of Belgium, etc. He
had the unusual habit of associating with himself various architects for different jobs. I have assumed, I hope correctly,
that Hood was the directing genius in the matter of design
in each of these. For instance, with K. M. Murchison, F. A.
Godley and A. Foulihoux on the Beaux Arts Apartments,
with Harvey Corbett and B. W. Morris on Rockefeller
Center. Andre Foulihoux was his partner at the time of his
death. In losing Raymond Hood in his prime, one wonders
how many a brilliant unborn concept the world has also lost.

In the fall of 1929 with skyscrapers shooting toward
heaven on every hand and amidst the rattle of the rivet-
ers and the roar of the stock market came the debacle.

Most unhappily depressions show a marked affinity for
architects second only to bankers. I can remember how, as
a boy hunting or botanizing, I would occasionally run into
a gaunt, paintless, windowless, mansarded and cupolaed
house, rising before me in the woods like a veritable House
of Usher. It was a monument to the fall of the House of
Jay Cooke and the panic of 1873. Again for two years
after the panic of '93 architects had little or nothing to do.
In 1897–98 building was in the doldrums. But never in the
history of America had anything approached the depression of 1930–36. Never before had architects and draughtsmen been the recipients of public relief. Never before had
architectural offices by the thousands closed their doors and
taken down their shingles. Never before had a large percentage of the profession sought shelter under the wings
of Washington, working in the capital or at home on public works, created, in part, for their aid; and never had

the government created before a nation-wide project for the aid of helpless draughtsmen, nor had it set up enormous funds to encourage home building, nor had it become, with its huge housing projects, a landlord in its own right. The five to six black years, therefore, which we call the Depression have not, in quantity certainly, very much to offer the historian and, to make it still easier, the few achievements stand out like peaks, each of a different kind, from a flat and arid desert.

The principal architectural achievements of the Depression seem to me to be the Cathedral of New York, the Century of Progress, Rockefeller Center, and the Restoration of Williamsburg. There were also certain architectural phenomena such as the growth of the New Architecture, called hereafter (occasionally) the International Style; the search for the "prefabricated house"; and government participation in architecture which is of three principal kinds—Government buldings, Housing, and the Historic American Building Survey.

THE CATHEDRAL OF NEW YORK

One of these stretches back to the far off time of the Romanesque Revival and that is the Cathedral of New York or, more particularly, of St. John the Divine. It is not yet completed nor will it be for many years. Its present architect, Ralph Adams Cram, writes in his absorbing and altogether too modest book, "My Life in Architecture": "The completion of the cathedral may cost an additional eight or nine million dollars. If there are those who question such an expenditure it might be well for them to remember that the total cost will be just about that of one super-dreadnaught battleship. The cathedral, engineers say, will easily stand for two thousand years. During that time it will serve, at the lowest computation, the spiritual and moral needs of, say, 350,000,000 people. The function of the battleship is the encompassing of death and destruction and its span of life is, at the most, some twenty-five years. The parallel should be conclusive." It had often occurred to me that the two greatest structural works of man were a great cathedral and a great ship, though I was thinking more of a super-liner than a dreadnaught. Both represent complete organization on a gigantic scale and a supreme skill that makes of their puny creator not so much a super-man as a wondering servant who can cry in his humility, "Not to me the glory, O Lord."

The building of this cathedral which, when finished, will be the largest in English Christendom and twice the area of St. Paul's, has run the gamut of human emotion and endeavor. Tragic disappointment as well as triumph lie in its granite heart, and its brow someday will tower over a city which may scarce remember the men who gave it birth.

The most curious thing about the cathedral is its early capitulation to the power of Fashion. It was won in competition by Heins and LaFarge, architects, on a Romanesque design. This was in 1887. How could the Bishop, the trustees, the jury, and the architects have foretold that the Romanesque Style would not only be completely outmoded within five years but so discredited that its retention would actually prevent the continuation of building operations! Accordingly, after twenty-five years of halting progress, in 1910 Cram, Goodhue and Ferguson were employed to remodel and complete the cathedral in the Gothic

Style. At that time the choir had been finished and the crossing roughed in and roofed with a temporary dome. At the present time the choir with its seven radiating chapels, the crypt, the baptistry, the nave, and the west front and towers (as high as the roof) are complete, all in Gothic guise. To my notion, the finest part of the cathedral is the nave, both internally and externally. Here Cram, now the sole architect, has equalled the architect of Liverpool with a brilliant tour de force. Accepting the square bays, planned for the Romanesque design, he boldly vaulted them with the early Gothic device of a six part vault. This calls for an intermediate pier which he made of a free column of granite over eighty feet in height and he raised the height of the major aisles (St. John is a five aisled cathedral) to the level of the nave vault, something like the *"halle kirche"* of Austria. Other scintillating features are the design of the baptistry, the work of Frank Cleveland of Cram and Ferguson, the proposed vaulting of the crossing, and the beautiful design of the chapels, one of which, at least, is by another architect. Various buildings of great beauty surround the Close (examine the Synod house) and, as a final commendation, especially dear to the heart of the architect, there is not a sham in the whole cathedral: all honest solid masonry and whatever it appears to be.

CENTURY OF PROGRESS, CHICAGO, 1933–1934

As a confidence between author and reader, a major difficulty in writing this book was the best way to treat the most interesting architectural phenomenon of the age—the "New Architecture," variously called the Modern Style, Functionalist Architecture, and the International Style. The difficulty lies in the fact that, if our thesis is correct, the birth of this movement lay a hundred pages back in the chapter on Louis Sullivan but its consummation (not its culmination) lies about us in the present chapter. Furthermore, any comprehensive history of the phenomenon would take us to Europe for a large number of pages. I have, therefore, adopted the course of describing it here and there as its head has bobbed up through the last forty-three years of American architecture. Sullivan, Wright, the Chicago School, Saarinen and the Tribune Tower competition, Hood and the new skyscraper all have called forth comment upon it. It was not, however, until the "Century of Progress Exposition" that the theory of the "New Architecture," particularly in its latest phase of Puritanism, was presented to the American people. I have, therefore, combined a further (absolutely the last) description with an account of the Exposition in Chicago.

The men who conceived and brought forth the International exposition of 1933, known as A Century of Progress, were fools for courage and a good many would say fools for luck. Not only was the time the depth of the Great Depression but the architectural style proposed was one untried and if not unpopular at least suspect. Moreover, the reputation of its great ancestor, the famous World's Fair of 1893, stood as an awesome challenge—a veritable God of the Mountain ready to crush with heavy tread any upstart pretender. But a new age cried for a showing and a new architecture demanded a tryout. A Century of Promise would have been a far better name, for prophecy not progress was its keynote.

In the thirteenth century no bishop nor master builder considered any style but the newborn Gothic for the proposed cathedral; so with the Century of Progress the commission of architects apparently regarded as inevitable that

the New Architecture—the architecture of function, the
International Style—would be the vesture for the new exposition. Several expositions had been held in Europe since
the War in the International Style, notably those at Brno,
Czecho-Slovakia, 1928, and in Antwerp and Liege in 1930,
but none in America.

The San Francisco Exposition of 1915 closed with a bang
the richly illuminated and gorgeously bound book of the
Renaissance, and it was not a new chapter but a new volume that was to be opened in Chicago in '33. This therefore is the best place to sketch in a paragraph, in places
repetitious, the progress of the New Architecture, because
at the Century of Progress it made its formal debut to the
American public.

Beginning in 1893 in Chicago as a functionalist movement, combined with secession from all precedent, glorified
by Sullivan's original ornamentation, and buoyed up by
its hope of becoming "the American Style," the New
Architecture has gone through the various stages of the
Chicago School, the Art Nouveau in England and Belgium, the Secessionism of Germany and the Nordic countries, the publication of Wright's designs in Germany, 1912,
the Exposition of Decorative Arts in Paris, 1926, with its
wealth of ornament, and the Puritanism of Corbusier and
his co-reformers in France and Germany in the last decade.
During this forty years, although the theatre of action had
shifted to Europe, Functionalist architecture had never
died out in the United States. Frank Lloyd Wright, George
Elmslie and one or two others had heroically kept it alive,
particularly in and about Chicago and on the western
coast. Suddenly, as we know, it reappeared—a pillar of fire
in Saarinen's Tribune design of 1922. Overnight almost it

became a conquering force, winning, in turn, the sky-scraper, the factory, the shop front, the moving picture theatre, the international exposition, and now it is thundering at the gates of the home and the church. Up to the Century of Progress it was a thing guiltless, it is true, of any Classic crimes or Renaissance misdemeanors but often loaded with ornament unpleasantly called "modernistic," almost all of which had first appeared at the Paris Decorative Arts Exposition in 1925.

About 1926 there was injected into the essence of the New Architecture a new element, the importance of which cannot be over-estimated. This was the Puritanism of LeCorbusier, Gropius, and the "New Pioneers." Cotton Mather denounced no more sternly the pretty brooch on the white throat of a New England girl than do these reformers condemn ornament on the fair surface of a modern building. I suppose red cheeks and blue eyes were tolerated in Boston in the seventeenth century, so even today ornament may be condoned provided it be "significant." What is significant ornament? Lettering is significant, a flag is significant, and so, I presume, would be a barber's pole, but no farther shall ye go. But Puritanism, whether it be of men or buildings, can never be more than a purge. Only for so long can the hand, especially the youthful hand, be restrained. Without a ribbon in the hair and a moulding on the wall life would not for long be worth living.

A more subtle but not less important element of this Puritanism is the complete expression of functionalism. A building is no longer an arrangement of "masses" but one of "volumes." Of other times a building was a sturdy thing of embrasures, of projecting buttress, of crowning cornice. Always the surfaces, lighted and in shadow, indicated the depth and strength of the wall. Assured by its mass of the everlasting quality of the building and pleased by its power, we were not so much interested in what went on inside those walls unless it pleased us to guess that the great window indicated a banquet hall and the oriel a lady's bower. But the Puritans of the New Architecture change all that for us. A building is no longer a hard-shelled mollusc but, in a sense, a thin-skinned vertebrate. Rooms like organs should be placed exactly where they are of the most use and they are to be covered with skinlike walls hung upon and about a skeleton of steel. Whilst Norman Bel Geddes, the streamline king, gives us clean and unknown forms, inspired, perhaps, by our rush through the ether.

How then can architecture in the sense of beauty of building be obtained? There is supposed to be beauty in any honest expression of a function (if you can't always see it so much the worse for you) and after all, according to the Puritans, it is ornament that makes a building ugly. But much can be done even with this stark program to make a building pleasing. The material of even a skinlike wall may have inherent beauties: the grain of wood, the texture of brick, the sheen of metal. Windows, which have been exalted to unprecedented importance, arranged in strips and turning corners with impunity are not unpleasing when you get used to them. And then there is color with which we are allowed pretty much to have our way provided, of course, we indulge in no sinful stenciling or other painted ornament. Proportion, the soul of Greek art and the jewel in the crown of every style since, is still a vague and shadowy thing in the limbo of the New Architecture. Despised by some and sought by others, it has not found its place but, at any rate, it is not yet anathematized. Approaches, terraces, receding and advancing planes, and varying heights indicate its possibilities. Certainly the beautiful proportions of the Science Building at A Century of Progress would argue for its use, while the monstrous awkwardness of some of LeCorbusier's buildings would forever condemn its exclusion.

Such a revolutionary program in aesthetics cannot be accomplished without a corresponding revolt in the engineering and mechanical arts. Of what are we to make our skinlike walls, our projecting terraces, our unified utilities? We will not attempt to answer here except to say that it is being done and that so far the engineers have met most of the demands of the architects. The Century of Progress, therefore, must be regarded as a vast proving ground for the New Architecture in all its aspects.

Nor can we, in the space left, catalogue or describe its buildings except in the briefest way.* The main divisions of the Exposition, architecturally considered, were the Exhibition Buildings, official and private, the Fountain, the Villages, and the Prefabricated Houses. The villages, excellently done, may be dismissed as having any influence on the future of architecture, but the others, all built in accordance with the principles described above, are heavy with portent.

Again that curious feeling comes over one that we are looking at living creatures instead of at inanimate buildings. You remember that Chesterton in coming suddenly upon the flank of York Cathedral saw in its buttresses and pinnacles a troupe of men at arms with banners flying— on the march. What is the Travel and Transport Building but a monstrous spider waiting in a web of steel? The Agricultural Building becomes a resplendent caterpillar,

* The members of the architectural commission who designed the Exposition were Harvey Wiley Corbett, Raymond Hood, Ralph Walker of New York; John Holabird, Edward Bennett, Hubert Burnham of Chicago; Paul Cret of Philadelphia, and Louis Skidmore, architect in charge of design and construction.

the Science Building, like an Amazonian butterfly, slowly unfolds its iridescent wings, while the Building of Exhibits marches upon us like a battalion of devouring locusts each with its gigantic antennae feeling its way through an unbelievable wonderland.

Space which I, perhaps, should fill with statistics—its area, 350 acres; its cost of construction, $15,000,000; its attendance (in 1933), 22,320,000, etc. etc.—I must devote to a note on color. No limitations of cost, precedent or conscience stayed the hand here. In the first year of the Fair Joseph Urban, using black as the *leit-motif* of the buildings on the lake side and white for those on the land side, spread broad surfaces of blue, red, green, blue-green and orange, and killed portions which he did not like with dull neutral tints. The second year Shepard Vogelgesang toned down the trumpet blasts to a lovely, almost a demure sonata of harmonious shades.

Now what of the lighting? There was nothing in flood lighting that we did not see in San Francisco. The advance was in the direction of general and decorated lighting from concealed sources, often from incandescent and gaseous origins aided by mechanical devices. Again the magician's wand waves as daylight fades and our Martian spiders, caterpillars and locusts are transformed into a host of luna moths opening their myriad eyes and spreading their damask wings over an enchanted scene.

THE PREFABRICATED HOUSE

The prefabricated house and the New Architecture, if not twins—identical or otherwise—are, at least, sisters under the skin. The prefabricated house may have been born of LeCorbusier's catch phrase, "a house should be a machine for living," but the early work and still the greater part of the work on the problem has been done and is being done by men such as Grosvenor Atterbury, A. Lawrence Kocher, Robert McLaughlin, Howard Fisher, and the Bemis Industries who have put aesthetics aside for the nonce and delved into the engineering and manufacturing part of the problem.

Immediately that the house-machine becomes a fixed idea one casts about for means to manufacture it like other machines. The machine with which the house is constantly compared, always to its disparagement, is the automobile. While the automobile may furnish us an example of design, untramelled by precedent, the comparison is unfair, one obvious reason being that the automobile has but one (legitimate) function and that is transportation, while the house has a countless number.

At present on top of foundations built in the old manner our house is assembled. The perfect prefabricated house would be one in which walls above the foundations, floors, partitions, roofs and utilities (heating, plumbing and lighting) could be shipped from the factory in complete sections of convenient size and these fastened together in some secure and simple way. (Why not by giant zippers?) As factory costs are much cheaper than site costs and as the time element to the owner might be reduced from five months to two weeks, the prefabricated house should cut in half the cost of ordinary construction. Furthermore, if it could be "unzipped" and moved about like other goods and chattels it might revolutionize our system of land values. Such a house has not been achieved but the difficulties are not insurmountable. Scores of architects and engineers are working on the problem and progress certainly has been made.

The difficulties are enormous. For instance, to achieve the primary aim of low cost, mass production is essential; the Depression, by removing the demand, killed that incentive; the great size and complicated functions of a house; the varying sizes of families and their modes of living; the varieties of sites with their different orientations seem to call for a multiplicity of models, nor can we expect organized labor in the building trades to applaud our efforts; in factory-made houses many familiar building materials must be scrapped and new ones invented and there is likely to be a menace in the fickleness of human taste and fashion.

Raymond Hood remarked that one of the functions of a building was to please the owner. Certainly the public can't be blackjacked into occupying some of the horrific examples that have been offered. Accordingly, the house must be pleasing in appearance to a majority of people without recourse to argument or persuasion and here the New Architecture stands ready to attack. Its skinlike walls, plain surfaces, square forms, and novelty of appearance agree exactly with the requirements of the prefabricated house. One large firm advertises prefabricated houses (made of sheet copper) in Colonial and Old English. Certainly within the law, but the idea seems impious.

What is the present status of the prefabricated house? In the "Architectural Forum" of December, 1935, thirty-six systems of so-called prefabricated houses were listed and described. They comprised materials of wood, of plywood, of slag slabs, of copper, of cork slabs, of steel in strips, in sheets, and in rolls; of gypsum lumber, of artificial stone, of panels in all sorts of synthetic and compressed materials—all sworn foes to cold, heat, wear and tear, termites; practically everything except death and taxes. Each of these systems is prefabricated only in degree, some hardly more than the old-fashioned house, where, after all, the windows and doors, furnace, and even bricks were prefabricated. Most, in fact, are little more than novel methods of construction, employing novel materials.

A tragic and unlooked-for result has followed in the train of the prefabricated house. The young architect has been the most ardent disciple of the New Architecture and the prefabricated house, but apparently he has dug a pit for his own adventurous feet, for now mail-order houses, manufacturers, realtors, contractors, and even a national weekly have jumped in the small house field and offer complete plans and specifications for small houses for every sum from nothing to $3.50. As the time-honored way for the young practitioner to get started is through the small house, what hope has the young architect against competition such as this?

Even if today, in its experimental stage, the prefabricated house falls short of its avowed ideals and brings professional distress in its train, yet those ideals are so revolutionary that the house stands as a portentous symbol of building and of living in the new era: it presages a revolution in construction through prefabrication, a revolution in manufacture through the development of new materials, a revolution in aesthetics through a new architecture, and a revolution in living through the house as a machine.

HOUSING

Any author should approach the topic of housing with wary steps if not with trepidation. No subject relating to building has called forth so much vitriolic ink spilling. A ten-foot table in the Burnham Library is covered with books (on edge) on this topic alone. The general tenor of most of them is—how much superior the Germans, Austrians, Swedes, Slovenes, Bohemians and Croates are to the simple-minded Americans when it comes to housing. Fortunately we are absolved from any necessity of discussing in this book the social aspects of housing or of apologizing for America, faced with the vastly superior culture of mittel-Europa.

In a word, we have had little housing in this country because our constitutions—federal and state—failed to foresee a proletariat descended upon us from middle and southern Europe. It was, besides, almost a national dogma that the American citizen had enegry, ability and ideals sufficient to build or find respectable shelter for himself and family, an effort which one writer refers to as "petty capitalism." It is, therefore, extremely difficult for nation, state or municipality lawfully to undertake housing. For the private investor housing for the poor classes—and that's what we mean by "housing"—is wellnigh impossible, owing to the high cost of land and the "exactions of the capitalists" (always emphasized), added to the high cost of labor and the exactions of the unions (seldom mentioned). The philanthropist, therefore, has had the field to himself and apparently the monopoly has left him a bit cold.

Nevertheless, a certain amount of housing had been accomplished previous to the New Deal. There are the Rosenwald (for the colored) and the Marshall Field Apartments in Chicago, and the Phipps Houses and Knickerbocker Village in New York City, and the Buhl Foundation's development in Pittsburgh. All of these and more were but drops in an empty bucket. The condition had become somewhat ameliorated by, say, 1930, owing to the sharp restriction of immigration and the growing prosperity of the slum dwellers who took to moving to the suburbs. The lower East Side of New York, for instance, had lost nearly forty percent of its population between 1920 and 1935. So, perhaps, there never would have been any housing on a grand scale in America if it had not been for one thing—the Depression. That, and not the goading of the town planners, the humanitarians, the settlement workers and the travelling students of a pinkish hue, caused the United States government to act; to act immediately and to act on a vast scale.

The agency of the government which has undertaken this work is the Public Works Administration, famous as P.W.A., and within it is its most spectacular and most discussed component, the Housing Division. Its job is the cleaning-up of American slums and the building of well constructed housing within reach of the lowest income group; a herculean task in itself if all went well but made doubly difficult by the man-made obstacles that are constantly arising. Some of these are the inability of the government, through court decisions, to condemn property; the unwillingness of private owners to sell at appraisal prices, often banding together for the purpose; political opposition and ridicule; and the high wage scale that unionized labor sees fit to impose.

The Projects in the Housing Division's program, when consummated, will be equivalent to a city of 130,000 inhabitants with streets, lawns, gardens, shrubbery and trees, rest and recreational areas. As a matter of fact, the program is divided between thirty-five cities and two insular possessions. This will provide for 25,000 families, will cost $130,000,000, and will have given 50,000 builders direct employment. In addition, seven housing developments, three of them of the first magnitude, have been built in various cities by Limited Income Corporations, financed by government money under the P.W.A.

The architecture of these buildings, after all, is our principal interest and here, again, the government has acted wisely. A board of local architects and a mechanical engineer have been selected for each project. Under the direction of its self-appointed chief they design the site plan, including layout of streets and utilities. Successively, they make sketches for the buildings, make the working plans, and write the specifications. Each step is approved by the Housing Division which takes charge from then on, taking estimates, letting the contracts and supervising the construction. Buildings, for the most part, are of three types—two or three story group houses (one family to the house); two or three story group flats (one family to the floor); and three or more story apartment buildings. The architects have a wealth of information to guide them, such as the unit plans, carefully studied at Washington, but they are not obligated to follow them. In regard to architectural style they are given the fullest liberty but automatically, in the aim at economy and efficiency, almost all embellishment has been eliminated save, perhaps, a softening touch about the doorways. This frugality in regard to the amenities of architectural style is not applied to landscape gardening, which the architects control, and no stint had been placed on the planting of trees, shrubs and vines. There is no doubt that America's essay in housing will achieve results far superior to their European predecessors, regimented and self-conscious as so many of them are; superior in convenience and in ease of living through more scientific mechanical equipment and most certainly superior in beauty.

There is no space, obviously, to list the fifty-one housing projects on the government program, but a few of the most important cannot be neglected. There is New York which heads the list with two projects, totalling $17,500,-000. Chicago is close behind with projects (one named for Jane Addams) costing $16,200,000. Boston's "Old Harbour Village" will cost $6,000,000. Cleveland's three projects will run to $10,729,000. "Laurel Homes" in Cincinnati will cost $6,500,000 and there are others in Cambridge ("Main Street," imagine it), Buffalo, Dallas, Detroit—$10,000,000, Atlantic City, etc., etc., ending with three projects on the Virgin Islands.

Not included in the Housing Division of the P.W.A. but pardonably confused in the public mind is the housing done at Norris by the Tennessee Valley Authority. This is entirely different in quality—detached and suburban in spirit, though simple enough for the middle income group, typical of the pioneer doctrine that an American should own and sustain a home.

As we rise higher in our income earning class we come to a very American institution, well known as the "restricted subdivision." The first and still, in some respects, the most impressive of them all is Roland Park, opened in 1891 near Baltimore. Every large city now has one or more of these restricted subdivisions. They are the answer to the realtor's prayer and there is nothing of altruism about them. Realizing that good design pays, many of these projects are the work of distinguished architects. Radburn,*

* As this book goes to press comes the news of the death of Henry Wright. Beside his work at Radburn, N. J. and other housing developments, his book on "Rehousing Urban America" made him the foremost of our housing authorities and town planners. He combined fervor, imagination and high technical ability.

New Jersey, and Sunnyside, New York, are famous examples; Coral Gables, Florida, Palos Verdos, Beverley Hills, and River Oak, Houston. Here, for example, are 1,000 acres. $10,000,000 has been received and an equal amount spent on the project. River Oak houses range from $12,000 to the sky. Its smallest site is 65 x 125 and its largest 14 acres. Golf course, tennis courts, parks, all the utilities are, of course, present. I suppose America's Restricted Subdivision is our riposte to England's Garden City. I wish our thrust were a little more convincing, but as the Garden Cities are subsidized and born of moral and social resolve quite likely the comparison is not in order. Undoubtedly, one of the great phenomena of tomorrow will be housing on a vast scale. What we are seeing today are but the portents.

THE HISTORIC AMERICAN BUILDING SURVEY

Of the many and varied projects of the government to provide relief and at the same time prime the pump, none was closer to the architect than the Historic American Building Survey. Its purpose was and is to use unemployed draughtsmen to measure, photograph, and record, by careful drawings, old buildings throughout the land. By old, anything before the Civil War, and especially to be favored were houses which by their beauty, historical interest, or liability to destruction made them worthy of preservation.

The project was proposed by Charles E. Peterson of the National Park Service of the Interior Department in November, 1933. It is still administered by this branch of government but its policies have been formed by a national advisory council of architects and educators of which the head is Dr. Leicester B. Holland of the Library of Congress.

The Survey has gone through various phases and as it

stands now it is, in a sense, a partnership of the Government, the Library of Congress, and the American Institute of Architects, actively assisted by various universities and by private individuals. A great part, therefore, of the administrative work is voluntary and without cost to the taxpayers. So far, over 1,400 structures have been surveyed and nearly 7,000 photographs made, and nearly a thousand needy draughtsmen employed.

A notable achievement of the Historic American Building Survey is the architectural survey of the pre-historic Pueblo of Acoma in New Mexico, and of the earliest English settlement in America at Jamestown, Va., but perhaps the most notable of all is the inculcation in the people's minds of the value as well as beauty of our early architecture and the great asset to the community in preserving it. Let us hope that the Survey will be made a permanent project of our government.

UNITED STATES GOVERNMENT WORK

It must be a genuine relief to Uncle Sam to turn from trying to build houses for his enormous and captious family to the building of some very nice ones for himself. Beginning with the Capitol in Washington and the White House, the government has been steadily building throughout the years. The buildings, sometimes by salaried government architects but for the most part by independent practitioners, have been on the whole dignified and creditable. They almost all lie within the limits of the Classic style. The exceptions like Gothic West Point are rare. In a way we have established an official style and I, for one, think we ought to stick to it. It is being employed now in the government's tremendous improvements progressing in Washington between Pennsylvania Avenue and the Mall and on Capitol Hill. These great buildings are done by private architects as are also the far-flung ranks of post offices and other federal buildings, except that the actual work must be done under the roof of the Treasury Department in Washington and the designs must be passed upon by a federal committee of architects.

THE RESTORATION OF WILLIAMSBURG

I find that without especial intent we are ending our story almost exactly where we began it, at the beginning of our architecture—our own endeared Colonial—the delicate fruit of our architectural springtime. I imagine for you, as for me, it is a very restful and a pleasant thing to come back to the old homestead after tramping the hard pavements of regimented architecture, from trying to follow the stern precepts of the Functionalists, and with eyes tired by the strange forms and sharp angles of "the machines for living." We may even with good grace admit that we are a bit over-fed with the air conditioning, the mechanical refrigeration, and the super-sanitary plumbing of those good-intentioned architects who insist that we be 100% comfortable when occasionally 50% would be a good deal more amusing and probably better for us.

It is the peculiar triumph of Williamsburg that after you have been there awhile you become one with the place and the old time and that it is the modern world that is unreal: an unpleasant, incomprehensible dream that you had last night in your four-poster.

In the fall of 1926 I was engaged in writing this book in its first form and after an expedition along the south shore of the James, including, of course, Bacon's Castle, ancient St. Luke's, Smith's Fort, I crossed the tawny river to Jamestown and on six miles farther to Williamsburg. Here I presented myself to the Reverend William A. R. Goodwin, D.D., rector of Bruton Parish Church. After an unforgettable day of picking out the treasures from the haphazard collection of architecture in the venerable town I stood with Dr. Goodwin, who had been my guide, on the steps of the George Wythe House. This ancient and historic house was owned by Bruton Parish Church and on it the Doctor had been doing a little amateur restoration himself. As we looked out over the somnolent village, glimpsing a Colonial gable here and a filling station there, Dr. Goodwin said,

"My dream and hope is to make this town exactly as it was in the eighteenth century."

"What?!"

He repeated it.

"But Doctor, how about all these war-time and modern buildings of various kinds?"

"We'll have to tear them down or move them off."

"How many are there?"

"Over three hundred, anyway."

"How many old houses would be left when you got through destroying the new ones?"

"About fifty-five but, of course, we would have to rebuild all those that have disappeared through the years."

"How about the new concrete pavement in the Duke of Gloucester Street and the cement sidewalks everywhere?"

"Up they come."

"And the telephone and telegraph poles and electric lighting standards?"

"Down they go," said the Doctor.

In my astonishment I now played my trump card. At the head of the Palace Green where now glows the loveliest of the Williamsburg restorations, the Governor's Palace, stood upright like a sore thumb the ugly but new and expensive Junior High School. I said,

"Well, the new high school will spoil everything, for you certainly can't tear that down."

"Oh," he said, "that is where we'll rebuild the Governor's Palace."

I laid my hand on his arm.

"Doctor, don't worry, get plenty of sleep and exercise and I'm sure you'll be all right in time."

Scarcely two years later every newspaper carried the story of Mr. Rockefeller's princely offer to restore Williamsburg.

To do more than record and summarize one of the most extensive restorations in history is impossible in this volume, but the following facts should be set down. The restoration covers a certain area only, about a mile in length and a third of a mile in width. It purposed the removal of all buildings since about 1810, the repair and restoration of all existing buildings previous to that date, and the reconstruction of buildings of the Colonial period that have disappeared. The restoration includes not only architecture but landscape gardening and interior furnishings; in fact, everything necessary to recreate the "Colonial Scene." With the exception of two or three "museum houses," all houses are homes with modern conveniences and continuously occupied. Williamsburg is no American Pompeii. Old material and even old methods of construction were employed as far as possible but nothing is made to look old artificially. An old resident remarked: "This is a funny place. They tear down new houses to build old ones!" The restoration is based on contemporary data and, in so far as locations are concerned, on the famous "Frenchman's map," made in 1782 by a French engineer in the entourage of Rochambeau. The exteriors of buildings were authenticated by contemporary cuts and sketches, certain drawings on old fire insurance policies, and, most important of all, by the deep study given by the architects of the Tidewater architecture of the eighteenth century. The department of research collected at home and abroad data of every kind pertaining to the problem. Particularly valuable was the Bodleian copperplate of about 1740 with contemporary engravings of the Wren Building, the Palace, and the Capitol. Exhaustive research was put on colors and the nature of the old paint used and numerous contemporary inventories supplied detailed information about furnishings and furniture.

Colonial Williamsburg restored comprises about a hundred buildings, not including the numerous outbuildings. Of these the most important are the Wren Building, designed by Sir Christopher Wren, built first in 1695, restored; the Capitol, built in 1705, rebuilt; the Governor's Palace, 1713, rebuilt; the Raleigh Tavern, before 1742, rebuilt; Bruton Parish Church, 1710, not included in the restoration; the Court House, 1770, restored; numerous houses of which the most notable are St. George Tucker, 1788, George Wythe, 1755, Paradise, about 1717, Bassett Hall, 1753, Peyton Randolph, etc., etc. The group of shops and civic buildings are not restorations of old buildings but, nevertheless, are pure "Tidewater" in style.

The architects of this tremendous operation are Perry, Shaw and Hepburn, who were assisted by a committee of advisory architects, members of the American Institute of Architects. To some the buildings will be but adjuncts to the gardens which, to my mind, are the loveliest in America. These, together with the mudless dirt streets, the meandering curbs, the wooden lamp posts, and countless touches here and there are the creation of Arthur A. Shurcliff who, as landscape architect, worked in close communion with the architects and the committee of consultants.

If, in this book, we must regard Williamsburg primarily as architecture, let it be architecture beyond the bounds of proportion and detail; let it be an all-embracing architecture that includes every lovely part in its arms and presents it all to America for the pleasure of the eye and the good of the soul. Let the restoration of a noble past become an inspiration for the future of architecture in America so that whatever form it takes it may be shaped as of old in beauty and in truth.

INDEX

INDEX